Raising Adopted Children

RAISING ADOPTED CHILDREN

A MANUAL FOR ADOPTIVE PARENTS

LOIS RUSKAI MELINA

A SOLSTICE PRESS BOOK

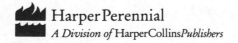

HarperPerennial
A Division of HarperCollins*Publishers*

A Solstice Press book produced at North Country Book Express, Inc., by Mary Schierman, Karen Doan, Patty McCauley and Richard Massey under the direction of Patricia Hart and Ivar Nelson

Cover design by Ken Yuhasz; photograph by Gerry Snyder

Library of Congress Cataloging in Publication Date

Melina, Lois Ruskai
   Raising adopted children.

   "A Solstice Press book."
   Bibliography: p.
   Includes index.
   1. Adopted children—United States. 2. Parenting— United States. I. Title.
HV875.55.M44 1986   649'.145   85—45648
ISBN 0-06-055044-X   98 97 96 95 94 RRD (H) 20 19 18 17 16
ISBN 0-06-096039-6 (pbk.)

*To my daughter, Emily,
and my son, Galen*

Contents

PART III. THE ADOPTEE GROWS UP

PART IV. SPECIAL ISSUES IN ADOPTION

Preface

Being an adoptive parent is immensely satisfying, as I know from personal experience. In addition to the other joys parents know, we who have adopted sometimes marvel at the serendipitous creation of our family—adults and children who probably would never have known each other have become a family with deep attachments to one another.

I believe our enjoyment is enhanced, though, by greater insight into our children's thoughts, feelings, fears, and experiences, as well as into our own psychological development as adoptive parents.

This book is intended as both a look at life in the adoptive family and as an ongoing source of information—a book parents will pick up again and again as their family progresses from adjustment to attachment to adolescence and to adulthood.

The need for a book like *Raising Adopted Children* was demonstrated more than thirty years ago by sociologist H. David Kirk. Surveying adoptive parents in the 1950s, Kirk found that some adoptive parents tried to view themselves as "just parents" and did not want to recognize the ways the adoptive family is different from the biologic family.

But there are differences. The primary difference is that our children have another set of parents. This is not typical in our culture, and children must struggle to understand what it means for them in their family and in society.

Just as our children grow up with the knowledge that most children live with the parents they were born to, we probably grew up thinking we would live with the children born to us. For most of us—fertile as well as infertile—the role-playing and fantasizing we engaged in about parenthood did not include adoption. As a result, we are functioning in a role we did not expect to have.

Kirk's research also showed that many people outside the adoptive family view adoption as a "second-best" way of becoming a family and even believe infertile parents are less "naturally" effective as parents. As false as these attitudes are, our awareness of them influences how we function as parents.

In his books *Shared Fate* and *Adoptive Kinship*, Kirk suggests it is vital for adoptive parents to acknowledge lovingly the differences between the adoptive family and the biologic family—including acknowledging our own pain and loss. By doing so, we can become more sensitive to the feelings of our children, more open to their questions, and consequently, more able to meet their needs.

Kirk was nearly alone in the 1950s in studying adoptive families. But in recent years, new research has given us more insight into adoptive parents and adoptees. Some of this research grew out of a genuine interest in the dynamics of the adoptive family, while other researchers, particularly those involved with heredity and environment issues, found adoptive families a convenient research sample. Whatever the motivation, we now know far more about adoptive families than we did even a few years ago.

This book provides adoptive parents with a comprehensive source of practical, reassuring advice, firmly founded on the available research as well as on the experiences of those involved with adoption.

Parents who adopt infants, older children, children of their own race, children of other races and ethnic backgrounds, disabled children, or children with serious behavior problems, will find the assistance they have long needed in recognizing and dealing with the special situations that arise when children are adopted.

While directed at the adoptive parent, this book is also useful for professionals such as social workers, psychologists, health care personnel, and teachers, who all need specific knowledge about the workings of adoptive families to serve them well. In addition, it is hoped that the adoptees who read this book will develop an understanding for the many factors influencing adoptive parents.

I have many people to thank for their contributions to this book. At the top of the list are the many adoptees, adoptive parents, and birthparents who have shared their stories with me over the years, giving me a greater understanding of the universality of adoption as well as the unique experiences of individual families. Their stories are in this book, unchanged except for minor details such as gender and age. But to protect their privacy, with few exceptions, their names have been changed.

I am also grateful to a few individuals who have repeatedly shared their remarkable knowledge of adoption with me and who have been supportive of my work: David Kirk, Reuben Pannor, and Barbara Tremitiere. David Kirk's work has profoundly influenced my thinking about adoption. I have also learned to count on him for thoughtful analysis of my work, which he provided after reviewing the manuscript of this book. Reuben Pannor has shared with me his years of experience in adoption, and has given me valuable feedback both on my writing in *Adopted Child* newsletter and on this book. I particularly appreciate the enthusiasm he showed for this project from the beginning. Barbara Tremitiere has made herself available to me whenever I needed information about special needs adoptions. She read parts of this manuscript and offered her thoughtful comments.

One cannot overstate Claudia Jewett's influence on contemporary adoption thought and practice. Her work on helping children deal with grief, helping children understand why they left one family to move to another, and her most recent ideas on how to help adolescents leave home in responsible ways are major influences on this book, and I thank her for her comments on those sections of the manuscript.

I appreciate Judith Schaffer's willingness to read this book in manuscript form and offer suggestions. Individual sections were read by Josephine Anderson, Robert Bilenker, Frank Bolton, Jr., David Brodzinsky, Dirck Brown, Remi J. Cadoret, Kathryn Donley, William Feigelman, Jim Forderer, James Mahoney, and James McLoughlin. I appreciate the time and care they took with it.

Thanks must also go to Sue Smith and her co-workers at Adoptions in Idaho, as well as to the staff of Holt Children's Services, who are always no more than a phone call away when I have questions, and who provided me with some of the information on children from the Philippines, Latin America, and Korea. Sue Smith has also been a helpful source of information on large adoptive families. Nancy Boucneau of International Mission of Hope detailed the experiences of children from India. Hyun Sook Han gave me a personal interview on the adjustment of Korean children. Dennis L. Murray offered helpful comments on the transmission of hepatitis B. Jim Forderer shared with me his insights into single parent adoption as well as the adoption of disabled children.

While I am grateful for all the help I received, I should make it clear that there are controversial issues in adoption as well as differing philosophies. Unless otherwise indicated, the views in this book are mine, and are not necessarily shared by all those who played a part in the book's development.

In Patricia Hart I found the thorough and demanding editor I always hoped to work with someday, as well as a friend who could be called upon for help with child care and other necessary support. I would also like to thank Ivar Nelson at Solstice Press who has been a valuable sounding board for ideas since the conception of the book, and Janet Goldstein at Harper & Row who understood the need for this book.

Final thanks are saved for my husband, Carl, who showed in ways both big and small that this book is as important to him as it is to me.

Lois Ruskai Melina
January 1986
Moscow, Idaho

Part I

Instant Family

Chapter 1

The Transition to Adoptive Parenthood

Adoptive parents often are told that they got their children "the easy way." Those who say that know little about the decisions and adjustments children and parents must make when they become "instant families" through adoption. Whether it is furnishing a nursery, buying school clothes for an older child, suddenly asking for a leave from work, dealing with parasites acquired before a child left her country or grief experienced because she left her home, adoptive parents often are hit with the full force of parenthood at once.

The first Sunday after our daughter arrived, we proudly took her to church with us, eager to share our joy with our friends. At the same time, I was somewhat reluctant to show her to people. I wanted everyone to see how beautiful she was, but she had begun to develop a rash on her face and scalp that we thought was probably an allergy to something new in her diet. Nevertheless, I was pleased to be sitting in the church "crying room" surrounded by other families—a mother at last. Later that day she spiked a high fever, and in another day it was clear she had measles. My husband, a family doctor, gave gamma globulin injections to all the children who had been exposed to the measles but had not yet been immunized, and our daughter recovered rapidly. But we were struck by the fact that within a week we had not only become parents, but parents of a sick baby who could have started an epidemic. Being unprepared for a baby who had contracted a disease that is practically nonexistent in the United States was our first indication that traditional sources of child care information often are inadequate for the adoptive parent. The majority of these manuals assume that the child was born into the family. They discuss the importance of a good birth experience for bonding and attachment, but don't talk about how to form an attachment with a child who was born to someone else. They advocate breast-feeding, but fail to mention how adoptive mothers can stimulate lactation. They tell parents the symptoms of teething, but not how malnutrition can affect a child's teeth. They talk about the awareness of sexuality that develops in adolescence, but not about the fear some parents have that their child may be at special risk for a teenage pregnancy.

Fortunately, the patience and persistence we develop to get through the often frustrating process of adopting and the trying process of resolving infertility are qualities we can use as parents. People come into adoption having had their decision to raise a child tested and affirmed. Couples often grow from the stress placed on their marriage by infertility. They learn how to identify their needs and solve problems together.

Adoptive parents, particularly infertile ones, have another advantage over other parents. One task of parenthood is reconciling expectations with reality. All parents have some fantasies about parenthood that are quickly dashed when faced with the real situation, and adoptive parents are no exception. But adoptive parents, especially those who are infertile, have already learned that parenthood can still be rewarding, though their original expectations of the role have changed.

ADJUSTMENT FOR PARENTS

Becoming parents in a way different from the norm can help prepare people for future adjustments, but can also be confusing. Sociologist H. David Kirk, in his books *Shared Fate** and *Adoptive Kinship,** says that when there is a contradiction between the way people have been culturally prepared for an expected event—such as parenthood—and the way it really happens, people experience a "role handicap." As adoptive parents, we experience a role handicap not only because we expected to become parents in a different way, but because our culture does not provide support for alternatives to becoming a parent other than through birth. We must adapt birth announcements to our circumstances, try to get our employers to make exceptions to the companies' maternity leave policies, and design our own ceremonies to mark the occasion. Having arrived at our role in a different manner, we may not be sure the role is the same. Without adequate role models, we may wonder if adoptive parents are different than biologic parents. And if we are unsure about our role, we may not perform well in it.

* See Selected References and Resources for complete citation of asterisked items.

In many respects, being an adoptive parent is no different from being a biologic parent, but situations arise in raising adopted children that are influenced by the child's history prior to joining the family, the parents' infertility (when that is the case), and information about the child that is missing.

Claiming

One of the first ways parents think of themselves as a mother or father is by identifying the ways their child is like them. Family members stand around a tiny, wrinkled baby expressing certainty that baby's nose is just like dad's. Even though adopted children have no genetic link to their adoptive parents, mothers and fathers find similarities between themselves and their children in mannerisms and personality characteristics, or sometimes even in physical appearance. This is an essential step in "claiming" a child as one's own. One study has actually found a connection between the degree to which adoptees and adoptive parents perceive themselves as similar and how satisfied they are with the adoption. When Kara saw a photograph of the one-month-old girl who would be her daughter, she immediately thought how much the baby looked like her younger sister at birth. She dismissed the impression, thinking it ridiculous that a Hispanic baby would look like her sister of Irish ancestry. But her sister's reaction to the photograph was the same. Chances are that the two babies' expressions were more alike than their appearance, but noticing the similarity was an important way of saying, "You're one of us."

Entitlement

Developing a sense that a child "belongs" in the family, even though she wasn't born into it, is a crucial task for adoptive parents. Unless parents develop a sense that the child is really theirs, they will have difficulty accepting their right to act as parents. In their book *How They Fared in Adoption: A Follow-up Study,* * Benson Jaffee and David Fanshel suggest that the amount of entitlement parents feel can be determined by looking at the extent to which they take risks with their children, deal with separation, handle discipline, and discuss adoption with their child and others. Extreme behavior in these areas may indicate that the parents do not feel "worthy" to act as parents. Parents who either overprotect their child or neglect their child's safety may not have come to grips with the risks and responsibilities inherent in parenting. Those who cannot bear to be away from their child may feel insecure about whether their affection (or their child's) is able to withstand separation, while excessive use of child care can indicate a lack of affection. Parents without a sense of entitlement may have difficulty disciplining a child, either believing they do not have the right to do so, or fearing their relationship is so tentative that discipline will alienate the child. Excessive talking about adoption, either to the child or to those outside the family, or excessive attempts to hide the fact that the child was adopted may also be signs of impaired entitlement.

Adoptive parents may not believe they have the authority to act as parents because in one sense, they don't. They must wait—often for six months—after a child is placed with the family before the adoption can be finalized. Parents are painfully aware that the child could be removed from their home during that time against their wishes, even though such occurrences are extremely rare. Adoptive families would benefit from changes in laws that would allow them to finalize adoptions, particularly of infants, shortly after placement.

Infertile couples may wonder if they aren't going against some kind of "heavenly plan" by adopting. They may wonder if infertility wasn't a "sign" that they weren't meant to have children. Consequently, these couples may have a hard time believing that it is okay for them to be a family and to function as a family. Feelings of inadequacy are usually fleeting, but when a couple believes their infertility was sent by God or fate, they may not have the confidence to act as parents.

Parents' sense of entitlement may also be impaired by guilt feelings, their above average income, occupational status, or "good connections" to a doctor or attorney having enabled them to adopt while other parents remained on waiting lists.

Sometimes the words society uses to differentiate between adopted children and children born into a family cast doubt on a parent's sense of entitlement. "Do you also have children of your own?" "What do you know about her real mother?" and "Do you think she'll want to search for her natural parents someday?" are questions adoptive parents hear often. These questions cast doubt on the parent-child relationship by implying that it is unreal, unnatural and somehow tentative. Adoptive parents are understandably sensitive about such terms, preferring to describe the child's ancestors as her "biologic mother" or "birthfather." But it's hard to educate society one person at a time, and many of us give up trying to explain to perfect strangers why we do consider these "our own children." (How to handle such insensitive remarks is discussed in Chapter 4.)

In *You're Our Child: A Social/Psychological Approach to Adoption,** social worker-educator Jerome Smith and attorney Franklin I. Miroff say that a sense of entitlement can be developed by recognizing and accepting the differences between adoptive families and families formed in other ways, by resolving feelings of inadequacy resulting from infertility, and by learning to handle the remarks of family and friends that betray a view that biologic parenthood is superior to adoptive parenthood. "Supporting an Adoption"* by Pat Holmes is an excellent booklet for parents to give people close to them that tells how friends and family can help support the adoptive family through the adjustment period.

Post-adoption Depression

Occasionally an adoptive parent, particularly the mother, becomes depressed after the child arrives. Post-partum depression in biologic mothers is caused by hormonal changes associated with pregnancy and birth. Adoptive parents do not have those physiologic changes, but may feel let-down after their child arrives. Post-adoption blues may occur because the adopting parents, who were excited about the arrival of the child, feel let-down when faced with the daily efforts involved in parenting a new child.

In addition, the parents may be grieving for the loss of an idealized version of the child they expected would arrive. One of the tasks that should be accomplished prior to adopting is grieving for the biologic child that will not be born. Couples who look forward to a little red-haired boy with freckles because that's what the husband looked like when he was small must let go of that image before adopting in order to accept the adopted child as he is. But even then, they may replace this wish with a fantasy about the adopted child. Perhaps they were offered a boy when they had been expecting and wanting a girl. Grieving for that girl is an important step in ultimately accepting the boy as their son.

Parents may be embarrassed to admit that they have the blues at this time. They think they should be happy and excited, and that because there was no pregnancy, there should be no depression. The adjustment period is a trying time for everyone in the family, and it is normal to have emotional highs and lows. That doesn't mean that the depression might not become severe enough to warrant treatment. But severe or mild, post-adoption blues is not necessarily an indication that the adoption was a mistake.

INFANT CARE CLASSES

Parents taking their new baby home may suddenly realize how little they know about diapering or feeding an infant. Learning how to care for an infant is built into the process of getting ready for the birth of a baby. Routine prenatal visits to the physician are often used to discuss child care questions. Childbirth preparation classes focus not only on breathing techniques during labor, but on how to bathe and feed a baby. There are additional opportunities in the hospital following the delivery of a baby for biologic parents to learn to care for their child. Adoptive parents do not have these same opportunities. The adoption process focuses on adoption issues rather than child care issues.

Ironically, adoptive couples who have had to prove they would make good parents often find themselves feeling inadequate shortly after becoming parents. We wonder if we wouldn't have a more instinctive idea of how to take care of a baby if the child had been born to us.

Caring for a child is a learned activity. It is not instinctual, even for the biologic parent. Much of what we know comes from having observed our own parents. Some learn how to care for children by being raised in large families, but most of us learn with our first child. Most parents report feeling much more relaxed with their second or subsequent children than they were with their first. They have learned what to expect, and how to handle the routine and the extraordinary.

Yet, caring for that first child can be made easier. Many communities now have infant care classes specifically aimed at adoptive parents. These are sometimes offered by an adoption agency, sometimes by adoptive parent groups or infertility support groups, and sometimes by individuals acting independently. They are each a little different, but most of them combine basic child care information such as feeding, safety, child development, and health problems, with adoption issues such as resolution of infertility and adjustment to adoption. If such a class is available, parents should consider enrolling in it, though it probably makes sense to wait until a baby is close to being placed with the family. This way the class is a pleasant experience rather than a reminder that it will be a long time before the information and advice will be put into practice. It is not too late to take such a class after a child's arrival. Many parents find themselves more receptive to learning about how to care for an infant after the child is in their home and they have a better idea of what they need to know. In addition to information on child care, parents will find an informal network of support and friendship through such classes. Parents who are adopting an older baby or toddler might want to check with the instructor of the class to see if the information presented will be pertinent to their situation.

Where there are no such classes available, parents might consider starting one themselves or encouraging their adoption agency to start one. *Our Child: Preparation for Parenting in Adoption* by Carol A. Hallenbeck (Our Child Press, 800 Maple Glen Lane, Wayne, Penn. 19087) is a guide for setting up such classes.

In putting into practice information from such child care classes or manuals, parents should keep in mind that all infants arrive with unique temperaments. Parents shouldn't expect their baby to cry, get hungry, or need stimulation the same way another baby does. Infant care classes, books, and grandparents are all helpful sources of information, but ultimately parents have to get acquainted with their own baby and respond to his needs.

CHOOSING AND CONSULTING A PHYSICIAN

Nearly every adoptive parent has heard a story about a physician who, upon diagnosing a serious medical condition in an adopted child, advised the parents to "send the child back to the agency." We are somehow more appalled to find this kind of attitude among the members of the medical profession than we are in the general population. But we should remember that physicians, nurses, and other medical personnel do not have any particular training in adoption issues. They bring to an interaction with an adoptive family as many of their own prejudices, misconceptions, and attitudes as any member of society. It is unfortunate, but they cannot be expected to be any more sensitive to adoption issues than are teachers, grandparents, or other individuals who have not been educated on the subject.

In her survey of attitudes among adoptive parents and those in the helping professions, Pat Holmes found that, like others not personally involved with adoption, medical personnel sometimes question whether the love between an adopted child and her adoptive parents has the same intensity and level of commitment as in a biologic relationship. Consequently, a nurse was overheard commenting about an adoptive mother who was staying in the hospital room with her son: "She's just like a real mother." And the physicians who have suggested "sending back" to the agencies the children found to have medical problems are showing that they do not understand the bonding and attachment process. Parents who have adopted "special needs" children may find that like their friends and relatives, their physician doesn't understand their motives for adopting someone with serious medical or mental problems.

This does not excuse insensitivity. But until the medical profession is educated along with the rest of society, its members will continue to practice medicine influenced by myths and misconceptions about adoption and the dynamics of the adoptive family.

Ideally, adoptive parents should select a family doctor or pediatrician who has some understanding of adoption issues. But if there are none in the community, they should select a physician who is open to being educated.

Choosing a Physician

Parents should set up an appointment with a physician before their child arrives so that they have time to make an evaluation and select another doctor if the first one they talk to does not seem right for them.

We will want to know a physician's qualifications, range of services, fees, and philosophy of medicine, and in addition, we will want to know his or her attitude toward adoption. The best way to find this out is to engage the doctor in conversation about adoption, or ask open-ended questions rather than specific ones; for example, "What has been your experience with adoptive families?" We should be more concerned with the attitudes expressed in response to the question than the number of families treated. We should press for explanations of any statements that seem to indicate an attitude that adoption is a "second-best" alternative, and find out if that is really his or her opinion, or if terms like "real parents" are being used because of inexperience with or ignorance of the preferred terms.

We also will want to know how the physician will deal with the lack of a medical history, if there is not a complete history of the adoptee. (See Chapter 6.) In addition, parents should discuss any particular concerns they might have, such as whether the physician supports the mother's decision to breast-feed the baby.

Even parents who already have a family physician should discuss the physician's experiences with adoption. They may find that the doctor who has been treating them for years has some attitudes toward adoption that they do not feel comfortable with.

Over-anxious Parents/Unconcerned Doctors

A common complaint reported by adoptive parents is that physicians tend to view adoptive parents as excessively anxious and sometimes ignore real medical problems. In fact, some adoptive parents do seem to be overly concerned about the health of their children. A study of Canadian children in the mid-1960s found that adoptive mothers took their daughters to the doctor significantly more often than biologic mothers. One explanation they suggested was that adoptive parents may have a greater reliance on the helping professions. People who have gone through intensive treatment for infertility and later found they needed the help of a physician, lawyer, or social worker to adopt a child may not be as reluctant to consult a physician for routine matters as someone who has seen a helping professional only occasionally. They also suggested that this may not reflect greater illness in the adopted girls, but a higher degree of anxiety in adoptive mothers about the health of their daughters. Adoptive parents are often intensely involved parents who have invested a lot of energy and emotion in achieving their role. They want to justify the "approval" of the adoption agency or birthparents by doing everything "right." (This subject is discussed in more detail in Chapter 5.)

Of course, sometimes physicians view adoptive parents as over-anxious and parents view doctors as unconcerned simply because they are not communicating adequately. We should not assume health care professionals are knowledgeable about the ways adoption affects a family just because they are well educated in many other areas.

ADOPTION ANNOUNCEMENTS AND RECORD BOOKS

Adoptive parents often have only a few days' notice that their child will be arriving. Even when the date is known, we fear that some last minute emergency, such as immigration problems or illness, will change the date of the child's arrival. We wonder if the birthmother will go through with the adoption as planned. We may be reluctant to tell more than a few close friends that we are adopting, or much less, when our child is expected. Or, in the flurry of last minute things to do, we may not have time to tell more than a few people.

Newspapers that print birth announcements receive their information from public records at area hospitals. Since notice of adoptions are not public records, newspapers do not have access to that information. Some newspapers may be willing to include the announcement of a child's adoption in the "births" column. If not, parents can always pay for an advertisement announcing the child's arrival.

There are commercially printed announcements specifically for adopted children, but these are usually designed for infants. Several adoptive parents have developed cottage industries designing announcements for adopted children, including foreign-born or minority children. (See the Merchandise section of Selected References and Resources at the back of this book.)

Parents don't need to be artists to develop their own announcement. Many parents have announcements printed at their local stationers. Others announce a child's arrival with a handwritten note on informal stationery. Either handwritten or printed announcements could read: Tom and Sally Joyful announce the May 24, 1986 arrival of their daughter Marie, who was born April 30, 1984.

Record Books

Baby books wherein parents are expected to describe the "ride to the hospital" and which parent the child resembles are clearly unsuitable for adopted children. There are commercially printed baby books specifically for adopted children, but even these are inadequate for all but those children adopted as newborns. Sources of record books for older children or foreign-born children are listed in the Merchandise section of Selected References and Resources at the back of this book.

Blank "Baby's-First-Year" calendars allow parents to write in the month and year that they want to start keeping track of their baby's development, presumably the month the child is born. But this format is easily adaptable to the adopted child with the first month being the month of the child's arrival. Parents then mark momentous events on the days they occur. Parents may also purchase blank journals in which to write narratives about the child's development, or even keep a similar record on a storage disk for a home computer.

"Life books" are different from record books in that their purpose is to show where a child has lived, whom she lived with, and why she was moved, prior to joining her adoptive family. Adoptive parents may want to add to that book mementos such as report cards and school pictures, or they may want to keep a record book of the child's progress separate from a history of her adoption. Life books are discussed more thoroughly in Chapter 4.

NAMING AND RENAMING

Choosing a name for a child is one of the first decisions parents make. Some have selected names years in advance. Others wait until they see the child to decide what name "fits." Parents usually want to select a name for their adopted child, even if he already has been named. The infertile couple who feels they have little control over becoming parents may feel particularly strongly that they have every right to decide what their child will be called.

Why we have strong feelings about choosing our children's names is unclear. Perhaps naming is one way that we make the transition from imagining to knowing a child as a real individual. The child is no longer an "it," but "Sam" or "Katie." Naming a child may also be a way of claiming a child—of signifying that the child belongs. Adoptive parents need to engage in such claiming so that they feel they have a right to parent their child. But while most experts advise parents to change the child's last name immediately, some think parents should be cautious about changing the first name of even a young child.

Changing the First Name

Before renaming a child, we should consider the age of the child, the importance of traditional or religious naming patterns in the adoptive family, motivations for changing the name, whether the child's original name is somehow undesirable, and sometimes the preference of the child.

Parents usually can feel safe renaming a newborn, even though the baby has a name on her birth certificate; the baby has not heard her name often enough to respond to it. But if the birthparents chose the name, adoptive parents might consider keeping it, at least as a middle name. Later on, the child might appreciate having "something" from her birthparents. One of the bits of information adult adoptees search for is their original first name. Retaining the original name as part of the new name can also indicate that the adoptive parents look at the birthparents as part of their child's identity and past. If the original name is not kept, adoptive parents should at least write it down and keep it in a safe place to be given to the adoptee at an older age. It is amazing how details like that, which we think we will always remember, are eventually forgotten.

Adoptive parents who plan to name their child after a relative should consider their motives for doing so and the message that this gives the child. For example, naming a child "junior" may be a way of pretending that the child was born to them. More likely, the parents are trying to show how much a part of the family the child is. They might want to consider other ways to communicate that, such as by giving the child a family heirloom. In an extreme reaction to claiming by naming, one adoptee, whose family traced its ancestors to the Mayflower, felt that being named for those ancestors was dishonest. He felt adoption attached him to a family, but not to a heritage that he had no claim to.

Pediatrician Vera Fahlberg cautions against giving a new first name to a child who already has learned to respond to a name—a task normally accomplished before the age of one. Although an infant will learn to respond to a new name rather quickly, it is just one more new thing for the child to adjust to at a time of many major adjustments.

A preschooler may have a particularly difficult time adjusting to a new first name. A young child's identity is so closely tied to her first name that changing it during the preschool years can cause a child to think she is not really the same person, or that one name goes with being a good person and one name with being a bad person. A name change can make it more difficult for the child to integrate her past life into her present.

Even foreign-born children do not necessarily have to be given an anglicized first name, particularly if the family is living in a multi-ethnic or international community. My daughter attended preschool with children with Arabic, Spanish, and Japanese first names. Keeping her Korean name would not have made her an oddity in the classroom.

Most parents recognize that a school-age child has lived with his first name for so long that it would be difficult for him to give it up. This is something that should be discussed with the child with care. Some children may want to change their names when they are adopted as a way of trying to get rid of their past. This may indicate that a child has unrealistic expectations about adoption. He needs to be helped to understand that his past is part of him, and that even if it was unpleasant, it doesn't make him bad. He is not a "new person" because he has been adopted.

Sometimes the adoptive parents are the ones who seek a name change as a way to leave the child's past behind. The past is always part of the child's history and parents shouldn't pretend otherwise. Even if the child was named for a parent who abused her, the effects of the abuse will not disappear with a new name.

Parents who want to change the foreign-sounding name of a school-age child because they think it will help her assimilate her new culture more quickly and be accepted more readily by her peers should discuss the proposed name change, perhaps with the aid of an interpreter. The child may prefer teasing to giving up what may be the last tangible remnant of her life in her country of birth. Adoptive mother Joyce Kaser has written about the naming dilemma she and her husband R. Kent Boesdorfer faced when adopting a six-year-old Colombian boy—a problem complicated by the fact that Kaser and her husband have different last names. They found that the boy wanted to keep his full name, and so became Christopher Jorge Cruz Kaser Boesdorfer. Parents adopting a child from overseas have until the time the child becomes a naturalized citizen to decide whether to change her name. A visa can be issued in her original name.

Parents who want to choose a name for their child may consider selecting a new middle name, incorporating any family or religious naming traditions into their choice. Still, it is important to call the child by the name that she identifies as her "self."

When a Change is Necessary

While adoptive parents may have to fight the urge to rename their children, there are some circumstances that warrant a change of first name. If there already is a child in the home with the same first name, the new child probably should be renamed. Or, if the name is likely to leave the child vulnerable to ridicule, it should be changed. If the first name is changed, parents should try to find a name that sounds like the original name; and the original name should be incorporated into the legal name, perhaps as a middle name. It isn't unusual for an adopted child to have more than one middle name as a result of efforts to keep her original name part of her legal name.

Parents who intend to change their child's first name can inform the foster family or agency and ask that the child be prepared for this, so that she doesn't have to make quite so many adjustments after placement.

Giving a Family Name

Adoption experts agree that the child's surname usually should be changed to the new family's name at the time of placement rather than when the adoption is finalized. The surname is one of the ways our culture defines who is a member of a particular family. One of the most important concepts to communicate to the adopted child, to friends, to teachers, and to relatives is that by adoption we are creating, or expanding, our family. That process begins when the child arrives, not when he legally becomes a member of the family.

The child's teachers and school personnel should know what he is to be called. The child's name will not be legally changed until the adoption is finalized, and some school officials are reluctant to allow a child to use a name other than his legal name. The fact that the child's records from his previous school are in his original surname makes the problem even more difficult. Starting school or moving to a new school is hard enough without teachers, principals, and bus drivers calling a child by the "wrong" name.

Occasionally, more often when a teenager is adopted, it is too traumatic for the child to change his last name. He may feel that changing his surname is being disloyal to his birthparents, or may simply be too accustomed to the name he has had for thirteen, fourteen, or fifteen years to change it. The child's feelings should be discussed and ultimately respected. While it may appear that his refusal to take his adoptive family's name indicates an unwillingness to become integrated into the family, he may resist becoming part of his adoptive family less if he knows it doesn't mean giving up important parts of his previous life. And with many blended families and women keeping their maiden names after marriage, it's not at all uncommon for a child to have a last name different from parents or siblings.

Chapter 2

Adjustment of the Family

Adopted children are forced to break some ties with people or surroundings to which they have become attached. The length of time children have been in another place, the quality of the relationships with the people who cared for them, the number of times they have been moved from one home to another, and, to some degree, their developmental stage can all affect how children react to a move. It is not uncommon for a child, even an infant, to grieve when separated from people he cares about or from a familiar environment—even if those people or that environment was considered to be detrimental to the child's welfare. It may not make sense to us that the child is mourning; but he must be allowed to grieve and be comforted while he does.

The adoptee is not the only family member who must make adjustments. Siblings must adjust not only to the arrival of a new family member, but perhaps to additional scrutiny of the family by outsiders. Extended family members have to welcome the new family member, too often without adequate preparation or a thorough understanding of adoptive relationships. There is likely to be some disharmony as family members learn how the addition of the new child affects them.

Perhaps the most difficult aspect of the adjustment period for those adopting for the first time is not knowing when—or if—it will end. The adjustment of our second child was not necessarily easier than the adjustment of our first, but our experience told us it was a temporary period. We were helped through our adjustment with our son by thinking back to incidents that happened with our daughter six months, one year, and two years after her arrival that were turning points in our development as a family. We should keep in mind that many of the most difficult times in the adjustment period are necessary for the development of attachment and a sense of belonging in a family, a subject discussed in Chapter 3.

ADJUSTMENT OF INFANTS

Many people believe that babies adapt rather quickly to their new caretakers and home. However, infants do notice changes in diet, color, odor, sounds, and other aspects of their environment, even if they don't perceive a change in the specific individual caring for them. Usually there is little need for adjustment if the infant is placed in an adoptive home immediately after birth because he hasn't been in one place or cared for by one person long enough to become accustomed to certain smells, sounds, and routines. But babies who have been in foster care or have been cared for by their biologic parents for even a few weeks will notice their environment is different, even though they may not be aware that a specific person is no longer caring for them.

Infant Grief

An infant reacts to changes somatically, usually with sleeping or eating problems. The baby may refuse to eat, spit up his formula, have an upset stomach, or have chronic diarrhea. Or he may have difficulty sleeping regularly or for extended periods of time. The baby may be generally irritable or cry for prolonged periods for no apparent reason, may fail to progress developmentally, lack vitality, have frequent illnesses and accidents, or lose weight or hair. The infant may also show his emotions through his facial expression, tone of voice and body language.

Lesley and Craig had never seen a baby show sadness other than by crying until their son arrived at seven months of age. His eyes and facial expression clearly showed that he was missing something or someone. Smiles were hard to evoke, and laughing was even rarer. He also had problems with eating and digestion and chronic illnesses. In the six months after his arrival he had three ear infections, influenza, bronchitis, pneumonia, eczema, and chicken pox. Some of his problems were undoubtedly due to his exposure to viruses and infections, but it is also likely that his psychological state either was directly responsible for some of the problems, such as eczema, or lowered his resistance to disease.

Adoptive parents who discuss the adjustment reactions their infant is having often will have their diagnosis belittled by non-adoptive parents. "My baby had problems sleeping for three years," or "All babies have bouts of unexplainable diarrhea," they may say. The implication is that the adoptive parents don't know what they're talking about because they aren't biologic parents, and that they are overemphasizing the effect adoption has on a person's life.

An infant who is having ongoing sleeping or eating problems, or is otherwise showing signs of distress, should be checked by a physician to determine if there are any medical causes for the irritability or indigestion. But social work educator Carol Williams suggests that in the absence of a medical explanation a parent should assume that the baby is reacting physically to subtle changes he perceives in the world around him.

Babies and Toddlers have Different Reactions

Psychiatrist Justin Call has identified the reactions that parents can expect when infants are moved from one home to another at certain stages of development. Call believes infants are most vulnerable to being distressed by a change in their environment between four and twelve weeks of age. Younger babies are concerned with having their bodily needs met and are not as aware of their surroundings. One- to three-month-olds are alert enough to respond to stimuli, but not sophisticated enough to modify them when they receive too much. They are easily overloaded. Three- to six-month olds are more adaptive to change. They are better able to use their bodies to modify stimulation, can handle more complex stimuli, and can adjust to changes in diet more easily. Six- to twelve-month-old infants are again vulnerable to change because their attachment to their primary caretaker is intense at this time. Besides noticing a change in their environment, babies of this age will perceive the loss of an individual. A baby in this age group may go through the stages of grief that older children and adults experience. This includes denial, often expressed by the "searching" behavior that indicates the child expects the previous caretaker to return; anger, expressed often by uncontrollable crying; depression, or withdrawal and distinterest in food or play; and restitution, or acceptance of the new situation. These stages may not be sequential and may repeat themselves. Two-year-olds show the same kind of reactions to change as younger children, but more dramatically, Call reports. Their clinging will be more intense, their withdrawal more striking. However, because they can express themselves better than infants, they can actively participate in resolving anxiety, for example, by making their food or activity preferences known, or by using words to express emotions.

Easing the Transition

Although it is not often done, an ideal way to ease the transition for an infant from one environment to another is for the adoptive parents to visit the infant prior to the baby's being placed in their home. This gives the parents an opportunity to observe the baby's routine and learn precisely how he is being cared for. Pediatrician Vera Fahlberg suggests that having the foster parents begin each task, such as bathing the baby, and having the adoptive parents complete the activity does more than help the new parents learn the baby's routine. It gives the infant permission from the foster parents to accept nurturing from the adoptive parents. With an infant old enough to recognize familiar faces and objects, visits by the adoptive parents and perhaps even visits to the adoptive parents' house prior to placement can ease the "stranger anxiety" that is typical of the six- to twelve-month-old. Spontaneous smiling and an interest in interacting with inanimate objects in the new environment are signs that the baby is ready to make the move.

If visits with the infant prior to placement are not possible, adoptive parents can make the transition easier by learning and following the routine and method of care and interaction used by the previous caretaker. It is important to maintain the infant's schedule as much as possible and to replicate the way the infant is used to being held during feeding, to being dressed, bathed, and even diapered. Some babies are used to being carried on someone's back, while others are familiar with a Snugli baby carrier. Some are massaged during baths. Some babies become more alert after feeding, while others are used to falling asleep with a bottle. Particular care should be paid to how the infant was soothed when distressed; even a baby who is well prepared for a move may show signs of grief. Even the same kinds of sounds can be important. New parents should try to make the same kinds of word sounds that the previous caretakers used with the child, such as those used in parent-child babbling games. Some social workers recommend wearing the same kind of perfume that the foster mother wore as a way of providing the child with an odor that is familiar, that the child associates with being taken care of.

It often helps a child six months or older if familiar toys or other objects are transferred with him to the new home. One mother said her eight-month-old son would grab his clothes with his right hand and put his right thumb in his mouth frequently after he arrived, causing her to wonder if he had been attached to a security blanket that wasn't transferred with him. She introduced one and he immediately became attached to it. Another child in the family can make the transition easier for an older baby by providing diversion and entertainment.

Using a familiar object to bridge the move from one environment to the next is particularly effective with a toddler, Call says. The two-year-old has begun to claim some space in the home as his own. His space in the new home should be made clear to him by the presence of toys or furniture. However, parents should take care not to introduce too many new aspects of the new environment at once. The child will take the lead in exploring the house. The backyard, siblings, pets, and other aspects of the new environment should be introduced one at a time, perhaps even on different days.

Of course, it is not always possible to communicate directly with the foster parents or birthmother to learn the child's routine. Nor is it always feasible to have the baby and adoptive parents visit each other several times before the placement. And some agencies are not aware of the importance of replicating a baby's routine. Parents may have to insist on knowing how the child has been cared for or on being given a written description of his schedule.

Even when it is possible to take the time to ensure a smooth transition, adoptive parents are understandably anxious to have the baby in their home as soon as possible rather than wait several weeks while the baby gets used to the new people and environment. And some parents may resent having to care for "their" baby the way someone else did. They may want to put into practice their own style of child care. Yet it is important to remember that we are only being asked to follow someone else's routine temporarily, until the infant gets to know us. Then, gradual changes can be introduced. Parents who strongly object to some way the baby was cared for—feeding on a set schedule rather than feeding on demand, for example—have to weigh the advantage of demand feeding against the advantage of minimizing changes.

Transcultural Changes

A child from a foreign country encounters even more dramatic changes in environment. Even though a baby is not talking or responding to verbal instructions, she is hearing new words and new sound patterns. She may have moved from a humid, tropical climate to a cool, dry one. Because of differences in foods, the adoptive parents may have different body and breath odors than the child's previous caretakers. And the foods the baby is given may taste remarkably different than the ones she is used to.

Travel alone may require a major adjustment. The baby may have jet lag, or have her days and nights mixed up as a result of changing time zones. While it is unusual, one couple discovered that their baby had been given a large dose of a tranquilizer to sedate him for the long plane trip. The first few days in his new home he was still "hung-over" from the tranquilizer; then he experienced a mild withdrawal and refused to sleep for two more days.

Parents should find out as much as possible about the methods of care in the country their child is coming from, for example:

— What was the child fed and when?

We had a very difficult time getting our Korean-born son to take his formula in the initial days of his placement. Finally, in desperation, I called the adoption agency to find out specifically what he had been fed. "Oh, just add a little Karo syrup to the formula," I was told. "The formula in Korea is sweeter." Babies in Brazil are given coffee and sugar with their milk, and seldom white milk or any cold foods. Parents may want to add smaller and smaller quantities of coffee and sugar, or even chocolate syrup, to the baby's formula until he gets used to the taste of plain formula.

Parents should continue to feed the baby with something close to the food he has been used to and make any changes slowly, perhaps mixing the baby's old formula with his new formula and gradually increasing the amount of the new formula in the mixture

— What have been her sleeping arrangements?

Korean children generally sleep on a mattress on the floor and, like Latin American children, may sleep with many people in the same room. These children may have difficulty falling asleep in a crib or in their own quiet room. Babies in India are accustomed to sleeping on their backs and may fuss if placed on their stomachs

— What methods of child care were used by the person who cared for her? How was she soothed when she was fussy?

Ann would place her infant on a blanket in the middle of the room, toys within easy reach, while she worked in another part of the house. She couldn't understand why her daughter wouldn't entertain herself for even a few minutes. Only later did she learn that Korean mothers carry their infants on their backs while they work.

Some cultures start toilet training in the first year; some dote on an infant, giving him freedom and attention that would be considered "spoiling" in the United States. Those parents who travel abroad to pick up their child should plan to spend some time if not with the child's caretaker, then learning how children in similar circumstances are cared for. The booklet *Understanding My Child's Korean Origins,** by Hyun Sook Han is valuable for parents adopting a child from Korea. Unfortunately, similar booklets for babies from other foreign countries do not seem to be available. However, some agencies may have information sheets that discuss infant care practices.

Variation in Adjustment Reaction

Some babies show adjustment reactions immediately after being moved into a new home. Others internalize their reactions to a move and develop sleeping and digestive problems months later.

Babies who have experienced more than one move may have either a minor reaction to the latest move or a severe one. If the baby was not attached to the last person who cared for him, or if the care was substandard, he may have few problems with the move. With other infants, a new move may recall all the previous moves and they may show intense reactions to the new environment.

There is little parents can do to help the infant who is grieving except give comfort and support. This may mean a lot of rocking and walking the floors, even though it may not seem to be doing much to soothe the baby. While it's difficult to try to comfort a baby who seems inconsolable, doing so not only lets the infant express her grief, but it shows her that this is an adult she can count on in times of distress.

When the child is in good physical health, eats and sleeps well, progresses well developmentally, forms relationships, and otherwise lacks signs of distress, parents can assume the baby is making an adequate adjustment to her new environment.

While infants can have problems adapting to a new environment, it is a mistake to characterize the adjustment period as an unpleasant time for parents and baby. The joy of falling in love with the baby is there, just as every parent hopes it will be. And it doesn't take too many months before the baby stops thinking of her new home and caretakers as strange. I remember the first time that my son cried when I left him at his play group. I was so pleased to see that instead of missing some other caretaker, as he had for weeks, he now was missing me.

ADJUSTMENT OF OLDER CHILDREN

When preschoolers and school-age children move into a new family, it is often described as a "marriage" in which the various members of the family must learn about each other and adapt to the different personalities. Older children typically go through a period immediately after placement of near-perfect behavior, often called the "honeymoon." This is followed by a testing period. The behavior of children during these two phases is tied to their grief over their separation from and loss of their foster parents or birthparents, and to the process of forming attachments in their new family, which is discussed in Chapter 3. Many adoption advocates believe parents who adopt older children should initiate family therapy prior to the child's placement or immediately after. Whether or not professional services are used at this time, it helps to understand the stages of grief that older children may be experiencing.

Grief in Preschool and School-age Children

Elisabeth Kübler-Ross, psychiatrist and authority on death, has identified five stages that people go through when dealing with death: denial, anger, bargaining, depression, and acceptance. Every time we experience a loss we go through these predictable stages of grief, although if the loss is a minor one, we may go through the stages quickly. Psychiatrist John Bowlby reports that children as young as four mourn much like adults, and that even two-and-a-half and three-year-olds can experience the stages of grief that adults do, provided their questions are answered and their memories not discouraged.

Denial, Anger and Bargaining

One of the first reactions to a loss is shock and numbness. Instead of collapsing or getting hysterical, people tend to function automatically, but report that the realization hasn't "hit them" yet. Children, too, may react seemingly casually to news of a loss, but later cry uncontrollably or lash out angrily at those around them.

Realization of the loss is generally followed by denial and disbelief. Children often show "searching" behavior that indicates they expect the person to walk through the door at any minute. A child may even stare out the window, looking for the significant person to return. The adopted child may believe that the birthparent didn't mean to place him for adoption; that he was "stolen" or that it was all a misunderstanding and the birthparent will return for him. He may deny the loss by denying that the person lost was important to him, making statements such as "I really didn't like that place anyway." Strong emotions such as anger are not uncommon at this time, and the child may reveal them verbally or through other forms of behavior. It is crucial that the parents let the child know that they recognize how he feels, that those feelings are normal, and that he is allowed to express them. He may be saying shocking things, or things that hurt, such as that he wants his "real" mom or that his real mom was bad and he wishes she were dead. Rather than stifling these feelings by criticism such as "Don't you like living with us?" or "Oh, you don't really wish she were dead," parents should let the child express them so that he can move to ultimate acceptance of his loss. Children need the support of their parents at this time, and holding or touching goes a long way toward reassuring a child.

At some point the child may try bargaining for a different outcome. They often believe they were to blame for what happened and if they change, they will recover the foster parents or birthparents who were lost to them. The child may decide to behave perfectly or to never love his new parents so that he can be rewarded by the return of the people lost to him.

The child in this stage of grief believes his loss can be reversed. Eventually he realizes that despite all his efforts, there is no hope of recovering his loss. That is when despair sets in.

Depression and Acceptance

One of the most difficult aspects of grief is the despair that accompanies it. The child has no hope of being reunited with the significant person that he lost, but still yearns for her as much as ever. The person may feel life is hopeless and have difficulty functioning. He may contemplate suicide. A child may lose his appetite or look to food as a source of comfort. He is likely to withdraw and become apathetic. Screaming and crying is replaced by a mournful wail. Parents want to spare their children pain and will have difficulty accepting the fact that there is little they can do to mitigate their child's sorrow. But allowing the child to express his feelings is what is needed. If despair continues beyond a few weeks, though, the child may need professional help moving on to the next stage—an understanding and acceptance of the loss, and the ability to move on with his life. As a child realizes that all the denial, all the searching, and all the bargains don't work to eliminate the loss, he will ultimately come to accept it.

Dealing with Grief

Bowlby points out that even though children mourn in much the same way that adults do, there are differences. Children have less control of their grief process—they may not be as able as an adult to get the information they need to help them understand their loss, and it is not as easy for them to seek comfort from other people if those that they depend on for support fail to provide it. Children are also more distractable and may seem to be having little reaction to their loss, when in reality their attention may have been diverted only temporarily. As a result, they may have sudden mood swings. Children need sustained comfort, an adult they can depend on, answers to their questions, and toleration of their memories. Claudia Jewett's book *Helping Children Cope with Separation and Loss** is an excellent discussion of how parents can help their grieving child.

One of the ways that a loss affects children is by demonstrating that relationships and situations they thought were permanent are not. Children then wonder what other seemingly permanent situation could be lost. Adoptees typically understand what it means to be placed for adoption years before they comprehend the legal system that makes adoption permanent. An awareness that they have lost their birthparents may be accompanied by a fear that their adoptive home is not permanent. This anxiety, according to Jewett, may show up as a fear of going to school, insomnia, nightmares or night terrors (in which the child screams and may appear to be awake even though he is sleeping), nail biting, increased allergic responses, increased risk of infection, or other physical ailments. Jewett suggests surrounding the anxious child with softness—having him wear layers of clothes or sleep next to something soft like flannel sheets or a quilt. Adjustments in the child's sleeping routine also may be necessary, such as allowing him to fall asleep with the radio going or the light on. Parents may worry about establishing "precedents" like this—believing that a child coming into a new home should understand "the way it's going to be." But some allowances do need to be made for the child experiencing grief. Adjustments in routine can be made when the child's needs change.

When parents and child must be separated during this stage, the parents need to be particularly reliable about returning when they said they would, or calling the child to let him know they have been delayed.

Even though children need to express their feelings, they may not be willing to do so, especially with "new" people like their adoptive parents. Parents may have to take the lead in initiating discussions of what the child might be feeling. Specific activities that parents and child can engage in that can lead to discussions about feelings of separation and loss are discussed in Chapter 5.

Adjusting to a New School

At the same time that he is adjusting to his new family and grieving for those he is separated from, the older child is also expected to adjust to a new school and make new friends—formidable tasks for even an emotionally stable child. If possible, the older child should be placed in his adoptive home during the summer so that he can start his new school in the fall, reducing his self-consciousness at being "new" at school. Because of the emotional turmoil in his life, the older child may need to be moved back in school or need special education classes. Parents should have their child evaluated as soon as possible—and insist on the results immediately—to minimize the number of classroom changes for the child. At the same time, they should take care not to overwhelm the newly placed child with batteries of tests but try to balance the need to adequately evaluate the child with an awareness that the adjustment period is a difficult time for him. (See the discussion of learning disabilities in Chapter 5.) In selecting an appropriate grade level, parents should keep in mind their child's level of emotional maturity, as well as his academic level, both of which may regress during this adjustment period.

Even with a carefully selected classroom, the adoptee may have difficulty with her schoolwork because she is using a great deal of energy to grieve and form new attachments. Claudia Jewett points out that the grieving child may have difficulty following directions or concentrating. She suggests giving children concrete suggestions to help them concentrate on their schoolwork, rather than the vague "buckle down." She also suggests giving them specific times, both at school and at home, when they can discuss their worries and concerns. They may then be able to push aside their feelings when they need to concentrate, knowing that there is a designated time when they will be able to think about their loss.

Parents should not put too much importance on the child's schoolwork, appearance, or other "learning" activities during the adjustment period, says psychologist Terrence Koller. It is more important for the child to concentrate on her new relationships. Of course, it will be difficult for parents to resist the pressure from teachers, relatives and friends to focus on the child's developmental progress. If friends and relatives have expressed doubt that someone can have an influence on a child adopted at an older age, parents are going to want to show them how quickly she has advanced in school and improved her appearance. This is a time when support from other parents of children adopted at an older age can be valuable.

Parents should insist on a conference with the child's teacher before the child begins attending classes to explain his background. While emphasizing that they do not expect special treatment for the child, parents should point out that the child may need extra attention as well as empathy for his intense feelings at this time. Psychologist Ann Jernberg points out in "The Special Student"* that the newly placed child needs stability in his life, and teachers should be advised to provide him with as much predictability as possible. The child who has recently experienced a move may need more preparation than other students for changes in routine such as a field trip or substitute teacher.

Teachers may also have little experience with children who do not readily form attachments and may need guidance in finding ways to get close to the child. (Attachment and the unattached child are discussed in Chapters 3 and 11.)

Most older children will want to reveal their adoptive status in their own way and in their own time. Parents should discuss this with the child and inform his teacher if he does not want his classmates to know he is adopted. Otherwise, the teacher may introduce him to the class with an explanation that he is new in school because he has just been adopted.

Because children are self-conscious about being new in school and about being adopted, we should be aware that a newly placed child may have a greater need than other children to blend in with his peers and be understanding if he seems to need to conform to the prevailing fashion or hairstyle.

Parents should not wait to enroll a foreign-born child in school until he learns English, but should try to find a school with an English as a Second Language (ESL) program. If none are available, parents should work closely with the school to minimize the child's frustrations.

Adjusting to a New Culture

Parents who adopt older children from foreign countries are hindered in helping their child through the adjustment period by the language barrier. The first thing parents should do to reassure the child is to let him know that the family taking him home is the right family. This can be done through an interpreter or by using any photographs of the family that were sent to the child before his departure.

Language is the most obvious, but not the only cultural change the child must adjust to. The foreign-born child may be experiencing both new foods and an abundance of food, different ways of expressing affection, alternative forms of discipline, and new values. Parents whose child is reluctant to be kissed or hugged sometimes think the child has never experienced parental love or is rejecting theirs. In fact, the child may just be unfamiliar with such a direct method of expressing affection. There may be other cultural differences. For example, in the Philippines, forcing a child to make eye contact demeans him. In Korea, the younger person is submissive to the older, and the oldest child may expect his younger siblings to wait on him. Without an understanding of customs such as these, though, parents may find their child's avoidance of eye contact suspicious or think they have adopted a lazy child or bully who expects his siblings to do his bidding. Some children will not be accustomed to having pets in the house, and others may not be familiar with bearded men.

While many of us expect a child who has lived in an orphanage to be passive due to lack of stimulation, parents report that these children often have very effective "survival" instincts. Like street-wise children, they may be aggressive about taking food or hoard it when it is available. One parent found that instead of needing a security blanket when she went to sleep, her daughter needed to clutch a piece of bread. It may take many years for these children to learn that food will be readily available. In the meantime, parents should leave food on the table day and night so that the child learns it is always available. Parents may have to monitor their child's food intake by serving him instead of allowing him to heap food on his plate, and by watching for the stashing of food in unexpected places.

Children from foreign countries are unlikely to have had the quantities of material goods that Americans are accustomed to. In her excellent discussion of East-West cultural differences, *Oriental Children in American Homes: How Do They Adjust?,** Frances Koh notes that children brought up in a Confucian-dominated culture highly value material goods. These children may be strongly status-conscious, flaunting their belongings and hoarding money. Of course, such behavior can also reflect a history of poverty in a child of any culture. Children who have not owned much in the way of toys or clothing may not be experienced with either the concept of "possession" or of "sharing," and thus may not hesitate to take something they want.

We can ease the transition for our foreign-born children in several ways:

— Unless they are fluent in the child's native tongue, parents should have an interpreter available whom they can call on, even at odd hours, when sign language and a bilingual dictionary aren't enough to facilitate communication. While many parents believe the child's adjustment will be much easier the sooner he learns to speak English, there is no need to rush his assimilation of the language. It will come quickly and easily as he is immersed in the new culture. In the meantime, they should tolerate his need to express himself in the way that is most comfortable for him. It is difficult enough for an adoptee to express his feelings, but more so if he is expected to do so in a new language. (For more on the benefits of bilingualism, see Chapter 10.) Parents should have the interpreter tell the child why he is there—a child is sometimes anxious when he meets someone from his country of origin because he fears this person is going to take him back to their country.

— Have some identification on the child, perhaps an identification bracelet. An older child sometimes runs away during the adjustment period and when found by the police, the foreign-born child may not be able to say his name or where he lives.

— Become acquainted with the customs of the country the child is coming from. Frances Koh's book and Hyun Sook Han's booklet (cited earlier in this chapter) are excellent guides to the Asian culture. *Gamines: How to Adopt from Latin America,* * by Jean Nelson-Erichsen and Heino R. Erichsen, focuses more on the adoption process than on customs, but is one of the few available sources of information on Latin American adoptions. Pamphlets and information sheets on other countries are often available from the adoption agency placing the child, and travel guides available in any bookstore are other sources of information about different countries.

— Do not require the child to become Americanized overnight. She will abandon her original customs so quickly and so completely in an effort to fit in that her heritage will be virtually lost. There is no risk that allowing her to sleep on the floor, speak her own language, or eat familiar foods will hamper her adjustment. (This is discussed in more detail in Chapter 10.) On the other hand, parents should know what the child has been accustomed to. One family took their five-year-old Korean son to a Chinese restaurant on the way home from the airport. Each time he would pick up his fork to eat the rice they had ordered for him they would indicate that it was quite all right for him to eat with chopsticks. Years later, the boy told them that in preparation for adoption in the United States, the staff at the orphanage he had been at encouraged the children to use knives, spoons and forks. He did not know how to use chopsticks.

ADJUSTMENT OF SIBLINGS

How children react to an adopted sibling depends a lot on the age of the new member of the family and his age relative to the other children in the family, and on the reactions of other people to the child.

The greatest adjustment will need to be made by the child who is most displaced by the arrival of the new sibling, for example, the child who had been the youngest and now is a middle child, or the child who was the only boy in the family and now has a brother. The displaced child will probably have some behavior problems as a reaction to the new child's arrival—regressing or becoming aggressive. While the last thing parents think they need at this time is inappropriate behavior from a child they have come to expect good behavior from, it is really a healthy sign. Pediatrician Vera Fahlberg says the displaced child will only engage in "testing" kinds of behavior if he feels secure in his family. If he does not show signs of jealousy or other behavior problems, the parents may need to find out why he doesn't feel safe enough to let them know he is upset as a result of the new child's arrival.

We often expect exemplary behavior from the children already in the home when a new child arrives. Parents would like to be able to concentrate their energy on the new child and the changes they must make to accommodate the new child. They want the rest of their lives to be predictable, including the behavior of their other children. Adoptive parents are not sure they can control the behavior of the new child, so they may try to increase control in an area where they know they have it—the behavior of the children who have been in the family.

Siblings will want to know how the family has been changed by the addition of this child and, in particular, how their position in the family has been affected. So, they test the rules and test their parents. Rather than seeing this testing behavior as normal, adoptive parents may find their self-confidence shaken. The problem is exacerbated if the new child is having a difficult time adjusting to the new home. Parents shouldn't neglect the children already in the home in their efforts to smooth the transition for the new child.

Reactions to Infants

When an infant is adopted, the reaction of siblings is much the same as it would be to a child being born into the family, but adoptive parents who try to prepare their young children for the arrival of a new baby may find that many of the books written for that purpose are unsuitable. Most of them discuss the mother's pregnancy, show pictures of a pregnant woman, or talk about the baby "coming home from the hospital." There are good books that discuss the feelings of jealousy and displacement children feel when another child comes into the house. Although they do not specifically deal with adoption, they do not show a pregnant mother: *One Frog Too Many*, by Mercer Mayer and Marianna Mayer (New York: Dial Press, 1975), a wordless book about the arrival of another frog that could be interpreted in many fashions; *On Mother's Lap*, by Ann H. Scott (New York: McGraw-Hill, 1972), a book designed to show that mothers have room for more than one child; and *Peter's Chair*, by Ezra Jack Keats (New York: Harper & Row, 1967), a book that focuses on the feelings of the older child when a baby arrives. *On Mother's Lap* and *Peter's Chair* are also good choices for families trying to avoid books illustrated with all-white families. *The Chosen Baby** by Valentina P. Wasson shows a family adopting a second child, but focuses on the adoption process rather than the feelings of the child.

There is a chance that an adopted baby can receive more attention than a child being born into a family. If the waiting period is so long that parents become preoccupied with it, if the family has not adopted before and adoption is a novel thing for relatives and friends, or if the child is of a different race or ethnic background, she can receive more attention than she might otherwise. People may be especially interested in seeing a child from a foreign country because they are curious about the child's skin color, hair texture, and features. They may fuss more about a foreign-born child's appearance than they would about a baby that looks (to them) like every other wrinkled baby or spunky toddler. Or people may pay more attention to the child because they are looking for signs of mental or physical problems.

It is a good idea to take a present for an older child when taking a present to a family with a new baby, or otherwise recognize that the older child is likely to feel jealous of the attention paid to a new baby. It may be even more vital to remember the older children if the baby is likely to receive undue attention.

Reacting to an Older Child

How children react to an older child depends on the age of the child and his age relative to the children already in the home, and on whether the child has emotional or behavioral problems. The children already in the home need some frank talk about what to expect when the new child arrives. They may be expecting a playmate and be surprised to find the new sibling stealing from them and competing for the parents' attention. Adoption activist Laurie Flynn says agencies should prepare children for the arrival of an adopted sibling. Too often, though, the job is left to the adoptive parents who usually are not well suited for the task. Parents expecting the arrival of an older child may be anxious about how the adoption will affect their family and want everything to go well. Rather than wanting to discuss the ways the adoption may be unpleasant for the children they already have, parents may look to these children to affirm their decision to adopt an older child. They may minimize potential problems because they hope those problems won't come up.

Some agencies and parent groups have preparation sessions for children whose families are adopting an older or special needs child. There also are support groups for children who have a physically or mentally handicapped sibling, regardless of whether or not the sibling is adopted.

When the child being adopted has a history of serious behavior problems, particularly inappropriate sexual behavior, the other children in the home need some additional preparation. But parents are sometimes justifiably reluctant to violate the new child's privacy by revealing his history to other members of the family. The best way to handle the situation is to discuss in general terms what kinds of problems any child might have who has been in similar circumstances. Instead of saying, "Jack was sexually abused by his father and made sexual advances toward the children in his last foster home," parents can say, "Sometimes children have been sexually abused by older people. When this happens, they sometimes try to engage in sexual behavior with someone younger or smaller than they are. This is not okay, and if this should happen, you need to tell us immediately. You won't get into any trouble."

When the new child has serious behavior problems, children already in the home may be embarrassed to be related to him. They don't always share their feelings with their parents. Children who previously have been welcome in all their friends' homes and who have been able to invite their friends to their house may find their friends' parents are reluctant to let their children visit a house in which there is a child with a serious behavior problem. And these children may be embarrassed if the new sibling lies, steals or otherwise gets into trouble—particularly if it's at school. Parents or school counselors can help these children understand that they are separate persons from other family members and not responsible for someone else's actions. It may be more difficult to help their friends' parents understand that.

During the adjustment period, children may observe that their parents seem to be tolerating behavior in the new child that they know would not be tolerated if they engaged in it. A child who has learned that his parents will not tolerate his shoplifting even a candy bar may see them apparently overlooking more serious stealing in the new child. Children may not understand that equal punishment for equal transgressions may be inappropriate when one child has serious behavioral problems. They may not understand that their parents may be pleased that the new child is doing less stealing than he was in his previous home, but only see that mom and dad would punish them severely if they were stealing at all. The lesson parents need to transmit to their children at these times is that life is not always fair. They can explain to their children that they have certain expectations of their behavior that may be different for each of them, just as they may expect one child to get straight A's but be happy that another one gets all C's, because each is performing to the best of his or her abilities. The problems that develop when each child is not treated the same are not limited to the adjustment period, but may be ongoing.

This is one of the most difficult dilemmas for families adopting children with behavior problems. Parents worry that if the new child is punished differently than are the other children, that the other children will think that standards have relaxed—that they can now "get away with" stealing or truancy. We must have some confidence that the values we are transmitting to our children will withstand some trial. Parents may see the normal testing behavior that children engage in when a new child arrives as an indication that the behavior of the new child is becoming a poor influence on their other children. Parents may need some professional assistance at this time, if they are not already involved in therapy. A therapist or the family's social worker can help parents decide whether the children who have been in the home are testing them to see how the family has been changed by the arrival of a new child, or if their behavior represents a more serious problem. One of the reasons placements of older children disrupt is that the parents perceive the child as having an undesirable influence on other children in the home.

ADJUSTMENT OF RELATIVES

The adjustment of an adopted child and the long-term adjustment of the family is affected by the level of acceptance and support given to the family by relatives and friends at the time of the adoption. Too often, though, adoptive parents expect their friends and relatives to give unconditional approval of the adoption without realizing that they too may need information about adoption. Not all couples share with their families the problems they are having conceiving a child or their reasons for considering the adoption of a foreign-born or special needs child. They forget that their relatives may have some of the same doubts, grief, and questions that they themselves had before deciding that adoption was the right choice for them. As a result, instead of giving the parents a wholehearted endorsement of their plans, the extended family may be resistant.

Accepting Adoption

Though most relatives eventually accept adoption, their initial reaction is not always favorable, perhaps because they have little experience with adoption. If they think adoptees do not love and respect their adoptive parents the way they would their biologic parents, the extended family may worry that the adoptive parents will be disappointed.

Sociologists William Feigelman and Arnold Silverman found that the more the child being adopted resembles a child the parents would have given birth to, the more accepting friends and family members initially are. Infertile couples who adopt infants of the same race receive the most support, while those who adopt older children, children of a different ethnic background, or special needs children receive less support—especially if they are able to have biologic children. Among those adopting transracially, people adopting Colombian babies receive about the same amount of support as those adopting Caucasian babies from the United States. The adoption of Asian children receives somewhat less support, and the adoption of older black children meets the greatest resistance.

Resistance diminishes as family members and friends get to know the child and see that despite the racial or ethnic differences, the family attachments are "real." Nevertheless, the initial reaction is important to the short-term and long-term adjustment of the family, and the more support adoptive parents receive, the smoother the adoption goes. Researchers at Rutgers University found that parents of transracially placed infants are often reluctant to leave their child in someone else's care, perhaps because they perceive a lack of support from friends or relatives. As a result, they may not take much time away from their child, though they may need rest from parenting as much or more than other adoptive parents.

Although relatives usually accept the adoption eventually, the initial lack of support continues to affect the family. Having gone through the initial adjustment period without the help of family and friends, parents may get used to being self-reliant and not turn to their relatives or friends even after they have accepted the adoption.

Adoptive parents should remember that while adoption may be meeting our needs, it may not be meeting the needs of our extended family. We want to love and nurture a child, and so adopt; but perhaps our aging grandparents want to know their genetic line will be continued after their deaths. Perhaps our children are grown and we want to extend our parenting roles by adopting special needs children; our parents feel their need for grandchildren to dote on has been met, and don't understand why we want to take on more work at a time when we could be taking life easier. Maybe the extended family has not had much contact with disabled people or people of different races and isn't sure how to act around them. They may need time to get used to the idea of infertility, adoption, or transracial families. They may also need a neutral forum where they can ask questions, express their doubts, and obtain information without it interfering with their relationship with the adoptive family.

We can help our families accept adoption in the following ways:

— Introduce the idea gradually instead of springing it on the family as a decision that has been made and that they must accept unquestioningly.

— Give them an opportunity to get information they need. Many adoption agencies and adoptive parent groups are recognizing the need for relatives and friends of adoptive families to become educated about adoption and so provide information sessions or invitations to attend adoption meetings geared to prospective parents. Relatives can then ask questions of a social worker or other adoptive parent that they might be hesitant to ask a family member.

— Provide them with an opportunity to see other adoptive families. Once relatives see that adopted children treat their parents the same way that biologic children treat their parents, many of their fears are assuaged.

— Provide them with an ongoing source of support and information. Holt Children's Services has formed an organization, The Loving Circle,* specifically for extended family members. They receive the agency's magazine as well as a newsletter written specifically for them. A subscription to *OURS Magazine*, *Adopted Child* newsletter, or whatever publication parents have found to be particularly insightful could be sent to extended family members. "Supporting an Adoption"* by Pat Holmes is an excellent booklet for relatives.

— If, despite having an opportunity to become educated about adoption, relatives still seem resistant, parents should initiate a candid discussion about the subject. Parents could be misreading their relatives' intentions, or there could still be some reluctance to accept the adoption that needs to be discussed.

— Forgive relatives for any insensitive remarks they made while they got used to the idea of adoption. Adoptive parents forget that there was a time when they, too, may have had doubts about adoption, told racist jokes, or thought there was no choice but to conceive a child. Relatives who ultimately accept the idea of adoption and embrace the adoptee as a complete family member should not be held accountable forever for earlier remarks.

— Finally, encourage contact between relatives and the adoptees as early as possible. Just because the adoptive mother is not recovering physically from a pregnancy does not mean she doesn't need help with the care of a new baby. And while it is not a good idea to overwhelm an older child with visits or gifts from relatives immediately after his arrival, some marking of his arrival should be made—a special gift, photograph, or family keepsake could be given to him. A visit can follow as soon as the family regains its equilibrium.

If parents find they cannot count on their friends and relatives for the support they need, they should not hesitate to set up a new support system, perhaps turning to an adoptive parent group. (For information on the nearest parent support group, contact the North American Council on Adoptable Children.*)

A Sense of "Clan"

In addition to giving the adoptive family needed support, extended family members have to remember that their relationship with the adoptee cannot be taken for granted. While adoption gives them a legal tie, there is not the biologic tie that usually bridges generations. The adoptee thinks of his adoptive parents as his parents because they raise him, but isn't always sure of his relationship to people who are referred to in terms such as "forebears," "kin," and "clan." As he grows up, particularly after his adoptive parents die, he may wonder whether he is an authentic member of the "clan."

Adoptees and their extended family members can and do develop deep, warm relationships, but they must be based on meaningful human interaction, and not on an assumption of kinship. Certainly there are biologic families in which grandchildren and grandparents are strangers because of geographical distance or other circumstances characteristic of today's families. But if the child does not know his grandparents well, at least he knows there is a connection—he's been told that he gets his determination from his "pioneer stock," or feels an obligation to show his Irish heritage by wearing green on St. Patrick's Day. The adoptee who doesn't know his extended adoptive family well has only a legal document—to which both the adoptee and the relatives were passive participants—to bind him to them.

It is important, then, for extended family members to make an effort to develop strong relationships with the adoptee. Parents and relatives should make sure the adoptee knows who comprises her extended adoptive family. One study of Scottish adoptees who were searching for information about their biologic families found that some were interested in their biologic origins because they did not have information about either their adoptive or biologic genealogy. One adoptee's family made her a book with a page for each extended family member containing a photograph of the person and a drawing of him or her doing a typical activity. The words on the page indicate the relationship between the adoptee and the person shown, and tell something about him or her. Especially nice is the theme running through the whole book: This is your family and all these people love you.

Extended family members should also be encouraged to write, make telephone calls if affordable, and send small gifts to the adoptee, especially if they don't see each other often. Children are easy to please. An interesting picture from the newspaper, wildlife or other stamps that are sent to every mailbox, or an inexpensive sticker or balloon are treasures to a child. Older children could be sent magazine or newspaper clippings on a topic that interests them. An inexpensive tape recorder can record stories about grandparents and great-grandparents, or best of all, stories about the adoptee's parents when they were little. Relatives can also read a children's book from the library into a cassette for a personalized present. These all show the child that his relatives care enough about him to do something special for him.

Although the adoptee and his extended family members do not share a heritage, they can build their own traditions. Relatives can try to develop particular activities to share so that Uncle Ralph becomes the uncle who always took the child swimming, and Grandpa is remembered for sharing his record collection. Eda LeShan's book, *Grandparents: A Special Kind of Love* (New York: Macmillan Publishing Co., 1984), helps children understand their grandparents, including problems such as senility. *How to Grandparent*, by Fitzhugh Dodson (New York: Harper & Row, 1981), is aimed at helping grandparents understand children and build relationships with them.

Chapter 3

Bonding and Attachment

My friend Julie was clearly exhausted from four consecutive nights with little sleep. Her newly arrived Filipino daughter had her days and nights mixed up, and Julie and her husband had been taking turns walking the floors with her.

"This can't go on much longer," she said to me.

I nodded. "It's even more difficult when you don't love her yet, isn't it?" I asked.

Julie looked at me in amazement. "I'm glad you said that," she said quietly, "I was beginning to think there was something wrong with me."

Julie and her husband lost many hours of sleep while their daughter adjusted to her new surroundings, but in the process she learned to depend on them, and they received satisfaction from meeting her needs. This grew into what is now a strong attachment between them.

ADOPTIVE FAMILIES DO FORM ATTACHMENTS

People do not adopt unless they believe they can love a child that was not born to them. Although love for a biologic child is the same as love for an adopted child, the attachment between a child and her adoptive parent develops under different circumstances than the attachment between a child and her biologic parent. But some theories of how bonding and attachment develop between a child and a biologic parent have raised doubts about whether adoptive parents and their children can form relationships that are as deep and secure.

Current child care manuals emphasize activities during pregnancy and birth as contributing to the "bonding" of mother and baby. This philosophy grew out of research published in the 1970s indicating that early contact between parent and baby was essential to the formation of a bond between parent and child.

Obstetrical practices were altered to allow fathers an active role in the baby's delivery. Hospital environments changed to allow babies to stay with their mothers and breast-feed immediately. Parents began to think that natural childbirth, rooming-in, and breast-feeding were essential for bonding. They believed that if these practices were used, then bonding would be virtually accomplished before the mother went home from the hospital.

All this has not been lost on the adoptive parent. Intellectually we know that natural childbirth, rooming-in, and breast-feeding are helpful, but not necessary for bonding. Still, we're anxious to form an attachment with our children as soon as possible so that we can dismiss our own doubts and those of our in-laws and friends.

Fortunately, there is now evidence of what adoptive families have known all along, namely that adoptive parents and their children bond, or form attachments, as successfully as biologic families. Researchers at Rutgers University and Yeshiva University found no difference between the development of attachments between mothers and infants when non-adoptive families were compared to adoptive families in which parents and child were of the same race. Nor was there any difference between adoptive families of the same race and interracial adoptive families. Interracially adopted infants were more anxious than non-adopted infants, but the researchers suggest that parents who adopt a child of a different race may need more time to feel comfortable with a child who looks remarkably different. These researchers conclude that adoptive families—even those adopting interracially—can be optimistic about the development of warm, secure parent–child attachments. Rather than needing immediate contact after birth to make this attachment, parents need confidence in their ability to take care of the child, and a warm, consistent atmosphere of caretaking that is based on the needs of the infant.

Early contact between parent and child can get attachment off to a good start, but experts on infant care are discouraging parents from thinking of bonding as something that happens instantaneously. The fact is, it often takes time before biologic or adoptive parents feel their child is an irreplaceable part of their lives; it takes time for the child to think of her parents as special people who are not interchangeable with any others.

BONDING AND ATTACHMENT

Although we often talk about the development of love between parent and child as "bonding," those who have studied the phenomenon differentiate between "bonding" and "attachment."

Bonding, as Frank G. Bolton, Jr. explains in *When Bonding Fails,* * is a unidirectional process that begins in the biologic parent—primarily the mother—during pregnancy and continues through birth and the first few days of life. It is the parent's instinctive desire to protect the infant.

Attachment takes more time and more interaction between parent and child. It is a reciprocal process between parent and child that develops during the first year they are together and is solidified throughout the relationship. It is the development of a mutual feeling that the other is irreplaceable.

Given these definitions, what most of us are talking about when we refer to "bonding" is actually "attachment." In fact, some people question whether the attachment behavior that humans engage in can be compared to the instinctive "bonding" activities of animals.

There may be some attachment taking place in the adoptive family prior to the arrival of the child. Many parents report feeling a closeness based on the photograph they have of their child and mourn if that child can't be placed with them for some reason. But in both the adoptive and biologic family, the feeling of attachment between parents and child develops after the child arrives.

WELCOMING THE CHILD

A positive experience at the time of placement is not necessary for attachment to develop in the adoptive family, but it can get the relationship off to a good start.

In open adoptions, adoptive parents often meet the biologic mother prior to the birth of the child and sometimes attend the birth or even act as the mother's childbirth "coach." This can be not only a special time that the adoptive parents and child have shared, but can make adoptive parents feel they were involved in their child's birth.

More often, however, placement of the child takes place at a public place—an agency, airport, hospital, or lawyer's office. This should be a private time for the family. Parents should have some place where they can hold the child, examine her, shed tears, and welcome her into their lives. They should not have to be concerned about whether the lawyer has another client waiting or the social worker is going to need her office back.

When our daughter arrived, we left for the airport without our camera. As we stood at the gate holding her for the first time, a businessman waiting for a plane approached us. He had a Polaroid camera in his briefcase and offered to take a photo for us. It is that stranger's acknowledgment that this was a special event that I remember when I think of our first meeting with Emily.

Airports cannot be designed for the convenience of adoptive families, and legal papers need to be signed. But in the absence of some kind of formal ceremony at the time of placement, some families are developing their own welcoming events. They invite friends and family to their home, or perhaps to their church, and formally acknowledge the arrival of their new family member, taking care not to overwhelm the new child with too many new people and situations too soon.

ATTACHMENT TO AN INFANT

Attachment between parents and child develops as the child learns that she can count on her parents to meet her physical and emotional needs. We as parents learn to take pleasure in subordinating ourselves to the needs of our children.

This process is the same whether the child has been born to us or is adopted.

A newborn's initial needs are for food and physical comfort. He can't begin to relate to people until he has the security that these needs will be met. A baby comes well-equipped to make people take care of him. With his large head, big eyes, soft skin, puffy cheeks, and short limbs, he looks helpless. Parents, especially adoptive parents who have waited a long time for a baby, respond because they want to be needed.

Reciprocal Relationship

At about three months of age, the child begins to relate to people and starts to develop a reciprocal relationship with her primary caretaker, usually her mother. She learns that if she smiles, mother smiles back. If she makes silly gurgling sounds, father does, too. If she cries, a parent comes running. By this age, she recognizes her primary caretaker and prefers that person to someone else. It is important for parents to be playful. The "coochie-coochie-coos" that embarrass some adults are an important way of interacting with a child.

The adoptive parent should be cautious about overstimulating the infant. We are often so anxious to be "good parents" that we overreact to the baby's signals and create anxiety rather than security in the infant. This is especially likely to happen when the baby has been abused or neglected and the parent is trying to compensate for the child's unpleasant experience.

Babies may respond to such intensity by withdrawing. The adoptive parent who misinterprets the baby's need for rest as rejection may try even harder to communicate with the baby, prompting even more withdrawal. Babies are made to tell us what they need; all we need to do is be open to the cues the child is giving us.

Gradually the baby learns it is not a coincidence that when he smiles, mom does too. He discovers he can make the grown-up do something for him. His actions begin to be intentional.

The first person whom the infant knows he can influence in this way takes on great importance to him. He is sure he can make his mother do something. He's not that sure about others. As a result, he gets upset when he and his mother are separated.

Separation anxiety is determined by the attachment process and not the child's age. Most child care manuals say an infant will fuss when she is left at about six months of age. That will be true for an adopted infant if she was placed at birth. Our children arrived at about seven months of age. They did not begin to show separation anxiety when I left them until they were perhaps a year old and the attachment process had progressed to the point where I mattered to them more than someone else. I remember a friend reaching for my eight-month-old daughter, and then drawing back to ask, "Does she go to strangers?"

"Of course," I answered. "She's living with strangers."

Exploring the World

Gradually (in the second six months of life for an infant who has been with her caretaker since birth), the baby feels more confident of her ability to make her parent do things, and begins to test other people. When she finds she can influence other people as well, she begins to feel powerful, and her dependence on her parent tapers off. The baby continues to test the degree to which she can make others do what she wants until she is about three years old. At times of stress, however, she will still turn to the person with whom she first felt safe.

The infant who formed an attachment to her biologic or foster parents prior to being placed may look for that person in times of stress. This doesn't mean she is rejecting her adoptive parents. In time, she will come to recognize them as her primary caretakers. Searching can be a good sign; the child who has been able to form attachments in the past will form new attachments more easily than the child who has never felt an attachment.

We must allow our children the opportunity to make attachments to other people, including those outside the family. These do not diminish their attachment to us, but demonstrate that they feel secure enough to try to test the rest of their world. A parent who thinks he or she is the only person capable of properly caring for a child or playing with her is fostering dependency, not attachment.

Ways of Interacting

Feeding, smiling, eye contact, and body contact are all ways that infants and their parents interact. Through these reciprocal activities, the child learns that he can affect other people, even though they may be bigger and stronger than he is.

Eye contact is a good way to communicate with a baby who cannot yet send verbal messages. Eye contact stimulates other interaction between parent and child. Few parents can look into their baby's eyes for very long without stroking the baby's cheek or picking the baby up. And when the parent moves away, chances are the baby will follow her with his eyes. It is a simple action, but it tells the parent she is important enough that the baby will want to see where she's going.

Very often eye contact between parent and baby will lead to an exchange of smiles. The smile is another small but powerful means of communication. A smile from the baby in the morning erases a lot of the resentment that parents may feel because the baby kept them walking the floors all night.

Cuddling, stroking, kissing, and other means of bodily contact are also ways of enhancing the attachment process. Positive messages are transmitted back and forth. Of course, not all children or all parents are cuddlers. Alex came from a foster home where there were several children. When his adoptive mother held him, he did not put his arms around her or put his head on her shoulder. His arms flailed about him. He has never been able to sit on his mother's lap for long periods of time, or snuggle in bed. However, they hug, hold hands, and sit close while reading books.

When a parent or child finds touching of any kind objectionable, a powerful message of rejection is sent. Professional help is needed to deal with this situation if it arises. In most cases, however, parents and child find physical contact pleasurable.

When a parent feeds a baby he is doing more than letting her know that when she's hungry she'll get what she wants. He is usually touching and having eye contact with the child as well. Parents who feed the baby according to their schedule rather than the child's needs, or who remove the bottle before a baby is finished nursing, are communicating that the child can't depend on them.

Length of Time for Attachment

It is not possible to predict how long it will take to feel that a child is irreplaceable. It may take weeks, months, or a year or longer. The mother and father probably won't form an attachment with the child at the same rate or in the same way. A child may take less or more time than the parents to feel they are essential. A parent should not feel a need to rush the attachment process, nor feel like a failure if it takes more time than expected. The important thing is that parent and child do develop an attachment, not how long it takes to do so.

A child's responsiveness to a parent and the parent's confidence in recognizing the child's needs are a good measure of successful attachment. Another sign of a secure attachment is the child's willingness to move away from the parent, returning to the parent during times of stress to regain the confidence she needs to be on her own again. Similarly, a parent's willingness to let go—to be enthusiastic about a child forming close relationships to others in the family or outside the family—is a sign that the parent feels the relationship is strong. Attachment is a never-ending process—parent and child will continue reinforcing the attachment that began in infancy throughout their lives.

BREAST-FEEDING THE ADOPTED BABY

Breast-feeding is one way to use feeding time to become close to a baby. Because the baby's sucking at the breast is the primary stimulation for lactation, or the secretion of milk, breast milk can be produced without a pregnancy.

While it is possible to breast-feed an adopted infant, breast-feeding is not the right decision for every mother and baby. Before making a commitment to breast-feed an infant, parents should consider the advantages and disadvantages and their motives for wanting to do so.

Some social workers are suspicious of adoptive mothers who indicate an interest in breast-feeding. They consider such interest an indication that the woman is trying to pretend she gave birth to the child. The vast majority of women are not trying to simulate a biologic experience by breast-feeding an adopted infant. Those who are probably show other signs of unresolved infertility such as unwillingness to openly discuss adoption. When that's the problem, the adoption might be better off postponed until the infertility issue has been resolved.

The woman who considers breast-feeding her baby is very likely trying to minimize the disadvantages to her child of being separated from her birth-mother. Today's child care manuals say breast milk is the best substance to feed a baby. They say nursing is the best way to form an attachment to a baby. (Some incorrectly imply that it's the only way.) Given this advice, some adoptive mothers may feel they are second-rate mothers if they feed their children the "second-best" choice of food—formula, and they may feel pressured to speed up the attachment process.

Nutritional Benefits

Breast-feeding an adopted child for nutritional reasons may be one of the poorest reasons for nursing. Adoptive mothers who breast-feed usually provide only 25 to 75 percent of their infants' nutritional needs. The average is about 50 percent. In one study, most adoptive mothers had to use supplements for the entire time the infants nursed. More than a third needed to feed at least two bottles of formula a day.

Because the composition of adoptive mothers' breast milk is slightly different than that of biologic mothers, the premature baby should not be breast-fed. The milk of women who have stimulated milk production without a pregnancy lacks colostrum—a protein and antibody-rich substance found in the first milk of biologic mothers. The first milk of adoptive mothers is comparable to the milk produced by biologic mothers after about ten days—it has a lower level of protein and a higher concentration of water than colostrum.

Babies will compensate for the lower concentration of protein by drinking more milk. However, some infants, especially premature babies, will not be able to tolerate the additional quantities of milk they have to drink to obtain enough protein. They may "spit up" or vomit after feeding. Formula-feeding is preferable in those cases.

Emotional Benefits

The foster mother of Pam's two-month-old baby neglected to tell her that she had been breast-feeding the infant. Pam struggled with the distraught child who guzzled bottles of formula, but remained dissatisfied. She was well nourished, but clearly missed the emotional benefits of nursing. It took nearly a year for the baby to adjust to that emotional loss and develop a strong attachment with her new mother.

Most adoptive mothers who want to breast-feed are trying to enhance the mother-child relationship. I remember holding my daughter one day and thinking that if I were breast-feeding her, I would be able to hold her even closer.

The closeness that develops during breast-feeding is realized regardless of the amount of milk produced. Of course, if the infant is getting so little milk that she is frustrated, or if mother feels she is a failure because she isn't producing vast quantities of milk, breast-feeding is unlikely to be a positive experience.

Adoptive mothers should breast-feed if they want to, but not because they think they will be depriving their child of first-class care if they don't. Formula still provides infants with a highly nutritious diet. And breast-feeding is only one of many ways to form an attachment with a child. What is more important to the development of a close relationship with a baby is not whether the infant is breast-fed or bottle-fed, but whether the mother is comfortable with her choice. The mother–child relationship is unlikely to be enhanced if the baby is being breast-fed out of a sense of duty rather than desire.

How to Breast-Feed an Adopted Infant

A mother who decides to breast-feed her adopted infant will not need injections of hormones or other drugs. She will need to prepare for the demands of a breast-feeding infant through proper diet, exercise, and rest. Pregnant women are constantly reminded to eat right and get enough exercise; and people understand when they say they need a nap. It may be difficult for the expecting adoptive mother to treat her body as though she were pregnant, or get the support she needs to do so. But this is necessary to meet the physical demands of nursing.

Milk is produced in women by the baby's sucking at the breast. Lactation is not immediate; it takes time for the stimulated breasts to produce milk. Babies are unlikely to keep sucking at a breast when hungry if they are not receiving any milk. Adoptive mothers can either manually stimulate their breasts prior to the arrival of the child, so that milk already is being produced when baby begins to suckle, or they can use a nursing trainer that provides the baby with milk from an external source while she sucks at the breast.

Breasts can be manually stimulated either by expressing milk from the breast by hand or by using a breast pump a few times each day. Two to six weeks of frequent stimulation is necessary to produce milk. This method is impractical in most adoptive situations, though. Adoptive mothers seldom know exactly when their infant is due to arrive, and because delays in even an expected arrival are not uncommon, this method is not recommended. A woman may be willing to rearrange her life to accommodate the nursing schedule of a demanding infant once that baby is in her arms, but she will probably find that sitting down with a breast pump several times a day in anticipation of the baby's arrival only increases the anxiety that adoptive parents feel during that waiting period.

The Lact-Aid® Nursing Trainer™ System* is a more practical way to accomplish lactation. Lact-Aid is a device developed for women who want to breast-feed an adopted infant. A presterilized bag that can contain up to four ounces of milk is attached to a nine-inch flexible tube about the width of a strand of spaghetti. The mother attaches the bag to her bra or hangs it around her neck, and positions the tube next to her nipple. As the baby suckles at the breast, she receives milk from the Lact-Aid bag, so she keeps suckling, which eventually causes the mother to produce milk. The disadvantage of the nursing trainers is that it makes the uncomplicated act of breast-feeding decidedly more difficult, and any plastic bag filled with liquid could leak.

Elizabeth Hormann, an authority on breast-feeding adopted infants, says adoptive mothers should use nursing first to pacify infants rather than feed them. Assuming the baby is on a four-hour feeding schedule, Hormann says to give her formula first, then the breast. Two hours later, just offer her the breast. In another two hours, formula again followed by the breast. It is a good idea to nurse the baby to sleep, as she will be less resistant when she is tired.

Adoptive mothers should not feel personally rejected if the baby refuses the breast at first, or even after several valiant attempts. Biologic mothers often have difficulty getting their babies to suck properly. Infants are conservative creatures who resist change, and those who have been bottle-fed may not want to work as hard as they have to for breast milk. The younger the baby is, the easier it will be for her to make the transition. Infants older than eight weeks are as likely to reject as accept the breast. La Leche League members can provide emotional support and technical advice to adoptive mothers who want to breast-feed.

It is important for an infertile woman who wanted a pregnancy but was unable to achieve it not to attach too much importance to her success at nursing. She shouldn't feel like a failure as a mother if her baby refuses the breast, or if she does not produce large quantities of milk. The goal is a healthy, well-nourished infant, secure in the love of her new parents, not milk production.

ATTACHMENT TO AN OLDER CHILD

The older the child being adopted, the more intensified are the parents' concerns about forming an attachment with him. As they grow, children's personalities, habits, likes, and dislikes become more established. Parents understandably worry about whether they will even like the child, much less love him. One mother said, "What worried me more than anything else about adoption was that I might get a child and just not like him. So I felt I had to get a kind of 'bonding' feeling with a picture of a waiting child. I needed some kind of immediate attraction to the child that would make me stop turning the pages of the adoption exchange book and think, 'Oh, I've got to check on that child.' "

An additional concern about the adoption of a child who was not placed at birth is the child's possible history of abuse or neglect that could make him wary of physical contact and new attachments.

The process of attachment between a parent and an older child is similar to infant attachment, but with a few twists.

The infant first learns to depend on a particular adult to meet her physical needs. Then she learns that she can make this adult smile or stop what she's doing to play with her. At that point, the attachment becomes reciprocal. A baby toddles over to her mom, who is reading the newspaper, holds out her arms and says, "Up, up, up." Mom somewhat reluctantly puts down the newspaper, lifts baby up, and is rewarded with a hug or a smile, making the interruption worthwhile.

This is significant because parents often expect the older child to be at a later stage in the attachment process when she arrives. They don't expect they will have to prove to her that there will always be a meal on the table at the appropriate time. They expect her to have more patience in her demands than a two-year-old who stands next to mom screaming, "Up, up, up," until she finally puts the newspaper down. They expect that the same kinds of activities that would reinforce the attachment between a parent and a biologic seven-year-old can be used to develop an attachment with the seven-year-old adoptee joining the family.

Initially, that seems to be the case. Older children typically go through a "honeymoon" period immediately after placement. Their behavior is appropriate, they seem to be accepting of their adoptive parents and siblings, and they may be responsive and responsible.

When attachment begins to develop, the honeymoon period is replaced by what is sometimes called the "testing" period. During this time, the child begins to behave in ways that threaten the developing relationship.

Attachment Ambivalence

The older child at the testing stage of attachment has some ambivalence about the close feelings she is experiencing. All her past relationships with adults have ended in separation; she may be worried that this one will too, and try to end it before she gets too close. At the same time, she is drawn to the parent. Sometimes this period is explained as a time when the child tests the parent to see if she's accepted as a family member only if she behaves well, or if she can be "bad" too. She wants to be a family member, but wants to find out how far she can go in her behavior.

The child may try to put distance between herself and the parent. This includes using abusive language, lying, fighting, refusing to make eye contact, or acting too grown-up for her age. The same child also may cling, whine, have difficulty eating and sleeping, and regress in toilet habits. For the parent, this is as frustrating as the lying and fighting. But while lying and abusive language are ways to push the parent away, clinging and whining are designed to draw the parent closer.

For example, a mother might think she has a serious problem if she discovers her child taking small items that the child couldn't even use, such as an earring, to school. The child isn't stealing. She is trying to take a part of her mother with her to school. Her actions are not much different from the toddler who has to take her favorite blanket with her to the day-care center.

Psychologist Terrence Koller says the older child often acts like a young child in the early stages of attachment. Whining, clinging, and baby-like behavior are acceptable ways for an infant to draw mother closer. They have the opposite effect for a seven-year-old, especially when combined with "disengaging" behavior like refusal to make eye contact.

We need to remember that a school-age adoptee can regress physically, emotionally, and morally. We don't expect a toddler to keep her pants dry, to go to bed without a fuss, or to know that it is wrong to take objects from mother's dresser drawer. We expect a seven-year-old to know these things. But the recently placed seven-year-old may behave like the toddler because that's where she is in relation to the family—she's not an infant in age, but she is an infant in the family.

It helps to learn to distinguish between behavior that is clearly designed to push parents away and that which attempts to bring them closer, and to respond as though the child was much younger, by allowing the seven-year-old to suck her thumb or ask for a drink of water three times a night.

The difference between "come close" and "go away" behavior is not always easy to see, especially when the child is doing both at once. A parent needs to look hard for the signals that the child wants to be close, and may have to find creative ways to meet the child's needs, especially for physical contact. The twelve-year-old who seems to be defiantly resisting instructions to go to bed may want to be rocked to sleep as an infant would. She may allow her parent to do so. However, she also may resist being treated "like a baby." Another way of giving her the comfort and physical contact she needs at that time may have to be found.

Attachment Following Arousal

Pediatrician Vera Fahlberg, who works with children at a Colorado psychiatric facility, suggests that children are most open to attachment after a period of high arousal. She believes children go through cycles of high arousal brought on by some physical or psychological need. Once that need is satisfied, a period of relaxation follows. During that time, the child is open to attachment. The calm period following a child's temper tantrum is one time when the child may be open to attachment, but parents may be inclined to want to leave him alone while they rid themselves of their own anger. Ironically, that may be a good time for a hug.

Seeing a child through an illness or injury also can enhance closeness. The child's defenses are down and he learns he can count on someone in times of stress.

As with an infant, parents should interact with the older child in a playful way, even playing baby games such as "patty-cake." It may be difficult to look on a child's sudden inability to control his bladder as a hopeful sign. But it is. He's letting his parents treat him as a baby so that their attachment can grow.

This testing stage is difficult. However, it may help to realize that much of the behavior that is making life chaotic is a sign that there is a future together as a family.

THE UNATTACHED CHILD

The attachment of parents and child does more than give the family a warm and fuzzy feeling—it creates order. The unattached child is a child who doesn't care what people think, and therefore one who can do as he pleases. Obviously, this can make life with the unattached child chaotic and even dangerous.

While there are many causes of learning problems, adoption specialist Josephine Anderson says both learning disabilities and conduct disorders can be signs of an unattached child.

The child may have a hard time differentiating between the present and the past, and therefore can't see how doing well now will help him in the future. He may not even be able to think in terms of a future. It is not unusual for the unattached child to have poor impulse control or a short attention span.

The child with a conduct disorder exhibits sociopathic behavior. He has no conscience and shows no remorse. If he doesn't care about anyone, there is little to keep him from hurting someone or to make him feel sorry when he does. Most of us can remember doing something wrong and seeing the disappointed or hurt look on our parents' faces. Such looks have no effect on the unattached child. He doesn't care about his parents, so why should he care if he lets them down?

Sometimes the unattached child demands excessive displays of affection, but fails to reciprocate. He has no concept of "proper" behavior, so he may behave inappropriately in social situations, such as opening all the presents at someone else's birthday party. He has a lack of regard for rules, so he doesn't comply with them, and sees no need to submit to punishment for breaking them.

The unattached child frequently will avoid making eye contact. With eye contact, he loses the distance he has put between himself and his parents. In losing distance, he loses control of the situation.

Parenting techniques based on making a child feel appropriately guilty for breaking rules will not work with the child who doesn't care. Methods for dealing with the unattached child are discussed in Chapter 11.

Just because the child doesn't attach to the parent doesn't mean the parent won't care about the child. Friends and relatives may encourage parents to "disrupt" the adoption—return the child to the agency. This is certainly an option that parents and their caseworker should discuss before taking any action. However, it is not unusual for parents to feel so committed to the child that they want to raise him regardless of his behavior. If that is the case, therapy to help him form an attachment is recommended. Failing that, professional help to cope with living with an unattached child is indicated.

The Lifelong Process of Becoming a Family

We don't need to be in a hurry to form an attachment; we should enjoy the process, have fun with the child, and build up a reservoir of pleasant experiences to draw on when there is friction in the family. We must try to identify and meet the child's needs without hovering over her. Especially with an older child who demonstrates her growing closeness in seemingly negative ways, parents have to learn to recognize signs of attachment and gather strength from them.

Part II

At Home with Adoption

Chapter 4

Talking with Children About Adoption

Years ago, adoptees were often kept in the dark about their adoption indefinitely, or were not told until they had discovered the fact themselves. Later, parents were told to tell their children sooner that they were adopted, but not to tell them much beyond what they asked. The child who asked no questions about his adoption was thought to be well-adjusted, while the inquiring child was thought to have problems. Today we know that many adoptees are reluctant to initiate a discussion of adoption with their adoptive parents. Many keep their questions to themselves, which can lead to fantasizing and even magical thinking—a belief that thinking about something can make it happen. We know now that discussions of adoption should be open and ongoing, and even be initiated by parents in some circumstances.

Parents sometimes wonder when they should tell their child he is adopted. That sounds as though talking about adoption is a one-time event with the parent doing the talking and the child doing the listening. It is more appropriate to question when to "start talking with" a child about his adoption—when to begin a dialogue about being adopted that will continue throughout the life of the adoptee.

Adoptee Betty Jean Lifton writes in *Lost and Found** about adoptive parents who try to find the "right" age to tell a child about his adoption, as though picking the proper moment will eliminate the doubts, fears, questions, and fantasies adoptees grow up with. Instead of worrying about the proper time to start talking about adoption, parents should be concerned about setting the right tone. Then when the doubts, fears, questions, and fantasies arise, the child will feel free to discuss them with his parents. No one can say when the timing will be right with one particular child; no one can give parents the right words to say. But we need to feel at ease with adoption so we will be prepared not only to answer questions, but to anticipate them and communicate our willingness to discuss our child's concerns. Before talking with our children about adoption, we should make sure we're ready to talk about issues such as infertility and why birthparents place children for adoption. To prepare ourselves, we can read about the experiences of adoptees and talk to our spouses and other adoptive parents. Unless we feel comfortable talking about adoption, the adoptee may be reluctant to talk with us again about adoption issues, or worse, may conclude that the reason there is tension during discussion is because adoption is something bad.

STARTING TO TALK ABOUT ADOPTION

Each of Kristy and Dan's children has a book that was made for them before they arrived. It tells the story of why each child was wanted, why the child needed a home, the process Dan and Kristy went through to adopt the child, and their first meeting. The pictures are simple but recognizable as their house, their family, and their dog. The text is brief enough for a preschooler; the pages—plastic-covered cardboard designed for holding photographs—are durable enough for toddlers. They began reading the stories of how their family was formed long before their children were able to understand what the stories meant. At first, the children just enjoyed seeing pictures of people and things they knew. Gradually the stories took on meaning and led to more detailed discussions of their adoptions.

Kristy and Dan are among those who believe in letting children hear the term "adopted" long before they can understand what it means. They believe that if "adoption" is part of the children's vocabulary from their earliest memories, their children will not be shocked when they realize they are adopted—it will be something they have always known, although the full meaning had yet to be revealed. Furthermore, there is no risk that the child will hear about his adoption first from someone other than his parents or in anything but a loving atmosphere. One of the best reasons to tell children from the very beginning that they are adopted is that it is honest. Delaying the adoption revelation for five to seven years almost inevitably will involve some deception that could work against the parent–child relationship.

This "early telling" theory is the prevailing philosophy on adoption revelation, but not everyone agrees with it. Some experts believe that the child should not learn he is adopted until he can understand what that means, usually at the age of five, six, or seven. Children can't fully understand adoption until they understand about conception and birth. They are confused by the idea of having two sets of parents. Children can't understand that they were the biologic offspring of another man and woman until they understand how babies are conceived.

Advocates of "telling later" fear that to label children "adopted" before that time may cause them to think there is something wrong with them. Psychiatrist Herbert Wieder is among those who believe that early telling is disruptive to psychological development. He points up the need for clinical studies to determine whether early or late telling is less traumatic for the child.

Parents of foreign-born children or children who are racially different from them have little choice but to tell their children as soon as possible that they are adopted. For although young children don't comprehend enough about genetics to realize children usually resemble their parents, other people will comment on the physical difference and ask if the child is adopted in the child's presence.

Even if my children were not Asian, I would subscribe to the early telling theory. I think it is risky for parents to pretend that their child is not adopted. We can't acknowledge and build on the unique aspects of our families while we are pretending that there is no difference between our family and a biologic family. Furthermore, it is essential for adoptive parents to develop an attitude of openness with their children on the subject of adoption. If children are sent out of the room so their mother can talk to the doctor privately, or hear their grandmother being hushed when she starts to mention something about them, they can imagine something terrible is wrong with them. And if children feel they were deceived about being adopted, it can affect the level of trust they have with their adoptive parents on that subject.

The fact remains, however, that these are just theories without clinical data to back them up. Experts can suggest what they think is the best time to start talking about adoption, but ultimately the choice rests with the parents. The best that parents can do is be informed about the advantages and disadvantages of each approach, and consider those along with the personality and reactions of each child.

ADOPTION CONCEPTS

Regardless of when parents start to talk with their children about adoption, there are certain concepts that need to be communicated. Naturally, the younger the child, the more simply these attitudes and ideas will need to be conveyed. More detail can be provided as the child matures. It is helpful, of course, if the child asks questions indicating what she wants to know. But adoptees sometimes are reluctant to bring up the subject of adoption because they may feel disloyal, or because they have somewhere received a message that the subject is off-limits. Parents can initiate discussions or seize opportunities to comment on something related to adoption. At the same time, parents can go too far in talking about adoption. Excessive discussion of adoption can indicate that the parents have not resolved their infertility or are not yet comfortable with the topic. It tells the child: "We're constantly aware of your being adopted." It tells her she's different. For example, a man whose home I was visiting introduced his five children by their first names. With the last he said, "And this is David. He's adopted." There is a fine line between talking about adoption enough that the child knows this is an acceptable topic for conversation, and talking about it so much that the child starts to think there's something wrong with being adopted.

When talking with their children about being adopted, adoptive parents should start at the beginning—the child's beginning. That means talking about the child's birth and places that he lived before being adopted. The child's life did not start with his adoption, although he may have no conscious memory of his life before his adoption, and his parents, perhaps, have little information. The birthparents should be referred to as real people—by first names if that information is known—who exist somewhere, though they may not be part of the child's current life.

Parents should discuss the decision to place a child with empathy for the birthparents: they were people caught up in their circumstances, who engaged in behavior without forethought about the consequences. When faced with the reality of the pregnancy, they made a difficult decision that they thought was best for the baby. Adoptive parents used to be told to convey the selflessness of the decision by telling their children: "Your birthmother gave you up for adoption because she loved you so much." Therapist Claudia Jewett points out that this is a confusing idea for a child who is told that his adoptive parents love him a lot, too. The child may worry that his adoptive parents will also love him "enough" to place him with another set of parents. As the child grows older, he may also have difficulty reconciling loving someone with placing someone for adoption. When he falls in love, he will want to be with that person, and he may have difficulty believing that anyone would willingly separate from someone they love. It is important to tell the adopted child his birthparents probably loved him, and that it was probably very difficult for them to place him for adoption, but that they thought that was what would be best for him. Jewett suggests that parents add that the birthparents probably think about him often.

A child should be reassured that his birthparents placed him for adoption because they weren't able to act as parents of any baby and not because there was anything wrong with him. As the child approaches adolescence, parents can talk about what is involved in raising children, what makes it difficult, and what kinds of skills parents should have. Then they can discuss the realities or probabilities of why his birthparents could not cope with a child.

It is important that a child know that there are thousands of children who are adopted or who do not live with both biologic parents. Children should know that they are not freaks because they were adopted or because their birthparents did not choose to raise them. They need to know there are many other children in similar circumstances.

The child should understand that even though he has two sets of parents, his adoptive parents are responsible for raising him, and that this is a permanent arrangement.

I am a naturally curious person, so I have no trouble understanding that adoptees are curious about their origins. But not every adoptive parent thinks such curiosity should be encouraged—and some people think there is something abnormal about an adoptee who wonders about her birthparents or circumstances of her life before she was adopted. While researchers have not come up with a clear-cut answer to the question of why some adoptees are interested enough to search for their birthparents and others are not, most experts agree that being curious about one's origins is normal. Adoptive parents need to let their children know that it is okay for them to have questions about their past, and to come to their parents with those questions.

When we tell our children about their past, we should be honest. If there is information that the parent does not think should be shared with the child, he can say, "Yes, I know your birthmother's name and I will tell you when you're eighteen." It's better to risk having a child angry at a parent because the child knows the parent is keeping something from him temporarily, than to lie to a child and later try to convince him that "I was going to give that information to you when you were eighteen."

When information is not known, parents should be honest about that too. But they can suggest what they think to be the case: "We don't know how old your birthmother was, but most women who place children for adoption are in high school or college. It's likely your birthmother was very young."

Not every mention of adoption requires a formal setting in which the parent pulls the child onto her lap and talks in serious, low tones. Sometimes it is better to handle the subject casually, with what may appear to be an offhand remark. For example, when a child's friend can't play on a Saturday because his non-custodial father is taking him for an outing, an adoptive parent could remark, "I guess Jimmy has two fathers, too." Depending on the child's response, a discussion could follow about how Jimmy might feel about having two fathers, or the subject may be dropped. It is similar to the way parents help their children understand other important concepts such as the danger of crossing the street without first looking for cars. Sometimes they have serious, formal discussions on the subject. But those are reinforced whenever an opportunity presents itself. When driving down the street, a mother might point out some children who are not playing safely, then resume the conversation she was carrying on in the car. If every mention of adoption turns into an intense analysis of feelings, children may avoid the subject.

POSITIVE ADOPTION LANGUAGE

The words parents choose to discuss adoptive and biologic relationships with their children are not only descriptive, they convey attitudes. Consequently, it is important to consider how a word is emotionally loaded before using it in a discussion of a sensitive issue such as adoption. In an article in *Child Welfare*, Marietta Spencer of the Children's Home Society of Minnesota offers some of the following suggestions on the appropriate words to use in describing the adoption process and adoptive relationships.

The Adoptee

Words used to describe the child who has been adopted should be positive and imply a sense of belonging to her adoptive family. Fortunately, not many people still refer to children born out-of-wedlock as "bastards," a highly derogatory term. But "illegitimate" is still heard, and it still carries a negative connotation. This term literally means "against the law." It is preferable to refer to children as "born to unmarried parents."

Although I use the phrase "adopted child" in this book for clarity, I don't use it in my home. Referring to a child as "my adopted daughter" seems to place a qualifier on the relationship—especially if there are biologic children in the family too.

The Adoption Process

Terms such as "put up for adoption," "adopted out," and "surrendered for adoption" were once popular, but now have fallen out of favor. They imply a negative decision rather than a positive one. It is preferable to use terms that indicate that adoption was a voluntary and deliberate decision by the birthparents. "Surrendered," "relinquished," and "given up" all sound like the child was taken from the birthparents against their wishes. "Adopted out" does not carry with it a sense of destination. "Put up for adoption" is a term that dates back to the turn of the century when orphan trains brought children to the Midwest where they were exhibited—literally put up on platforms—to be selected for adoption. Phrases like "made an adoption plan" or "transferred parental rights" or "placed a child for adoption" convey an orderly, deliberate, thought-out decision.

Genetic Relatives

The phrases "natural mother" and "real father" are often used to describe the woman and man responsible for the conception and birth of a child. Adoptive parents object to these terms because by inference they make the adoptive parents the "unnatural mother" and the "unreal" or "pretend father." Adoptive parents prefer to call the other set of parents the "birthparents" or "biologic parents." "Birthmother" and "birthfather" are acceptable to people in those roles, but birthparents sometimes object to "biologic parents" because it sounds too clinical, as does "genetic parent." "Birthgiver" also has been suggested as an appropriate term, but is not yet widely used. All those terms may be too technical for a young child. "Your other mother," "your first mother," or "your Colombian mother" are often used when talking to preschoolers.

Marietta Spencer believes a child's other genetic relatives should be described by their relationship to the child's birthparents rather than to the child. Rather than "biologic aunt," one would say: "birthmother's sister."

Adoptive Family

An adopted child assumes full family membership in the adoptive family. Therefore it is unnecessary to qualify these relatives by their legal status, such as "adoptive mother" or "adoptive grandmother." They are the child's sister, father, aunt, and cousin. In this book I refer to "adoptive parents" for clarity, but I never introduce myself as my child's "adoptive mother."

WHAT CHILDREN UNDERSTAND ABOUT ADOPTION

Researchers at Rutgers University, including psychologist David Brodzinsky, found that children have similar levels of understanding about adoption at roughly the same age, whether or not they are in adoptive families. Children seem to develop a general understanding of what adoption is and how it works from their social environment rather than by accumulating facts and pieces of information from their parents. Adopted children learn what it means to be adopted whether or not their adoptive parents tell them about it. The job of the adoptive parents, therefore, is not to explain the social concept of adoption so much as it is to provide information about the child's particular situation. Parents also should provide emotional support and reassurance for the child, and create an environment where the child's questions can be discussed.

The Rutgers researchers found that children's knowledge and understanding of adoption change in predictable ways with their development. As a child's understanding of family, reproduction and birth, social relationships, values, and legal and social institutions increases, so his understanding of adoption and adoption matters grows and changes. Children, then, need to have the adoption story repeated because they will focus on certain aspects of it at different developmental stages. At one age a child is concerned with how old his birthparents were; at another age he is more concerned with the legal process of adoption. Fortunately, we now have some understanding of what children especially need to know at certain stages of development.

Preschoolers—A Little Information Goes a Long Way

Dawn was delighted that her four-year-old son Kevin could recite the story of his adoption. She was pleased that he seemed to accept his adoptive status and was proud of it. Then one day she heard him saying, ". . .and Jeremy's adopted, and Ben's adopted, and Adam's adopted, . . ." naming all his friends who were born into their families. Kevin accepted his adoptive status so well because he had no concept of it being unusual. Sure, he grew inside another woman before coming to live with mommy and daddy. That's how it's done.

While I do advocate the "early telling" theory, one problem of talking to preschoolers about adoption is that they often appear to understand more than they really do. The researchers at Rutgers found that preschoolers usually cannot differentiate between being adopted and being born into a family. The two concepts are fused in their minds. Preschoolers simply do not understand the concept of a "blood tie." To children that age, anyone who lives with them is part of the family. The reason they seem so willing to accept their adoptive status is because they don't understand it. When preschoolers tell the story of how they joined the family, they are usually just parroting what they've been told, not showing a real understanding of the circumstances of their lives.

Parents who talk with preschoolers about being adopted should think of their discussions as a foundation for later elaboration. The goal should be for children to hear some of the adoption terms rather than to absorb adoption concepts. Parents should use this time to create a positive atmosphere in which adoption can be discussed, and to become comfortable with talking about it.

Talking to children about their adoption is considered stressful by many parents, and the preschool years offer an opportunity to practice. Three-year-olds are not going to ask any tough questions. And because children are not really gathering information during these years, parents can make mistakes that can be easily corrected later. When Kristy and Dan made their first "welcome home" book, one page read: "Then Kristy and Dan heard about a baby who didn't have a mother or a father." They read this to their daughter for a couple of years before they realized they were ignoring the existence of the birthparents and avoiding the issue of why she was placed for adoption. They changed the page to read: "Then Kristy and Dan heard about a baby whose mother and father couldn't take care of a baby." Their daughter didn't seem to notice the change in the story line, but in a few years she would have.

No matter how many times parents have gone over the story with their preschooler or how well their preschool child can recite the story, the child probably does not have a real understanding of being adopted. The job of talking about adoption has not ended, nor are parents "safe" from uncomfortable questions about adoption just because discussions with preschoolers have seemingly gone so well. They cannot respond to the five-year-old who asks: "Did I grow inside you, mommy?" with a curt, "You know you didn't.

Remember, you were adopted." The five-year-old who asks that question may be thinking about it for the very first time, even though he seemed to understand the circumstances of his birth at the age of three or four.

Since preschoolers are not going to be picking up much actual knowledge, it is hard and perhaps unnecessary to suggest what they should be told. It is probably adequate to say: "Mommy and daddy wanted a baby very much but couldn't make one themselves. Your Chicago mother and father (or your other mother and father) couldn't take care of a baby, so you came to live with us. We were very happy."

Ages Five to Seven—Awareness of Life and Death

Children in this age group are interested in life and death issues such as "Where do puppies come from?" and "Where is heaven?" Around the age of six, the Rutgers researchers found, most children can differentiate between birth and adoption because they understand conception. Even parents who have talked about adoption before may have to start from the beginning of the story with children in this age group who are just beginning to realize what it means to be adopted.

Social work educator Carol Williams says children in this age group need to know that they were born just like every other person. So often adoptive parents talk about adoption by saying something like: "You know your friend Ben grew inside his mommy. But you didn't grow inside me. Mommy and daddy couldn't make a baby so we called an adoption agency and they found a baby for us, and that was you." This story, while accurate, skips an important step—the birth of the child. It is not unusual for the adopted child to conclude that "adopted" means being hatched or born through some other non-normal process. Karen, a 38-year-old adoptee, said that because her adoptive mother never talked about her birth, she never thought of herself "of woman born." As a result, she never thought of being naked ("as a newborn babe") as her natural state. She thinks this is why she was excessively modest and sexually reserved. Now that she's met her birthmother, she feels less inhibited about her body.

When information about the child's birth is available, it should be shared with him. Knowing the actual circumstances of his birth can help a child understand that his birth was normal and had nothing to do with becoming available for adoption. Adoptees sometimes believe they were placed for adoption because they were "bad from birth." Although the practice is less common today, some adoptive parents, uneasy with the idea of illegitimacy and the existence of birthparents, have told their children their parents died in an accident shortly after the child's birth. Rather than comforting children, these stories made children feel guilty about surviving.

There are other reasons for starting to talk with a child about adoption by talking about how he was born. Talking about the child's birth leads naturally into talking about why he was placed for adoption. And talking about the child's birth acknowledges that the child has a history that began before he joined the family, and communicates that it is okay to think and talk about that time.

The birthfather shouldn't be ignored in discussions about adoption. The mother of five-year-old Kelly explained to her daughter that being adopted meant that she had grown in the uterus of another mother. When Kelly asked her how babies were made, she responded accurately and matter-of-factly. It didn't occur to her to discuss those two topics simultaneously, but Kelly put them together. Eventually it became clear that Kelly thought her adoptive father had impregnated her biologic mother. That was the only explanation Kelly could come up with, given the information she had. Like many adoptive parents, Kelly's mother and father had never mentioned her birthfather.

Although the birthfather is as essential to a child's existence as the birthmother, he is often left out of the story. It is impossible to talk about how a child came to be adopted without mentioning the birthmother—the birthmother got pregnant; the birthmother couldn't take care of a baby; the birthmother made a plan for the baby. However, we often ignore the birthfather because we look at his role as merely sexual. In our uneasiness with that subject, we leave him out of the explanations. The result is that many adoptees fantasize, like Kelly, that their adoptive father is really their birthfather.

A scenario for talking with a five- to seven-year-old might be: "A man puts his penis into a woman's vagina. Sperm from the penis joins with an egg from the woman and out of that a baby grows. It was sperm from your other father and an egg from your other mother that made you. You grew inside your other mother. When it was time for you to be born, you came out through her vagina." Parents can add that this is usually a loving thing that happens between a man and a woman. *Our Baby: A Birth and Adoption Story** by Janice Koch discusses how babies are conceived and how they are adopted, and is a good way to discuss an adopted child's origins.

If the circumstances of the child's birth are not known, the likely circumstances can be discussed ("You probably were born in a hospital. . ."), along with what probably or actually happened after birth and up until the time he was placed for adoption. Parents should not say anything to imply that the child was responsible for being placed for adoption, but that the birth-parents "for some reason" couldn't take care of any baby. Parents might want to ask the child why he thinks parents might not be able to take care of a baby. The Rutgers study found that four- to seven-year-olds who had an idea of why parents place children for adoption thought children were placed for three main reasons: because of some negative characteristic of the child, because of the parents' financial problems, or because of lack of time to care for the baby. This is a good time to correct any misconceptions a child may have about why he was placed for adoption. The child who says he became available for adoption because his parents died could be told, "No, your other parents are still living, but they were still in high school and didn't know how to be parents yet"; or if the information is not known, "We don't know if your other parents are alive, but they probably are. They probably were very young and didn't know how to take care of a baby." Children in this age group believe their relationship to their adoptive family is permanent, but they aren't sure why. They believe it is permanent because they have faith in whatever their mother and father tell them. They will soon come to question that belief.

Ages Eight to Eleven—Feelings of Separation and Loss

Children eight to nine years old are beginning to have a notion of "blood relations" and how they differ from other kinds of relationships. These children can now have a fuller understanding of birth and adoption. However, the Rutgers team found that most children cannot understand the legal system that makes their adoptive status permanent until about age eleven. This greater awareness of blood relations and adoption but lack of understanding about the legal system may cause the eight- or nine-year-old to feel unsure of his place in the adoptive family. It isn't uncommon for children this age to think the biologic parents could possibly reclaim them.

Because the realization that someone made a decision to give them up for adoption hits children at age eight or nine, they may have a normal grief response at this time. Their reaction may be mild or severe, although it probably won't be comparable to the way a child would react to a death. Still, parents may not expect their child to grieve for his biologic parents eight or nine years after he was separated from them, and may not recognize that the child's sad feelings are a reaction to his growing awareness of adoption. The child is rapidly increasing his knowledge and understanding, but is unable to keep up emotionally with the new information and awareness. Parents should encourage their child to express his feelings and let him know that it is not only okay to feel sad, but perfectly normal. They should also let their child know they understand what he is feeling sad about, and that it is okay to talk about his birthparents if he wants to. It also is important to tell the child that the feelings eventually will go away, and that's normal too.

By age ten or eleven, children understand that somehow the legal system ensures the permanence of their adoption, although it still isn't as clear as it will be in a few years.

The Rutgers researchers found that the older the child, the more likely he will be to focus on financial problems as a reason for placing a child for adoption. Children also consider the marital state of the parents, parental immaturity, family disharmony, and parental death as reasons for placing a child for adoption.

Children eight to eleven years old usually are concerned about how they measure up to their peers. They compare material possessions, rules, and activities. Carol Williams says a child at this age wants to know if being adopted makes her different from her friends. She needs to know she is not the only adopted person in the world and that even though she's adopted, she's like other children. Because of their increasing understanding of various relationships, eight- to eleven-year-olds may want to know about the relationship between the birthparents, particularly whether or not they were married. The child may want to know if being conceived out-of-wedlock makes her different from other children. If they don't already know, children at this age will be curious about where they were born.

It is important to be honest at all ages when talking with children about their adoption. Children eight to eleven may ask difficult questions that parents may be tempted to avoid or answer evasively. Let the child take the lead. If she is asking a question, she probably is prepared to deal with the answer. In fact, she may be more able to deal with the answer than the parent.

Adolescents—Exploring Who They Are

By the age of twelve or thirteen, children understand that adoption involves the legal transfer of parental rights and responsibilities from the birthparents to the adoptive parents. They also have a better understanding of the reasons children are placed for adoption.

The teenager's job is to become a separate person from his parents. To do this, he has to learn who he is in relation to his parents. The adopted child must learn who he is in relation to two sets of parents before he can fully develop his own identity. It isn't unusual for teenagers to become more curious about their birthparents. Because adolescence is such a critical time for the adoptee, Chapters 7, 8, and 9 discuss teenage adoption issues in more depth. In general, however, parents need to communicate at this time that the child's interest in his birthparents is all right. They also need to let the child know that they are open to talking about the subject of adoption, perhaps even initiating such discussions.

Explaining Parents' Motives for Adopting

Amy grew up with the "chosen baby" story that was told to so many adoptees. In this story, the adoptive parents walked up and down the aisles of a hospital nursery or orphanage until they found the perfect baby for them. In Amy's case, her mother compared it to looking for the "perfect tomato" in the grocery store's vegetable case. Adopted children were told that other parents were "stuck with" the children they got, but that adoptive parents chose their children.

Adoptive parents are no longer encouraged to use the chosen baby story to explain their motives for adopting. In the first place, the story is no longer valid—if it ever was. Parents who adopted after the "boom" of available babies began to decline in the 1970s did not have bassinets full of babies to choose from. Many parents have waited years, perhaps circumventing the adoption system, to get a baby. Instead of choosing the "perfect" baby, prospective parents tell agencies that the sex of the child won't matter, perhaps that the race or ethnic background of the baby isn't an issue, and perhaps that they would even accept a child with disabilities.

In addition, that chosen baby explanation of how the child came into the family places an enormous burden on the adoptee. If he was chosen because he stood out from all the other babies, he has an impossible image to live up to. He was chosen because he was perfect. He could be unchosen if he reveals himself to be imperfect.

In his book *Shared Fate,** sociologist H. David Kirk encourages adoptive parents to become closer to their children by acknowledging that they were all in a painful situation: the parents wanted a child and couldn't conceive or carry one; the child could not be raised by his birthparents; adoption was the best solution for all. In this view of the adoptive family, parents are not the rescuers of their children who have to feel eternally grateful.

Parents should, therefore, be honest about telling a child why they decided to adopt. When parents feel the child is ready, he can be told that mommy and daddy couldn't make a baby (or that mommy and daddy's babies died before they were born), but that they wanted a child to love and take care of.

Like their understanding of adoption in general, children's concepts of why people adopt change with age. Four- to seven-year-olds who were studied by Rutgers researchers saw adoption in terms of the parents' needs: the needs to love a child, to choose a specific type of child, and to increase family size. Older children, eight to thirteen, were more likely to see infertility, concern for the child's welfare, and the joy of watching a child grow as reasons for adopting.

Books and Other Resources

Many parents find children's books help them discuss adoption issues. Norma Simon's books *Why Am I Different?* (Niles, Ill.: Albert Whitman & Co., 1976) and *All Kinds of Families* (Niles, Ill.: Albert Whitman & Co., 1975), along with Meredith Tax's book *Families* (Boston: Little, Brown & Co., 1981), discuss adoption as only one kind of non-traditional family or one way of being different. There are also several books specifically for adopted children that explain the adoption process and explore adoptees' feelings. Some are directed at transracial and older child adoptions. These are described in Selected References and Resources at the back of this book. While books are often helpful, parents should use them as a point of departure for discussions and not as substitutes for talking with their child about his particular situation.

Group sessions offered by some adoption agencies and therapists help children understand that their feelings about being adopted are natural and shared by other adoptees. Similar adult sessions are effective in helping parents realize the questions and concerns their children may be having. Adoptive parent groups provide support for parents, but also provide an informal social setting where adopted children can meet other adoptees. The North American Council on Adoptable Children* is the most up-to-date source of adoptive parent groups.

Agencies and parent groups sponsor summer camps—day camps and resident camps—for adopted children. Some of these are designed to give children from foreign countries an opportunity to learn more about the culture of their countries of birth and to share experiences and feelings they may have as a member of a minority.

TALKING ABOUT THE UNPLEASANT PAST

Adoptive parents are encouraged to be honest, open, and complete when talking to their children about their pasts. This is often difficult, and even more so when the child's mother was an alcoholic, when the child was physically or sexually abused, or when the child was moved from family to family while an attempt was made to find parents willing to adopt her. The past cannot be changed. As much as adoptive parents would like to have prevented those events from occurring, they cannot do so by pretending they didn't happen. Eventually, the full story of her past will need to be shared with the child.

Naturally, children shouldn't be told unpleasant information until they are able to understand it without being confused and without feeling responsible. Sharing too much too soon can give the child a negative image of her birth-parents and a negative self-image. For example, a child may have difficulty understanding that a mother might neglect her child unless the child was somehow unworthy of being cared for. There is no magic age at which parents should share unpleasant information about the child's past. It depends on the child and the nature of the information. During the child's early years, parents should speak positively about the birthparents and their decision to place her for adoption. But they should not say anything that might later be contradicted when the full story is revealed. Whatever information is shared with a child should be shared with the idea of building on that information later.

Children are perceptive, and at some point it will become clear to them that there are gaps in the information they have been given. When this happens, they often imagine something far worse than the actual circumstances. Therapist Claudia Jewett says that the information parents are reluctant to share with their child is often the piece that makes the whole situation make sense to him. For example, she says an adoptee who has been told that his birthmother placed him for adoption because she "couldn't take care of him" eventually will want to know why. He may assume it's because he was a difficult baby to take care of. Because of the stigma attached to mental illness, adoptive parents may be reluctant to tell him that his birthmother was committed to a mental insti-tution. Rather than being embarrassed by this information, the adoptee may be relieved. It makes sense to him that his birthmother couldn't take care of him if she was mentally ill.

Even though it can be difficult, parents are the best people to share unpleas-ant information with the child because they can be there to provide comfort and reassurance. Being honest doesn't mean being harsh. Even painful information can be softened. Parents can reassure the child that the events in his past didn't happen because he was bad, and he is not bad now because something bad happened to him.

As responsible adults, parents may be furious at the behavior of the child's birthparent or foster parent. But the adopted child is attached in some way to the people in his past. By attacking them, parents attack the child and jeopardize their relationship with him. Social work educator Carol Williams and therapist Claudia Jewett encourage adoptive parents to discuss the birthparents and foster parents empathetically and to help children comprehend the adult responsibility for their separation from their birthparents by incorporating the child's own experiences into the explanation. For example, a child can better understand how overwhelmed her birthmother felt by the responsibility of caring for a baby if she can remember a time when she was asked to do something that was too hard for her. This helps the child understand the situation without feeling responsible for it. Much of the material in the following sections is derived from Jewett's book *Helping Children Cope with Separation and Loss**

Abandonment

Like many children adopted from foreign countries, eleven-year-old Tiffany has little information about her background. Her adoptive parents were told that she was "abandoned" as an infant and that her biologic mother and father are "unknown." Her adoptive parents have told her they don't know who her birthparents are, but are unsure of what to tell Tiffany when she asks more specific questions that will lead to the information that she was found at a market and taken to an orphanage. They want to talk about the birthparents in a positive light and think telling Tiffany that she was abandoned will sound like her birthparents deserted her with little concern for what would happen to her.

We have difficulty understanding abandonment because we misunderstand customary adoption practices in other countries. Some countries do not have established procedures for formal adoption. And not all societies have the tolerance for unmarried motherhood that has evolved in our country. Until 1976, when it became legally possible for Koreans to adopt non-relatives, "abandonment" was the only way a child could be placed for adoption by a non-relative. Even in Korea today, and in other countries, a child is sometimes abandoned so that an unmarried birthmother does not have to answer embarrassing questions. But this doesn't mean the child is left without concern for his welfare. For example, one orphanage in the Philippines had a "revolving cradle" on which a child could be placed from the outside, then swung around to the inside of the orphanage where he would be taken care of without anyone questioning who the child was or why he was being taken to the orphanage. Sometimes a friend or relative of the birthmother takes the child to an orphanage or police station so that he can be placed for adoption, but to avoid questions, says she found the child abandoned. Some children have been placed in care supposedly temporarily, but the parents had no intention of returning. In some cases "abandonment" is a legal technicality—the child does not have any legal documents saying who his parents are, therefore cannot be placed for adoption any way other than by being declared "abandoned."

Tiffany's parents could tell her that it probably was very hard for her birthmother to leave her, but that she probably did so in a way that ensured she would be taken care of.

An abandoned child may fantasize that his birthmother just left him "for a minute," and that when she returned for him, he was gone—taken to an orphanage for adoption. Parents can say: "I'm sure you would like to think that your birthmother didn't mean to leave you. It was probably very hard for her to do so, but she knew she couldn't take care of a child and arranged for a way for you to be taken care of."

Certainly there are cases of real abandonment, both in foreign countries and in the United States. Children can be helped to understand this by comparing the difficult task the birthparents faced to something frustrating they have had to do. Parents can point out that one way we respond to difficult tasks is by avoiding them. Children can then see their birthmothers as frustrated by their responsibilities and unsure of their abilities. They reacted by abandoning the children. It's important to emphasize that the birthmother was frustrated because she couldn't be the kind of parent she wanted to be, not because the child's behavior was too hard to deal with. Even the child who was found in a garbage dumpster can be helped to understand that his birthmother probably was very scared at the thought of raising a child, and maybe afraid that people would be angry with her, and so she hid the baby. This can be compared to a child who breaks an expensive watch and hides it, hoping his mother and father will never notice it's gone.

One woman told me that when her children are particularly disruptive she tells them, "Better shape up. Garbage day is tomorrow." That's the kind of off-hand comment that many parents make to their children in frustration. To the child who has been abondoned, however, statements like that can imply that children are abandoned because of their failures. The emphasis should be on the birthparents as frustrated and scared.

Death

There are more adoptees who have been told they became available for adoption because their parents died than there are actual orphans. Adoptees have told me how amused they are when they get together and discover the rash of airplane and car accidents that supposedly happened to their parents. Although it is not as common a practice today as it was in the past, adoptive parents have told their children they were orphaned because they wanted to spare the children the stigma of being born to unmarried parents and spare themselves questions about the birthparents. Too often, however, the story of "adoptee-as-survivor" leaves the adoptee feeling guilty over being alive when the rest of his family is dead.

Children sometimes do become available for adoption after the death of the birthmother or both birthparents. When the child is told about it, he may feel guilty that he survived or even responsible for the death, especially if his birthmother's death was due to a complication in childbirth. Carol Williams suggests separating a discussion of the child's birth from a discussion of the parent's medical problems so that he doesn't feel responsible.

Physical Abuse

A child is hit not because he is bad, but because the adult is out of control. If there is anything children have experience with, it is being out of control when they are angry. Parents can try to explain why someone would abuse a child by relating it to the child's own experience with anger: "When you are really frustrated and really angry, do you sometimes hit somebody or something, even though you know you shouldn't?" Most children have. Parents can explain that grown-ups are supposed to be able to control themselves when they are angry, but that some people haven't learned what to do with their feelings. They hit. And because they are bigger than the children, it hurts. They probably knew that they shouldn't hurt a child, but they lost control. This doesn't excuse the behavior, but can explain it in a way that places responsibility for the abuse on the adult and not on the child. An abused child often thinks that if only he had been better, he wouldn't have been hit and would still be with his birthparents. The child should be helped to understand that he wasn't abused because he was bad, but because the adult did not have the experience or skills to handle a child.

Sexual Abuse

Children who have been sexually abused need to be assured that it was not their fault. A child usually can understand that adults need to be close to someone and don't like to be rejected. Parents might ask the child to talk about her own experiences of wanting to be close to someone and not wanting to be rejected. She can be told that the adult who touched her just wanted to feel close to her; but that while it is okay for two adults to get close by touching each other that way, it is not all right for a grown-up to touch a child that way. It's important to make a distinction between the inappropriate sexual exploitation of children and the appropriate expression of sexual feelings between adults so that the child doesn't grow up thinking sex is always bad. The child can be told that the grown-up knew what he was doing was wrong and probably gave some clues that showed he was aware of it, for example, having the child promise not to tell anyone and never touching her that way when anyone else was around.

The child whose sexual abuse is discovered because she told about it may have a particularly difficult time believing that she did the right thing revealing it. While telling stopped the abuse, it also probably resulted in either her or the abusive parent's removal from the home—something she might view as a "punishment" for telling. The other parent may have reacted angrily and acted as though she didn't believe her. These children need to know that the other grown-ups probably were angry because they couldn't make the abuse stop, and that telling was the right thing because it helped the grown-up deal with the problem.

No child enjoys being abused, but some receive secondary gains from it. She may become the favored child, or be rewarded with treats or special privileges for keeping silent and submitting. It can be particularly difficult for the child to sort out her feelings about the abuse when part of it frightened her and part of it seemed to be advantageous. The abused child needs therapy to sort out these ambivalent feelings and deal with other results of being molested. But adoptive parents don't need to consult a therapist to answer an abused child's questions about why she couldn't continue to live where she had been living. They can answer these questions honestly, empathetically, and without infusing a child with guilt.

Substance Abuse

Most children will not have experienced anything comparable to intoxication or addiction, so they cannot draw on their own experiences to understand a parent who was an alcoholic or drug addict. If they are old enough, though, they may remember what it was like to live with that parent. If they were removed from the home when they were young, they can be told what other people observed. They may remember that meals weren't always prepared, or that they were sometimes late for school because mom or dad couldn't wake up in the morning. Or they can be told that other people noticed their parents were only taking care of their own needs and not those of their children. The reason for this was that the parent was taking drugs or drinking too much and wasn't able to make the appropriate decisions or function as a responsible parent. A child may think, "If they loved me they would have stopped what they were doing and taken care of me." Adoptive parents can say they don't know why the birthparents didn't stop what they were doing—even doctors don't know why—but that it had nothing to do with how much they loved the child. Even though alcoholism and addiction are considered diseases, children younger than adolescents cannot distinguish between diseases of the mind and those of the body. To tell them their birthparent was "sick" can encourage them to think that anytime somebody gets sick, the children need to go somewhere else to live. (For information on the inheritance of alcoholism, see Chapter 6.)

Mental Illness

Just as they probably have not had feelings that parallel addiction, children usually have not had any experiences similar to being mentally ill. Again, they are best able to understand the mentally ill parent if they are asked to remember behavior in the parent that they observed or that someone else saw. If the parent is schizophrenic, the child might be able to understand how people can be frightened of something that other people tell them is not fearful, such as the dark. They may have had the experience of not knowing if they were dreaming or awake, or of thinking they heard someone talking when no one was around.

They can be helped to understand that it was not easy for the parent to control herself. If it is true, the child should be told that the parent had these problems before the child was born. Children may hear their parents saying, "You're driving me crazy." Children need to know that this is not what happened to their birthparent. (Chapter 6 discusses the inheritance of certain mental illnesses.)

Difficult Behavior

While parents try to explain why a child was moved from one family to another without placing the blame on him, sometimes children are moved because of their behavior. Some children set fires, run away, abuse members of the family, break the rules, and otherwise create chaos in a household. There's no way to ignore the fact that a child's behavior had consequences—a move to another home. But he can also be helped to understand that his behavior was the result of choices that he made and that he can make other choices in his new family. It can also be pointed out that his behavior made the adults he was living with scared and angry. As a result, he needed to be moved to a family where the adults were not as frightened of that kind of behavior. This tells the child that his behavior carries consequences, and that he has choice as to what kind of behavior he demonstrates. If he doesn't want to move again, he can avoid the behavior that precipitates it. But it also takes some of the blame off him by pointing out that some adults have an easier time than others living with children who behave as he did.

Mental or Physical Disability

Children should not be made to feel unlovable because they are in a wheelchair or have some other disability. Parents can engage the child in a discussion of what is involved in taking care of someone with their condition and explain that their birthparent did not feel capable of doing it. The birthparent is not condemned for her lack of ability, nor is the child responsible for the birthparent's inadequacy. Parents can say: "Maybe your birthmother didn't have friends at church who would be willing to build ramps in the house," or "Perhaps your birthmother didn't know how she could take care of a blind child because she lives alone."

Incest, Rape, or Prostitution

When a child was conceived as a result of rape, prostitution, or incest, parents can explain that when two people are close, sometimes it feels good for one person but not for the other. But discussions about the child's conception should be kept separate from discussions about his being placed for adoption. As the child grows in his awareness, he should be reassured that the act that resulted in his conception is not his responsibility.

While we should not give our children disturbing information about their birthparents until they are emotionally ready to handle it, we should keep in mind that what is disturbing to us may yet be helpful insight to the adoptee. (A discussion of the medical importance of knowing that a child was born of an incestuous relationship is found in Chapter 6.)

LIFE BOOKS

One way to initiate discussions about the child's past is to make or read a life book—a chronological outline of where the child has lived, who the people were that she lived with, and why she moved on. While these are most helpful to older children who have lived in many places and may be confused about the various people and houses in their pasts, life books are also useful with children adopted as infants.

The life book reconstructs each important episode in the child's life, starting with her birth. The text is written by the child, with assistance from an adult to ensure accuracy. Photographs, when available, or pictures drawn by the child illustrate the story. The life book can also be a record of the child's life, not just her adoption, and include such items as when the child first walked, what her first word was, and other milestones. Mementos, such as a hospital identification bracelet or airplane ticket, can also be included.

By working on a life book with their child, parents can discover the child's own theory of why she was adopted or moved from one family to another. It is an obvious time to provide information to the child that she doesn't already have, or help the child separate her fantasies about an experience from the facts. The parent can say, "I know that's how you would have liked that experience to be, but this is what really happened." When information about the child's past is missing, parents can discuss the likely possibilities: "We don't know why your mother couldn't keep you, but most mothers who make adoption plans for their children are young and don't know enough about how to raise a child."

It isn't difficult to initiate the construction of a life book. Parents can start by saying, "Let's talk about everything that happened to you before you came here." Once the child gets involved in the cutting, drawing, writing, and pasting, she will enjoy the activity. A four-year-old is mature enough to become involved in creating a life book.

Parents can be creative about the media used in making a life book. It isn't necessary for the life book to be a storyline illustrated with drawings and photographs; diagrams, letters to people the child knew before, and tapes of discussions may be more appropriate with some children.

Parents shouldn't try to make a life book in one day—to reconstruct the child's life one episode at a time is sufficient. Parents should also remember to let the child do the work. This is her story; let her tell it. We are there to guide her and make sure that the final product is an accurate record, not a work of art.

Reconstructing one's past can be so emotional that the child may only be able to tolerate the activity for fifteen to thirty minutes and may need to run off steam afterwards. Reliving painful memories may also cause some children to regress in their behavior. But parents shouldn't assume that because working on a life book makes their child feel sad or angry the activity should be discontinued. Even though it may sometimes be painful, understanding the past is important for the adoptee.

Parents looking for guidance in making a life book can consult *Making History: A Social Worker's Guide to Life Books,* * by JoAnn Harrison, Elaine Campbell and Penny Chumbley.

TALKING TO OUTSIDERS ABOUT ADOPTION

People who would never think of asking an acquaintance: "Is there any history of mental illness in your family?" will ask remarkably personal questions about a child who has been adopted. Complete strangers and casual acquaintances want to know how much the adoptive parents know about their child's background and how they will react if the child wants to search for his birthparents. Some of the people demonstrate an amazing ignorance of child development and heredity, such as the person who asked the mother of an Indian baby being raised in the United States whether the child would speak Hindi or English first. Often these questions are asked in front of the adoptees, as though they weren't there.

Nobody outside the immediate family has any right or need to know the private details of the child's life or background. No parent is obliged to tell people whether the child's birthparents were married or where the child lived before the adoption. Some adoption experts argue that adoptive parents do not have the right to tell others about their child's background even if they want to. This information belongs to the child. They suggest answering personal questions with, "That information is private in this family." While I am sympathetic to that attitude, I am also concerned that children who hear this response may conclude that their background is something to be ashamed of. That does not mean that I recommend telling the world that a child was sexually abused or that he was covered with scabies when he arrived. The parents who are asked, "Why did his mother give him up for adoption?" need not respond "Well, she was a heroin addict," but could simply reply (as they would to a young child): "She couldn't take care of a child." And then change the subject. Most people would see that the parents don't intend to discuss the matter in great detail. We can also learn to give polite replies that really give no information. Judith Martin, in her humorous, yet useful book, *Miss Manners' Guide to Rearing Perfect Children*, (New York: Penguin Books, 1985) suggests "a small laugh and the observation, 'My, we had no idea how curious people are about where babies come from,' " in response to the question about an adopted child's origins.

I am amazed at the number of adoptive parents who not only talk about their children's histories to strangers, but tell strangers information that they have not told their children. I have been at adoption conferences where parents have informed rooms full of people about something in their children's pasts that they have not told their children. People have given me information for publication that they have not shared with their children. Unless the person is a physician, lawyer, minister or someone else obliged to keep information confidential, parents should not give information to others that their children do not have. The risk of the child finding out the information may not be great, but it is there. If the child learns that his parents have kept something from him that they've been willing to share with the world, it could seriously damage their relationship.

Insensitive Remarks

Adoptive parents are often astounded at the ignorant and insensitive remarks many people make about their children, and in front of their children. People who are not involved in adoption sometimes view adoptees as some kind of alien species; therefore, they think it is all right to talk about them as though they were clinical specimens. My reactions to these kinds of questions and remarks vary depending on my mood, how well I know the person making them, and what I perceive to be their level of interest. To the stranger who looked from me to my Asian daughter and back to me again before remarking quite confidently, "Looks like her daddy, huh?" I replied, "Yes, she does." Sometimes, though, a seemingly insensitive remark is made by someone who seriously wants information about adoption but has not been involved in it enough to be sensitive to the preferred vocabulary. I normally ignore references to the "real" or "natural" parents rather than jump down someone's throat for using those terms instead of "birthparent" or "biologic parent." I think the question that surprised me the most was from a woman who had observed our two Asian children playing together at the park. "Are they really brother and sister?" she asked. I wanted to reply, "What difference does it make to you?" Instead I said, weakly, "Just legally." Next time I'll reply, "Yes, they really are." Unfortunately, adoptive parents usually get a second chance to reply to an insensitive remark.

Medical Personnel

It is probably impossible, and certainly undesirable, to refrain from discussing a child's adoptive history with his physician. Physicians need an accurate medical history on each of their patients. This may include information that the parent is not yet willing to share with the child, such as that his birthparents were closely related. Parents need to make it clear to the physician, however, when information is being given to him that the child does not know. (A more complete discussion of the importance of the medical history is found in Chapter 6.)

School Personnel

There is some controversy over whether school personnel should be told that a child is adopted. I was a bit startled when we enrolled our two-year-old son in a day-care center and one of the questions on the application was "Is the child adopted?" Immediately defensive, I wondered what difference it made. Was the staff going to have different expectations of him because he was adopted?

Parents are often concerned that if the teacher and school administration know that a child is adopted, they will expect less of the child academically. They also fear that any behavior problems will be blamed on adoption. They don't want their child treated differently because he has been labeled "adopted." Yet they expect the teacher to be sensitive enough to adoption issues that she wouldn't assign her class to a "family tree" project or to trace the origins of the color of their eyes.

After the initial shock of the day-care center's question, I realized that a child's adoptive status is part of his social history. And schools need to know the social histories of their students. Parents should make school personnel aware that their child is adopted. (Chapter 2 discusses some of the considerations parents and teachers should have when a newly adopted older child starts school.) At the same time parents have a right to investigate whether knowledge of the child's adoption is prejudicing the teacher or school counselor and to make sure adoption is part of any curriculum involving families or heredity. The Social Science Education Consortium (855 Broadway, Boulder, Colo., 80302), together with Children's Home Society of Minnesota, has prepared curriculum materials for use in elementary, high school, and adult education classes to improve public awareness of adoption.

If a teacher assigns a class to chart their family tree or trace an inherited trait, parents should talk with their child about how she wants to handle the homework. Parents who rush up to the school to complain about the teacher's insensitivity may cause their child more discomfort than the assignment. Children should be encouraged to come up with their own way to handle the dilemma, and may surprise us with their creative and insightful solutions. If necessary, though, we can suggest that the child draw a genetic family tree and graft a psychological or adoptive family tree onto it, or chart how her eye color might have been inherited, given what she knows about genetics.

THE IMPORTANCE OF ATTITUDE IN COMMUNICATION

Every time I make a mistake as a parent, I am sure I have done irreparable psychological damage to my children. So I understood the feelings of a group of parents, described By Betty Jean Lifton in *Lost and Found,** who first heard a talk on the benefits of the "telling later" theory of adoption. They had all conscientiously discussed adoption with their preschoolers only to discover that some people think early telling will confuse their children. They were distraught. Parents who have neglected to mention the birthfather, who have occasionally introduced their child as their "adopted son," or who have talked to their bridge group about their child's abusive past need not feel like failures as adoptive parents. What is important is that adoptive parents make an effort to know what it is that adoptees need to know as they grow up and provide their children with that information. In many respects it is the attitude we convey to our children, not the words we use, that is most important in discussing adoption. That attitude should be open, empathetic, and honest.

Chapter 5

How Adoption Affects the Family

Once the family and the adoptee have adjusted to one another, and that first discussion of what it means to be adopted has been successfully handled, is being an adoptive family any different than being a biologic family? Some people think not; they suggest that the only time adoption is an issue is when discussing how the child joined the family or whether the adoptee should have contact with the birthparents. "Once she's in your home, forget she's adopted," they tell adoptive parents.

Adoptive parents do forget their child is adopted, in the sense that they do not think daily about the way their child joined the family. Yet infertility, the adoption process, the way people outside the family respond to the child's being adopted, and the knowledge that there is another set of parents responsible for the existence of the child all affect adoptive parents and their children. These internal and external factors shape us as parents and adoptees as children. The dynamics of the adoptive family are different from those of biologic families because the family was formed differently.

ADOPTIVE PARENTS: INTENSELY CONCERNED

When asked to characterize adoptive parents, most professionals—as well as most friends and relatives—describe them as intensely concerned, deeply committed parents, who believe strongly that they can make a difference in their children's lives. Some might argue that only people with that attitude toward raising children are likely to adopt, or be approved for adoption. That may be true, but I think there's also strong evidence that infertility, as well as the adoption process, and the reaction of people outside the family to the idea of adopting contribute to parental attitudes. Adoptive parents bring their attitudes to every aspect of their role. For example, we might not recognize a parent's eagerness to help a child with her homework night after night as an adoption issue. We might be inclined to describe that parent as a caring mother or father. But it is entirely possible that the parent's extra effort is the result of the great weight he places on the role of environment in academic achievement—a philosophy that may be directly influenced by the parent's experience with adoption.

Caring and Commitment

Adoptive parents make the decision over and over again to become parents. Even when parents adopt one of the many older or disabled children "waiting" for families, adoption is a lengthy, complicated procedure. The pregnant woman and her husband who have doubts about parenthood, or discover that an expected promotion didn't come through, or develop marital problems find that it isn't easy to rescind their decision to become parents. Prospective adoptive parents know that a simple phone call can halt the entire process. People who proceed with adoption repeatedly commit themselves to becoming parents. Those who have decided on adoption because of infertility have spent years trying to have children, deciding each month that they want to be parents. Certainly many biologic parents make conscious decisions to have children and are committed to their roles. Most, however, have not had their decisions and commitment tested to the extent that adoptive parents have.

Some adoptive parents do manage to adopt without this level of commitment; the husband goes along with the adoption to please his wife, or both husband and wife think a child is the solution to their problems, and they are able to fool not only themselves but their social worker. But most professionals characterize adoptive parents as highly committed to the decision they have made to adopt and to carrying out their responsibilities. Committed parents are naturally caring and concerned. They want to do a good job. One strength of the adoptive family is the adoptive parents' concern for their children. Sometimes, though, parents can become overly concerned and too intense in their commitment. When this happens, caring becomes hovering; concern becomes control; and as a result, parents don't give their child enough room to explore or make mistakes.

We must learn to temper our concern so that we are not overprotective. Nobody wants their child to get hurt, but the child who gets no bumps or scrapes probably isn't exploring her surroundings. It's hard not to intervene to settle an argument between children, but sometimes children need to be left alone to work out their own solutions. We resist letting a child go to school without a coat when the weather is chilly, but sometimes we have to let him learn to make decisions and take the consequences. It is a delicate balance—caring without going overboard. Just recognizing the tendency to err on the side of overprotectiveness can help adoptive parents achieve that balance.

High Expectations

Many people go into parenthood with idealized visions of what they will be like as parents and what their children will be like as a result. For adoptive parents, though, infertility and the adoption process, as well as the attitudes of those outside the family, can combine to raise their expectations of themselves and their children.

Because infertility puts parenthood out of reach for a couple who desires that role, the goal becomes all the more valuable. Couples often fantasize after years of attempted pregnancy about what their lives will be like with children. Often they become obsessed with getting pregnant. If they do decide to adopt a baby—most infertile couples who decide on adoption prefer an infant—because of the high demand for healthy babies and the small supply, their goal is once again put out of reach. They may become preoccupied again with becoming parents. It's hard to think about the realities of raising children at this time. I remember a nurse at my physician's office who said, "You want to adopt? I've got a fifteen-year-old you can have." But I wasn't in a frame of mind to hear about how difficult it was to be a parent.

All expectant parents idealize to some degree what it will be like to be parents; but some infertile couples waiting for a placement are in such distress they begin to think all their problems will be solved by the presence of a child. Couples who expect such a high degree of satisfaction from parenthood are likely to be disappointed.

In addition to expecting parenthood to bring them a high degree of happiness, adoptive parents often believe that they are expected to be "superparents," and that they have the ability to live up to those expectations. Those who are "competing" for the few healthy babies who are available believe they have to present themselves—to the social worker, birthparents, physician or other intermediary—as the best possible choice of parents. The home study that "approves" them, plus the letters of recommendation from their friends required by many agencies, reinforce the idea that they are above average parent material. Sometimes couples believe that since the birthmother decided she wasn't able to raise her baby and chose instead to have her placed with people who could, the adoptive parents are not allowed any mistakes.

Liza adopted her daughter as an infant after six years of waiting for a child. She felt that because someone entrusted her with a child, she had to rear her perfectly. Mother and daughter were constantly together; for two and a half years, Liza refused to leave her daughter with another caretaker. "I went overboard," Liza said. "If we talked about leaves, I'd show her twenty, not two." She gradually recognized that her intensity was not beneficial.

People who are properly prepared for the adoption of a child with "special needs" are less likely to have idealistic visions of what it will be like to raise that child. Yet some may have unrealistic expectations of what raising such a child will take, or unrealistic expectations of their own limits.

As a result of their experiences, adoptive parents often jump into their roles with eagerness. There is nothing wrong with an enthusiastic parent; indeed another strength of the adoptive family is that parents take their roles seriously. But there is a danger that adoptive parents can expect too much of themselves and too much of being parents. Couples may expect that after all they went through to adopt, they will not have any doubts about the decision once the child is taken home. They may think they should be capable of dealing with any situation. Adoptive parents may expect that because they chose to adopt, had plenty of time to reflect on it, and made the decision over and over again, that they should be able to meet all the challenges of parenthood willingly and happily.

Being aware of the pitfalls in adoption that can lead to unrealistic expectations can help us avoid them. Adoptive parents shouldn't expect to be more patient than biologic parents would when raising children becomes overwhelming. Just because they wanted the child very much and waited a long time for her doesn't mean they are resistant to the rigors of parenting. All parents sometimes long for the freedom and more carefree days of childlessness. But adoptive parents, especially the infertile, may have a difficult time acknowledging those feelings.

One way to keep expectations realistic is to carefully select sources of child care information. Joseph Procaccini and Mark W. Kiefaber, in their book *Parent Burn-out,** are critical of the child care manuals that focus only on the needs of the child and imply that deviating from the "correct" methods of childrearing will have disastrous consequences. Parents should also avoid those manuals professing that a certain goal, such as toilet training or reading, can be attained if only the parents follow the guidelines exactly. Parents should choose child care guides that are realistic, humorous, and talk about the needs of parents as well as children. My favorites have been the Gesell Institute of Child Development series of books written by Louise Bates Ames and Frances L. Ilg. With titles like *Your Three Year Old: Friend or Enemy,* and *Your Four Year Old: Wild and Wonderful* (New York: Dell Publishing Co., 1976), these books let parents know that some obnoxious behavior is both normal and transient. David Elkind's Books *The Hurried Child* and *All Grown Up and No Place to Go* (Reading, Mass.: Addison-Wesley, 1981, 1984) discuss the disadvantages of pushing children to mature too fast.

Observing other children the same age as one's own is another way to ascertain what behavior is appropriate to a certain stage of development. Unfortunately, because they are typically older when they become parents for the first time, adoptive parents often find that friends their own ages have children much older than their own. Parents may want to look for other opportunities to associate with families who have children the same ages as their own.

Emphasis on Environment

Another reason adoptive parents may expect too much of themselves is because they may place too much faith in the capacity for a child's environment to influence her development. People not directly involved with adoption sometimes blame heredity for whatever goes wrong with an adoptee and credit the adoptive environment for the adoptee's successes. Adoptive parents often don't view their child's outcome in the same way. To commit themselves to raising a child born to other parents, adoptive parents must have a strong belief that the environment they have to offer the child will make a difference in her life. Claudia Jewett, writing in *Adopting the Older Child* (Harvard, Mass.: Harvard Common Press, 1978), says parents who choose to adopt may see themselves as having a more active role in manipulating the child's fate than biologic parents do. Consequently, they may expect to be able to solve all the child's problems. In addition, some adoptive parents try to deny that the child has any genetically determined qualities at all because they would prefer to ignore the existence of the birthparents.

Those who adopt infants usually want to adopt a baby so that they can have as much opportunity to influence the child as possible. And even those who adopt older children, whose personalities are already formed, place a high degree of confidence in environment. With another teacher, the right therapist, and enough love, they think, they can overcome any negative factors in the child's past.

All this effort and concern is important, but adoptive parents cannot and should not forget that their child comes with a genetic code that influences more than the color of her eyes and the texture of her hair. Researchers are finding that genetics plays an influential role in the development of intelligence, personality, and even vocational interests. By accepting the role of heredity in child development, parents are not relinquishing the responsibility they have to provide a good environment for their children. There is a complex interplay between nature and nurture. A child may inherit her intellectual capability from her birthparents, but will never realize her potential unless she is challenged and motivated by her adoptive parents and teachers. A naturally sensitive child who is belittled for not being tough enough will develop a personality quite different from the child whose parents find her sensitivity to be charming.

Recognizing the limitations of environmental influences can help parents be more unconditionally accepting of their children. It also can go a long way toward relieving pressure parents feel that any problem the child has is the result of inadequate parenting. Adoptive parents are not responsible for the ultimate outcome of a child—nor is any parent. We need to allow our children to be who they are and accept them as unique individuals rather than try to mold them to fit some preconceived ideal. One of the joys of parenting is the discovery that continues as our children grow. One of the joys of adoptive parenting is the differences we are able to experience by raising children with different genetic backgrounds.

Outsiders' Reactions

Even when adoptive parents recognize that they do not have a perfect family and are sometimes dissatisfied with their roles, they may feel a need to project an image of a family devoid of problems. If their friends and relatives expressed doubt about their decision to adopt, adoptive parents may feel pressure to show these people that all is well. For instance, adoptive parents may respond to others' doubts that adoptive parents and their children love each other as fully as do biologic parents and their children by trying to project that they have a warm, loving relationship with their child. Even though they may recognize that parents who love their children sometimes lose their tempers or resent the responsibilities of parenthood, they may feel they have to hide these feelings.

When adoptive parents are honest about the difficulties they are having, friends and relatives are not always supportive. In particular, those who adopt children with emotional problems find that others are not always sympathetic to their situation. The single career woman who chooses to have a child on her own is in a similar situation. Because she chooses a situation with predictable difficulties, she is not allowed to complain about them afterward. She is expected to be a "superwoman."

On the other side are those who believe adoptive parents are angels. "You are wonderful to take in a child without a home," they tell us. Who can tell a person who makes that kind of statement that the child has been intolerable all week? If we are labeled as "wonderful," we must live up to the expectation.

Some people complain about the day-to-day hardships of parenthood without worrying that their complaints make them appear to be dissatisfied with being a parent. Others are more sensitive to outside opinions. But everyone needs someone with whom she can be honest about the problems of daily life. At the very least, a husband and wife should not be hiding their doubts and dissatisfaction from each other. They may also need close friends who can listen to them without passing judgment. Some adoptive parents turn to adoptive parent support groups to have this need met. There they can talk about what it's like to be parents without feeling defensive about having doubts or problems after so deliberately choosing to become parents. They also get feedback and understanding from couples who may be experiencing the same doubts or problems.

Reconciling Expectations with Reality

The picture that emerges is of adoptive parents who care deeply about the responsibilities that they willingly and knowingly undertook. These people believe they have the skills, talents, or intuitive abilities to be good parents. They have waited a long time and gone through a difficult process to become parents, and they are anxious to begin their roles as mothers and fathers. They are full of enthusiasm. Another strength of adoptive parents is their belief in themselves and in their ability to overcome problems. But, at the same time, if they fail to adjust their view of themselves as "superparents" to the realities of raising children, they may put too much pressure on themselves and on their children. Ultimately, they may become disillusioned with parenthood and, perhaps, adoption.

Procaccini and Kiefaber say parents who have high expectations about how they would perform as parents and the amount of satisfaction and happiness that would result from parenthood are at risk for "burning out." When the realities of family life set in, these parents begin to feel fatigue, disenchantment and self-doubt—that parenthood isn't quite as ideal as they thought it would be. Some parents respond by adjusting their expectations to the realities. Others try twice as hard to make their family life perfect. Unless they eventually change their expectations, parents are likely to retreat from their jobs as parents, withdraw from their families and friends, and feel angry and resentful.

Parent burn-out is estimated to affect about half of the parents in the United States in some way and perhaps as many as 20 percent seriously. It can affect any parent, but adoptive parents may be at risk because of the many factors that influence them to expect more of themselves.

Ironically, the adoptive parents least likely to burn out are the ones most people think have the toughest jobs—those who have adopted large numbers of "special needs" children. They tend to have more realistic expectations and are aware of the limits of their children. And the more children in the family, the more the parents' intensity is diluted. With disabled children, the more severe the handicap, the less likely that the parent will burn out. Apparently, parents realize that the probability of substantial change in the child's condition is slim, and they adjust their expectations accordingly.

Procaccini and Kiefaber suggest that one way to avoid becoming disillusioned with raising children is for parents to take care of themselves. Parents need to take some time for themselves, perhaps just a half hour, to exercise, meditate, work on a hobby, or enjoy some other favorite activity. Parents who put everyone else's needs before their own are setting themselves up for feeling angry and resentful. Parents also need to take time for each other, nurturing their relationship as well as the relationship with their children. Because children are so impatient, and their needs so pressing, it is often easy to insist that the spouse wait to have his needs met until the children are taken care of. Husbands and wives must let each other know that they still consider the other a priority.

ADOPTEES: SEEKING PERFECTION

Adoptive parents sometimes falsely assume that if their children are not talking about having been adopted, they aren't thinking about it. How much an adoptee thinks about being adopted depends on the individual personality, how much factual information she has, and the attitude in her home toward her past. But we do know that a person who has been adopted will sometimes feel insecure about her adoptive home, will fantasize about what her life would have been like had she not been adopted, and may grieve for the people she has been separated from or never knew. Unless the adoptive parents establish an atmosphere in which the adoptee feels that she can express her feelings, they may not realize that their child's "moodiness" is related to her adoptive status.

Pressure To Be Perfect

One way that adoptive parents with high expectations of themselves gauge how well they are meeting those expectations is by evaluating the behavior of their children. Although there are a number of influences on children besides their parents, we tend to believe that children's behavior is a good indication of the quality of parenting. Parents who have unrealistic expectations of themselves are likely to have unrealistic expectations of their children. Strong believers in the influence of environment, adoptive parents may put undue pressure on their children to achieve more than they are capable of, or push them into activities or situations that the children are not interested in.

In addition, adoptees sometimes think they must be model children to stay in their adoptive homes. Results of a study by psychologists at Rutgers University confirm what adoptees have been telling us for a long time: adoptees sometimes believe they were placed for adoption because they were "bad" or in some way defective. They believe that if they had only been better their birth-parents would have kept them. The logical outgrowth of this belief is that they must behave very well to stay in their adoptive home.

Although it has fallen out of favor, some adoptees have been told that biologic parents have to keep the children they have, while adoptive parents wanted their children and picked them out because they were special. This puts pressure on the child to live up to whatever extraordinary qualities they had that led their parents to select them instead of another child.

While adoptive parents seldom want to be thanked by the child for adopting her, society implies that gratitude is required. And children express gratitude to their parents by being the kind of children their parents want. Not only is this an impossible expectation to fulfill, it is an unfulfilling expectation. As Betty Jean Lifton points out in *Lost and Found,** how can the adoptee possibly be perfect enough to repay her parents for rescuing her from being an orphan?

Adopted children may also feel pressure to behave exceptionally well for a reason that is peripherally related to adoption. Because adoptive parents typically are older than parents of children the same age and may be less patient or flexible than younger parents, they may expect better behavior from their children.

The pressure that adoptees put on themselves and that society puts on them can be eased by ongoing discussions of adoption. Adoptive parents, knowing that younger children tend to think they were placed for adoption because they were imperfect, should ask their child, perhaps in the course of making a life book, why she thinks she was placed for adoption. Misconceptions that she was placed for adoption because she cried too much, was messy, or was otherwise defective can be discussed. Frank discussions of why the parents chose to adopt can also communicate to the child that the adoptee was not the only one in need; the parents had needs that were met by adoption.

Family Romance Fantasies

Most of us can remember a time as children when we were angry at our parents and decided they were being mean to us because they were not our "real" parents. The only explanation for what we saw as horrendous parental behavior was that we had been adopted. Our "real" parents would have been more understanding, because they would have really loved us. We may even have fantasized about who these other parents were—a Juliet who fell in love with a Romeo but couldn't marry because the families were opposed to the marriage.

These family romance fantasies are neither unusual, nor abnormal. Psychiatrists, beginning with Sigmund Freud, have suggested that they serve several purposes: to express disappointment with the parents, to reduce guilt associated with incestuous feelings, or to meet other defensive needs.

The adoptee, also, has fantasies about her birthparents. Thinking, as all children do at some time, that her adoptive parents aren't letting her have her own way because they don't love her, she may imagine a set of birthparents who are every child's ideal. They are everything her adoptive parents aren't—young, attractive, understanding, and rich. Psychiatrist Herbert Wieder suggests that some adoptees have difficulty reconciling this ideal image with people who would "give away" a child. If she was so rich, she wouldn't have had to place a child for adoption, for example. At the other end of the spectrum, the adoptee may fantasize that to place a child for adoption, the birthparents had to be horrendous; and the adoptive parents were the saviors. Of course, this explanation is also flawed because she knows her adoptive parents are not ideal. Or she may decide that the birthparents didn't intend to place her, that she was stolen from them or that the placement was somehow beyond their control. Once they find out where she is, she thinks, they will rescue her.

Whatever the fantasy, it is more difficult for the adoptee to solve her temporary disappointment with her adoptive parents by fantasizing that she was adopted. The fantasy is mixed up with reality. While the biologic child can let go of the fantasy as soon as her anger or resentment at her adoptive parents subsides, the adoptee's thoughts about her birthparents do not go away so easily. And there is a danger that she may start thinking of one set of parents as "bad" and one set of parents as "good."

Jill Krementz's book *How It Feels to Be Adopted,** along with *The Adoption Triangle,** by Arthur D. Sorosky, Annette Baran, and Reuben Pannor, and books written by adoptees, such as Betty Jean Lifton's *Twice Born** and *Lost and Found,** can help adoptive parents understand that many adoptees think about their birthparents and what it means to be adopted far more often than most of us would imagine. Once we understand the kinds of thoughts that adoptees might have, we have a basis for discussion with them. We can tell them about the family romance fantasies we had as children and ask if they ever think their birthmother was a princess, using that as a way to initiate a discussion of their feelings and correct any misconceptions. Parents could say, for example, "It is nice to think that your mother is very wealthy and will someday buy the toys for you that we can't afford. Probably she would want to buy nice things for you, just as we want to. But she probably isn't very rich." Adoptive parents can also help their child understand that her ambivalent feelings toward them are quite natural and do not threaten their relationship. She can be angry at them, be disappointed in them, and think they are doing something wrong, just as they sometimes are angry at her and think she's making an incorrect decision. Those feelings don't diminish the fact that parents and child love each other and are a family.

Knowing that ambivalent feelings and fantasies about the birthparents are normal doesn't always eliminate the sting that adoptive parents sometimes feel when their children compare them to their birthparents and find the adoptive parents wanting. We must remember: this doesn't mean we've failed to communicate how much we love them, or that they don't love us. It is normal for children to think some other mother and father would be better to live with. Most importantly, however, adoptive parents can't let their children know that a comparison between them and the birthparents is a vulnerable point or children may use it to manipulate the adoptive parents.

UNRESOLVED OR RENEWED GRIEF

Adoptive parents often expect their children to need some time to adjust to a new family and to grieve for their birthparents or foster parents. But they may be surprised to find the children grieving for these losses years after the move.

The adoptee may never have seen his birthfather at all and may have been separated from his birthmother immediately after birth, but our society values biologic connections. He may not have formed attachments to his birthparents, but our society tells him he has lost people whose relationship to him is a valued one. When he realizes that, he is likely to grieve. Psychologist David Brodzinsky and his colleagues at Rutgers found that children don't understand this loss until about the age of eight. At that time, they may show signs of mild or even severe grief.

It may not make sense to us that the child is grieving. But a child who shows signs of grief must be allowed to express his feelings, whether or not they make sense to the parents, therapist Claudia Jewett believes. Unless parents are aware of the signs of grief and the reasons that children may grieve for a loss they suffered years ago, they may not even recognize a child's sad, angry, or aggressive feelings as symptoms of mourning, she says. (These signs of grief are discussed in Chapter 2).

Parents may have difficulty recognizing symptoms of grief when they aren't severe. Is John fighting more with his classmates because he's grieving or for some other reason? It can be hard to tell. And parents may not want to believe that the cause is adoption-related. They may want to believe that since they have formed an attachment with their child and told him he's adopted, adoption issues are behind them. Or they may think it's too simple to blame every problem on adoption. Perhaps they prefer to look for explanations of problems that they can have more control over so they will have a better chance of solving them.

Adoption issues are never completely put to rest. While it is unfair to blame every problem on adoption, it is unrealistic to think adoption will never be a factor in a situation. And adoptive parents are not powerless to deal with the aftereffects of separation and loss. Parents who maintain an open atmosphere in which the child feels comfortable discussing his feelings and talking about adoption are less likely to have to guess at the causes of problems. When the problem is grief at the loss of the birthparents, the parents who validate their child's feelings, allow him to express them, and provide unconditional support can help him through his mourning toward acceptance and understanding.

One of the most important ways to support grieving children is to provide reassurance that their needs will be met and that they will be taken care of. This may seem obvious to the adoptive parents who know how firmly committed they are to the child. But the child has been forced to deal with the reality that relationships aren't permanent. He needs some consistency in the relationships that still are available to him.

Triggering Memories of Past Losses

Children often grieve for past losses because they were not allowed or able to mourn at the time of the loss. But sometimes children who have resolved a loss find themselves repeating some of the stages of grief when they experience a new loss, on an anniversary of the loss, or on holidays. Their reaction is not likely to be as severe as it would be if the loss were recent, but it is equally real. Sam had an early history of foster and adoptive families. He was placed again for adoption when he was seven years old. His foster mother, unwilling to deal with Sam's reaction to another move, told him he was only going to stay with the new adoptive family for Christmas. After the holiday, she would come pick him up. Sam had a lot of behavior problems in his new adoptive family, but never more so than at Christmas time each year. His mother believes he was deliberately trying to destroy Christmas for the family. One year he damaged all the Christmas presents. Another year he shot out the windows of the neighbors' houses. Yet another Christmas he stole a checkbook and wrote a series of bad checks. The money it took for his parents to cover the bad checks almost eliminated the possibility of their buying any Christmas gifts. The double stress of the anniversary of his placement in the home, for which he had been poorly prepared, and the holiday season, combined to trigger extreme behavior problems.

Adoptive parents often celebrate the day their child was placed in their home—and they should. That anniversary marks the start of their life together.

It is a happy occasion, and entirely so for the parents. But a child may have mixed feelings about the anniversary, especially if she is old enough to remember having to leave another place to join her new family. The adoptee may feel that she should not think about her birthparents on a day when she is supposed to be celebrating joining a new family.

The adoptee may have similar ambivalent feelings when the adoption is finalized, or when celebrating other events that emphasize family, such as a birthday, wedding day, or family reunion.

Sometimes the exact day of an anniversary does not trigger remembrances of the loss as much as the time of year, Jewett says. Children may associate the loss with the feel of the air in a particular season, or the lengthening or shortening of days. Lorraine Dusky, a birthmother who wrote about her experience in *Birthmark,** associated the loss of her daughter, born in April, with the blooming of forsythia.

Holidays are other occasions when memories of past losses can haunt us. This is especially true when the loss was a relative, because most holidays emphasize being together as a family. People are usually sensitive to the way a widow feels on Thanksgiving or how a mother might feel on Mother's Day after her child has died. But we often don't expect the adoptee to think of her birthparents or foster parents on "family" holidays. That's probably because the birthparents or foster parents don't belong to our past—but they do belong to the child's.

Because Christmas is generally the biggest holiday of the year, it is often particularly stressful for the adoptee. The emphasis on being together as a family and on the birth of Jesus combine to remind adoptees that they are separated from some significant people. Adoptees may wonder if they would have been placed for adoption had they been as perfect a baby as Jesus, and may engage in other fantasies of what might have been. In Jill Krementz's book *How it Feels to be Adopted,** an adopted boy talks about his feelings at Christmas. If he had been bad, he would think Santa wasn't going to bring him presents, would put coal in his stocking, and his mother would take him back to the adoption agency. Unusually good behavior or unusually problematic behavior can be warnings that a child is having a holiday grief reaction. Unusual tension in the child is another sign.

The key to working through grief is to allow the child to express her feelings, but that may be more difficult at Christmas when the emphasis is on being happy, Jewett says. She points out that even the Christmas song "Santa Claus Is Coming To Town" tells children they'd better not cry or pout. For the parents who recognize that their child needs to discuss her feelings at this time, Christmas provides a lot of opportunities. Christmas stories about Rudolph the Red-nosed Reindeer or Charlie Brown's scrawny Christmas tree are good starting places for talking about feelings of rejection because of being imperfect. And the story of Mary and Jesus can be used as a starting point for discussions of mother–child relationships.

In Jewish homes, the High Holy Days of Rosh Hashanah and Yom Kippur emphasize family connections and the linkage of the family unit to Jews elsewhere and to history. The solemn evaluation and personal scrutiny that are part of these holy days may result in some thoughts by the adoptee about how she fits in with the family and with the history of her family. She may even wonder if she is "really" Jewish.

New Losses

Subsequent losses, even minor ones, can trigger memories of past losses, especially if the person has not fully grieved for the previous loss. Psychologists believe that anyone who experiences a significant loss is likely to feel new losses more acutely. The death of a pet, a broken toy, or a friend who moves away can provoke grief in a child that may seem out of proportion to the actual loss, Jewett says. This may indicate that the child is mourning for more than just the broken toy or absent friend. Psychiatrist John Bowlby suggests that when a person loses someone or something to which he is attached, he turns for comfort to an earlier attachment figure. If that person is not available, the loss is felt again. (For a discussion of how adopted children react to divorce or the death of a parent, see Chapter 12.)

Whatever the loss, a child's response may seem more severe than the loss would warrant. That may be because he is grieving for more than the immediate loss. Allowing the child to grieve, rather than implying that he shouldn't be feeling the loss so intensely, is essential.

Permission to Love Again

Parents can choose some concrete activities to help children resolve their feelings of separation and loss, either at the time of placement or later when they are experiencing renewed grief. Life books, discussed in Chapter 4, are designed to help a child understand where she has been and why she had to leave those places. Feelings the child has as a result of having to move can be discussed at this time quite naturally.

Claudia Jewett believes it is important for children to have a chance to say "good-bye" to the people she has lived with and receive a blessing from them—permission from someone she cares about to be happy in the new family, to be loved and to love. Even children who never knew their birth-parents learn from society that there's a certain loyalty children should have toward their biologic parents. At some point, they may need to know that it is okay for them to love their adoptive parents. The letters that some birthmothers are now writing to their children at the time of placement can explain to a child why she was placed for adoption and can give her the permission she needs to love her adoptive parents. In the absence of such a letter, Jewett suggests that the adoptive parents help their child write a letter or place a phone call to the people she needs to say good-bye to or receive a blessing from. If direct contact isn't possible or desirable, "make-believe" can be used. The child can be encouraged to make a phone call on a toy telephone, or use puppets or dolls to act out the event, with the adoptive parent playing the role of the birthmother or foster mother. The adoptive parent can direct the activity by saying, "What do you think you would say to your birthmother if you called her?" "How do you think she would respond?" "I think she would say, 'You sound like a fine, strong girl. This family must be the right place for you.' " The adopted child then has had an opportunity to say good-bye and move on with her life. We have funerals to say good-bye to loved ones who have died because we recognize that as an important part of the mourning process. But there is no such ceremony to help the adoptee deal with her grief.

ADOPTEES AT RISK?

News accounts of crimes will often mention whether the arsonist or murderer was adopted, as though this somehow explains the events. This reflects a belief held by some people—including many professionals—that adoptees are more vulnerable to psychological disturbances than non-adopted persons. While there is some evidence that adoptees may be at greater risk for emotional and behavioral problems, the risk is not as great, or as inevitable, as we are sometimes led to believe.

Behavioral or Psychological Problems

We are not surprised when children adopted at an older age have behavioral or psychological problems. Neglect, abuse, failure to set appropriate limits, frequent moves, and failure to form attachments affect a child and are likely to continue to affect her to some degree after placement in an adoptive home. In these cases, it isn't adoption that causes the problems, but factors experienced before she was placed for adoption. Nevertheless, one of the most important and controversial questions in adoption is whether adoption itself is so traumatic as to cause lasting psychological damage—even in those adopted as infants. Research into this issue has yielded conflicting results and a variety of interpretations of those results. Discontinuous mothering, unresolved grief at the loss of the birthparents, failure to make an attachment to the adoptive parents, confusion about the meaning of adoption, and feelings of rejection and abandonment may put an adoptee at risk for emotional problems. But not all adoptees develop problems, and enlightened attitudes on adoption and an awareness of its effects may prevent or mitigate problems. It is too simple for parents, relatives, or professionals to explain away any behavioral or emotional problems an adoptee has as being related to her adoption. But it is also unwise to ignore the fact that the adoptee has experiences in her life that children who have been raised by their biologic parents do not have. The effect of these may become apparent long after the adoptee's initial adjustment to the adoptive home and attachment to the adoptive parents.

Psychiatrist Marshall Schechter is often credited with starting the controversy more than twenty-five years ago when he published an article noting that he had a higher percentage of adoptees in his practice than were in the general population. He apparently received more publicity than his critics who challenged his statistics. Other critics have wondered if he took into account that he might have had a large number of adoptees because he had a reputation for working on adoption issues. Yet some studies since that time have also found that adoptees are overrepresented among children referred to mental health clinics and residential treatment centers. (Some adoptees have used these findings to justify opening their sealed adoption records. The higher incidence of psychological problems, they believe, is due to their lack of information about their biologic relatives.)

Other studies have found that adoptees do not seek mental health counseling any more frequently than non-adopted persons. And some experts have suggested explanations other than a greater degree of psychological problems for whatever overrepresentation there may be by adoptees in clinic populations. Adoption is generally a middle-class phenomenon, as is the practice of consulting mental health professionals. Perhaps a higher percentage of adoptees use counseling services because they come from a class of people who value their use. In addition, people who adopt are accustomed to using the helping professions. If they are infertile, they have had to enlist the aid of the medical profession in helping them achieve a pregnancy, or may have had counseling to help resolve their feelings about infertility. With an agency adoption, they have been assigned a social worker who has probed their reasons for adopting and their parenting skills. Even with an independent adoption, parents have needed the assistance of a doctor or lawyer. It is, perhaps, easier for these people to turn to a counselor for help than it is for someone who has never been in a state social services office or discussed parenting issues with a professional. While some people have no idea who to call for needed therapy, the adoptive parents may know a social worker by name or belong to an adoption support organization that refers families to counselors specializing in adoption issues.

It may also be that the intensity and concern that adoptive parents bring to their roles cause them to intervene sooner than other parents. Parents who have unrealistic expectations of themselves and their child may see anything but near perfect behavior in their child as a sign of psychological problems. Or perhaps, having been influenced by family and friends who believe they are going to have more than their share of problems with their adopted child, adoptive parents seek help at the first sign of trouble.

Other studies have looked at children outside of mental health facilities to evaluate adoptees' behavior to see if they have more problems than non-adopted children. Here too, the results are conflicting. Some studies have failed to find differences between adoptees and non-adopted children, while others indicate that school-age adoptees—including those adopted as infants—have more behavior problems. There is also some indication that adopted boys have more problems than girls. Some of the discrepancies among results can be explained by poor research methods—not all of which are the fault of the researchers. The secrecy that surrounds adoption has made it very difficult for social scientists to obtain representative samples of adoptive families and adequate information about adoptees' biologic backgrounds. Nevertheless, some studies are worth looking at.

One large study in Great Britain, which followed children from birth, found that behavior problems of adoptees increased between the ages of seven and eleven—the period when adoptees begin to comprehend that their first parents placed them for adoption, but before they understand the legal system that makes adoption permanent. This study also found that boys had more problems than girls. In a recent study that deserves attention because of the way its sample was selected and compared to a control group, researchers at Rutgers University found that adopted children six to eleven years old were rated by their mothers and teachers as having more psychological and school-related behavior problems and more difficulty getting along with their peers. Both boys and girls were equally at risk for behavior problems.

The findings of yet another study raise the question of whether adoptees are more at risk for psychological problems at certain times of their lives. The study, which looked at all patients registering for their first psychiatric services at a particular clinic, found that 5 percent of the children seen were adopted, but less than 2 percent of the adults were adopted.

Learning Disabilities and Hyperactivity

Adoptees are often said to have more learning disabilities than non-adopted children, but some people describe any school- or learning-related problem as a learning disability. Technically, learning disabilities are disorders of the basic psychological processes involved in understanding, perceiving, or expressing language or concepts. They include such conditions as dyslexia, but do not include learning problems that are the result of visual, hearing, or motor handicaps, or those due to mental retardation. Children with learning disabilities are often of average or above average intelligence, but seem to have a discrepancy between their intelligence and their ability to learn.

What adoptees seem to be at greater risk for are behavior problems such as hyperactivity, impulsivity, and inattentiveness, which are often associated with learning disabilities. Why adoptees may be at greater risk for these problems is not known. The origins of specific learning disabilities are still unclear but include such genetic, emotional, and environmental factors as chromosomal anomalies, metabolic abnormalities, neurologic damage, maturational delay of the neurologic system, nutritional deficiencies, and sensitivity to environmental substances. Neurological damage, and emotional and environmental factors are some of the causes of behavioral problems such as hyperactivity. In adoptees, grief and excessive pressure to succeed might be responsible for some learning problems. Or, adoptees may be showing a higher incidence of problems that result from poor prenatal care or birth trauma—both of which are risks with teenage mothers, who also have been the traditional source of infants placed for adoption.

Parents should not be overly concerned that their adoptee will develop hyperactivity or learning disabilities. However, because the adoptee may be at

greater risk for these problems, the parents who suspect their child is having them should have their child evaluated. Some early signs in the child include:
— Significant delays in language development
— Difficulty in expressing herself, including remembering the names of familiar objects or people
— Coordination problems or other signs of poor spatial judgment
— Inability to follow directions
— Lack of organization
— Being easily distracted by background noise
— Failure to use common sense
— Extreme restlessness or moodiness
— Dislike of school or physical complaints related to school
— Poor memory.

A child with one or more of these complaints is not necessarily having learning problems; he may simply be immature, for example. But parents who think their child is having learning problems should insist on having him evaluated and not be put off by lack of concern on the part of their child's teacher or physician. If no problem is found, the parental reassurance can be an important benefit. Diagnosis of learning problems will be aided by information about learning problems in the child's biologic relatives as well as information about complications the birthmother may have had during her pregnancy and delivery. (The importance of a complete history is discussed in Chapter 6.)

Parents who want their child's apparent learning disability diagnosed should first consult his physician, who may refer the family to other community resources. Parents of a school-age child can also use the resources of the school system, such as a school psychologist and learning disability specialist. Organizations such as the National Council for Learning Disabilities (P.O. Box 40202, Overland Park, Kan. 66204), and the Association for Children and Adults with Learning Disabilities (4156 Library Road, Pittsburgh, Penn. 15234) can help parents learn how to get evaluation and treatment for their children. Betty B. Osman's book, *Learning Disabilities: A Family Affair* (New York: Random House, 1979), contains helpful information for parents on identifying and dealing with learning disabilities; and because learning disabilities can affect a variety of living skills, including communication, the book *No One to Play With: The Social Side of Learning Disabilities*, by Betty B. Osman in association with Henrietta Blinder (New York: Random House, 1982), is also recommended. For parents of the hyperactive child, *Raising a Hyperactive Child*, by Mark

A. Stewart and Sally W. Olds (New York: Harper & Row, 1973), contains useful suggestions.

While getting help for their child is essential, adoptive parents may also need help to understand the child's limitations and prognosis. Learning disabilities often run in families, and when, for example, the father has had a learning problem, he can not only empathize with his child's problem, but may be able to show how he was able to compensate for it, or how it has not impeded his success as an adult. If the adopted child is the first person in the family to have a learning disorder, the parents may be more anxious about the long-term effects of the disorder or may not understand the child's frustration. In addition, adoptive parents who place great emphasis on the ability of environment to overcome problems may think that with the right diet, tutor, or extra help at home, they can compensate for the learning disorder. That may happen, but adoptive parents should also take care to communicate to the child that they are satisfied with the progress the child is making. Adoptees shouldn't feel they are a disappointment to their parents just because the parents asked for a "healthy child" and received a child with a learning disability.

It is advisable for parents who adopt an older child to wait until the child has adjusted to her new school and her new family before deciding whether any problems she is having at school represent actual learning problems or temporary adjustment or grief reactions. Even if her history indicates she has had learning disabilities in the past, parents should not be overzealous about having her evaluated immediately. She could get the idea that her remaining in her adoptive family is somehow tied to overcoming her learning problems.

Academic Expectations

Despite evidence that adoptees have more school-related behavior problems and are at risk for certain types of learning disabilities, research indicates that as a group, adoptees' school performance is acceptable. Studies of adoptees show that while their school achievement is slightly below that of non-adopted children in comparable environments, they do as well or better than children in the general population.

Studies in Britain and the United States that looked at thousands of children at birth and continued to evaluate them for many years found that the adoptees did as well as or better than non-adopted children, particularly in such areas as reading and language use. Results of mathematical ability varied.

But when adopted children have been compared to children in similar environments, they appear to be performing less well academically. In the British study, for example, adopted boys were not doing as well in mathematics, and the adopted group as a whole was doing slightly less well than children in comparable environments. In a Rutgers University study of 260 adopted and non-adopted children six to eleven years old, adopted children were rated somewhat lower in academic achievement than closely matched children who were not adopted. This could reflect genetic differences in intelligence or a preoccupation with adoption issues associated with pre-adolescence that distracts the adoptees from their schoolwork. In any case, while academic performances may show some statistical differences between adoptees and non-adopted persons raised in comparable environments, those differences may not be meaningful to most families. That is, we may be talking about the difference between a B-plus and a B average in school.

Putting Research Into Perspective

It is important to look at research into adoption issues, but it is also necessary to put scientific findings into perspective. If adoptees make up 2 to 4 percent of the population, but researchers find that, for example, 10 percent have psychological problems, they are going to conclude that adoptees are more likely to have problems than non-adoptees. Even if that is true, that still leaves 90 percent who are well adjusted. An increased chance that an adoptee will have behavioral problems during childhood may be one of the risks in adoption, but it may not be a great risk.

Furthermore, the factors in adoption that put an adoptee at risk for greater problems do not doom them to those problems. For example, just because the birthparents decided not to raise their child does not mean that the child must go through life feeling rejected. The way that adoption is explained to her, the degree to which she is allowed to discuss her feelings about being placed for adoption, and the amount of information she has about her birthparents can help her understand and accept the decision.

Thanks to those adoptees who are now adults and have shared their feelings about growing up, adoptive parents now have a much better idea of how children react to being adopted and know the kind of information and support adoptees need. Years ago, the fact that a child was adopted often was hidden, and the child was not encouraged to talk about it. It makes sense that the child who couldn't ask a question about her birthparents without her adoptive parents responding, "Why do you want to know that? Don't you love us?" might have more difficulty reconciling her adoption than the child whose parents are open and not threatened by discussions about adoption or birth-parents. Years ago, adoption workers gave parents the advice that they thought was best, and parents followed it believing it was best for their family. We now have other theories about adoption, based on research and experience, that seem to result in healthier families. There is certainly evidence that the more comfortable parents are with infertility (if that is an issue), adoption, and parenting in general, the more support they receive when adopting, and the more open and empathetic they are in discussing adoption with their child, the better adjusted the child will be.

Chapter 6

The Important Family History

Ellen developed vaginal cancer at the age of 24. An adoptee, she did not know until later that her birthmother had taken the synthetic estrogen diethyl-Stilbestrol (DES) during her pregnancy, and consequently, she did not know to have the more thorough screening for cervical and vaginal cancer recommended for daughters of DES mothers. She believes her cancer could have been diagnosed earlier had she known her medical history.

Adoptive parents should have a complete medical, social, and psychological history of their child, including information about the pregnancy of the birthmother and the child's birth. Too often, though, this information is not provided to adoptive parents or is incomplete. Even more often, the information is not updated when new conditions in the birth family are discovered. In some cases, the information in the family history is vital to making a diagnosis of a disease or to providing genetic counseling. More commonly, the information is helpful, but not essential. Perhaps the most important reason for having a complete family history is peace of mind for the adoptee and his parents.

Trying to get accurate information is a burden for the agencies or intermediaries involved. Dealing with the knowledge that the adoptee may inherit a physical or mental disorder is a burden for the adoptee and the adoptive parents. But not knowing is also a burden. Not knowing about schizophrenia or hemophilia in the adoptee's biologic family is not going to reduce the adoptee's chances of developing those problems. But the lack of knowledge can interfere with an early or accurate diagnosis.

There is no excuse for not providing this information to adoptive families. Perhaps years ago when there were more healthy babies than adopting families, news that there was mental illness in the biologic relatives of the adoptee could have kept that child from being adopted. That is unlikely to be the case now, since the demand for infants is so great. And even those who believe adoptees and birthparents should not know each other's names and whereabouts should be able to support the sharing of vital medical and psychiatric information, which can be done without identifying anyone.

While it may be troubling to know the physical and mental illnesses that a person may inherit, most people know their medical and psychiatric histories. The purpose of adoption is not to "protect" people from unpleasant information about their genetic heritage; that is a side effect of sealed records. Adoptees have a moral right to information they would have had if they had not been adopted, especially when the information is related to their physical or mental health.

THE MEDICAL HISTORY

Physicians and hospitals typically request that a patient provide his family medical history on lengthy forms. But when an adoptee or adoptive parent indicates such information is unavailable, the health professional may be quick to reassure the patient or parent that the history probably won't be needed. One is left wondering why such a long form is provided if there really is so little need for it.

Most health care personnel are trained to take a complete medical history. In practice, though, some use such histories more than others, depending on their own style of practice, the complaint of the patient, and the physician's specialty.

Inherited Medical Conditions

Most people recognize the importance of a family medical history when there are inherited diseases in the family such as sickle-cell anemia, Tay-Sachs, cystic fibrosis, hemophilia, or Huntington's chorea. Fortunately, the incidence of inherited diseases such as these is relatively small. While the physician should be able to diagnose these problems without a family history, it is helpful to the physician to know whether the condition he suspects the patient of having has been diagnosed in other members of his family. Even when the person does not have the disease himself, he may want to know if he is a carrier.

People with a chance of inheriting a medical condition should know how the disease is transmitted, what their chances are of developing the disease or being a carrier, what their chances are of passing the disease on to their children, if there are tests to determine whether the person is a carrier or whether the person has the disease before developing symptoms, and if the disease can be detected in the fetus.

— *Dominant genetic traits.* If either parent has a gene for such a disease, the child has a 50 percent chance of having it. Since symptoms for some dominant traits, such as Huntington's chorea, do not show up until middle age, a person should know whether he is at risk for developing the disease before he reproduces and possibly passes the trait on to his own children. While screening tests are not available for all dominant traits, a person who knows that he has a fifty-fifty chance of developing the disease is in a better position to make reproductive decisions than the person who does not know.

— *Recessive genetic traits.* Children of parents who both have a recessive gene for a disease have a 25 percent chance of having the disease and a 50 per cent chance of being a carrier without having any symptoms of the disease. With some diseases, such as sickle-cell anemia, a test can be performed to determine if the person is a carrier—information that may influence that person's decision about whether to have children. It is also possible to detect certain diseases, such as Tay–Sachs disease, in an unborn fetus using amniocentesis, if a parent is known to be a carrier.

— *Sex-linked recessive traits.* With conditions such as color blindness and hemophilia, the male offspring of a carrier mother and non-carrier father will develop the condition while the female offspring will not. For the daughter to have the disease, she must be the offspring of a carrier mother and father with the disease.

If there are inheritable genetic conditions, both the birth family and the adoptee need to know. For example, if an adoptee is discovered to have cystic fibrosis, a recessive trait, his birthparents should be contacted through the adoptee's social worker or other intermediary and told that they are carriers, for the sake of other children they might have. And even though an adoptee may not develop a genetic disease, he should know if there is a possibility of his being a carrier for one, for the sake of his children.

Familial Medical Conditions

The medical history is often helpful, but not necessary, in diagnosing medical problems that run in families but are not directly inherited, such as cancer, diabetes, heart disease and many other problems. While the diagnosis might be made sooner if the medical history is known, the physician probably will uncover the problem without it.

The medical history is also helpful, but not essential, in determining the cause of learning problems, including language and hearing disorders. Some learning problems are genetic or familial. Knowledge about the mother's pregnancy, such as whether she consumed alcohol or took certain drugs, can also help determine the cause of some learning problems.

Sometimes the absence of a history of rare or inherited diseases is not as frustrating as the absence of common knowledge about the birthparents. For example, if a child appears to be growing slowly, it helps to know whether both birthparents were short. Without that information, the physician is more likely to order tests for the child to discover if some disease is retarding the child's growth.

A pregnant adoptee is often curious about her birthmother's experience with pregnancy. Although decisions about the care of the pregnant adoptee will be made based on her individual physical and medical condition, it can help to know, for example, if the birthmother had a narrow pelvis or a history of short labor.

The medical history is most useful in preventative health care. For example, if a family has a history of heart disease, a physician may be more aggressive in ordering annual tests that could predict future heart problems, and in advising the patient on diet and exercise that could prevent heart disease. Once a person has a heart attack, however, knowing that the family has a history of heart attacks doesn't alter the treatment.

Children of an Incestuous Relationship

Adoptive parents should be told if their child's parents were closely related so that they can have their child evaluated for genetic abnormalities that may result from incest. Some of the problems can be diagnosed before any signs or symptoms appear if geneticists know to look for them. Since the diagnostic and evaluation procedures are the same whether the parents were first cousins or father and daughter, it isn't necessary to know the exact relationship between parents.

Geneticist Barbara McGillivray believes a history of incest should be suspected more often than it is when a girl decides to place a child for adoption, particularly if the mother is very young and unclear about the identity of the father. Agencies should probe for a more definite indication of the relationship of the parents whose child is being placed for adoption so that the adoptive parents can be told if there is a need for a medical evaluation. While there are no statistics showing that children born of an incestuous union are more likely to be placed for adoption, the family of a pregnant girl is probably less likely to absorb a child born of a brother–sister or father–daughter relationship than it would a child born under other circumstances.

McGillivray and Patricia A. Baird, also a geneticist, found that of twenty-one children referred to them by an adoption agency because of a history of incest, nine had serious abnormalities thought to be genetic, including mental retardation, cleft lip and palate, congenital heart defect, neurofibromatosis, and delayed development. This is a much higher number than would be expected in the general population. Some of the nine had no outward symptoms of the problems. Three of the twenty-one had abnormalities not thought to be genetic, and nine were normal.

Children born of an incestuous relationship have a greater chance of having an abnormality because their parents have a greater chance of having the same recessive gene for an abnormality. If they do, their child has a 25 percent chance of being affected.

Parents with a child suspected of being the offspring of an incestuous relationship should have the child evaluated by a geneticist. The family doctor or pediatrician can refer families to the closest medical center for genetic evaluation. Such evaluations should be done soon after birth, and the child should have more thorough medical observation as he grows. Most of the children in the study done by McGillivray and Baird appeared normal, and some diagnostic tests would not have been done on them had it not been known that their parents were closely related.

Obtaining a Family History

The National Commmittee for Adoption* has designed a form for obtaining a complete family medical history for an adopted child. Ideally, these are used by adoption agencies, physicians, and others arranging an adoption. They can also be used by adoptive parents as a guideline for information to be requested if a complete history has not been provided. However, it is sometimes more effective to have the child's physician request a medical history. One pediatrician, for example, reports about a 50 percent success rate in obtaining medical histories by making a personal appeal to the adoption agency. The American

Academy of Pediatrics supports efforts to obtain a complete medical history. In a 1981 statement, it said: "The pediatrician should encourage the adoptive parents to obtain as much medical and background history of the birthparents as possible at the time of adoption. . . . This complete information is required to enable the adoptive parents to provide essential answers as the maturing adoptee inquires about his or her background." Naturally, parents and physicians have a greater chance of obtaining the information the sooner the agency is contacted after placement.

Fortunately, those in a position to obtain complete medical histories of children being placed for adoption are recognizing the need for sharing that information with the adoptive parents. This recognition has come through the publicized efforts of adoptees and birthparents to find each other for the purpose of sharing medical information and through the willingness of adoptive parents to raise children who have medical problems or a medical history that puts them at risk for future problems. Those adoptees and adoptive parents whom agencies and health professionals sought to "protect" from negative information in the adoptees' backgrounds have made it clear that they prefer knowledge—even of something unpleasant—to ignorance.

When the Family History is Unavailable

Heather's pediatrician told her parents to bring Heather in each year for extensive laboratory tests because Heather did not have a family medical history. While some physicians advocate more vigorous screening tests, others think no screening is necessary. Still others advise parents to have inexpensive tests for hearing, vision, anemia, and urinary tract disorders, but to save the time-consuming and expensive tests until there is some sign that they are needed. Certainly the physician should have an increased index of suspicion if there is no medical history on a patient and should not dismiss the possibility that the person may have a rare or unusual condition.

Adoptive parents may want to set up an appointment with their physician aside from their regular visits just to discuss how the physician intends to deal with the lack of medical history—how important he feels it is, whether he is willing to contact the agency for additional information, and whether he thinks some screening tests are indicated periodically.

THE PSYCHIATRIC HISTORY

Psychiatric conditions such as schizophrenia, depression, manic–depression, and Alzheimer's disease are known to run in families and are thought to have genetic components.

Alzheimer's disease and the similar but less prevalent form of dementia, Pick's disease, are inherited as dominant traits, giving a child with one parent with the disease a 50 percent chance of developing it himself. There is currently no cure for Alzheimer's disease or other dementias—disorders of the brain that typically strike after age forty and are characterized by disturbed memory, difficulty in reasoning and cognition, deterioration of judgment, and personality change.

The inheritance of other psychiatric diseases is not as clear-cut. In many cases, scientists do not know how these diseases are inherited and what environmental factors—if any—must also be present for the diseases to manifest themselves. And because there may be different forms of the same general condition, not all of which are genetically controlled, professional diagnosis and genetic counseling are necessary.

Schizophrenia is thought to have a genetic component because schizophrenics who were adopted in infancy have been shown to have a higher rate of schizophrenia in their biologic parents and siblings than adoptees who were not schizophrenic. In addition, the adoptive relatives of schizophrenics have not been found to have a greater incidence of schizophrenia than the control groups or the general population.

A similar trend has been found among people diagnosed as having depression, although the results are not as conclusive. There is general agreement among psychiatrists that some manic–depression is influenced by genetics. There are indications that there are two kinds of manic–depression—one is inherited as a sex-linked dominant trait, and the other has an unclear method of transmission. However, they both manifest themselves in the same way. When symptoms of two diseases, or two forms of the same disease, are identical, and diagnosis is inconclusive, the risk of inheritance in a particular family cannot be determined.

Environmental influences may also be involved in some forms of schizophrenia and depression, but the interaction between genetics and environment in these diseases is not clear.

The Psychiatric History in Perspective

It may be difficult to accept the idea that mental illness can be inherited. We know it often runs in families, but we are more likely to credit that to the family environment than to genetics. If we change that family environment by adopting the child, we don't expect those disorders to surface.

Mental illness is frightening because disturbances of the mind are closely tied to who we are; indeed, mental illness alters a person's personality, thoughts, moods, and behavior. We think of mental illness as a disorder of the mind rather than a disorder of that physical gland, the brain. We expect to be treated for a physical illness, and probably cured. But many people still think mental illness is not treatable or curable.

We need to overcome our fear of mental illness and particularly the fear that a genetically inherited factor in mental illness will predetermine the fate of the afflicted. Furthermore, we have to remember that just because these diseases may be inherited doesn't guarantee they will be. Even when a disease is inherited as a dominant trait, the offspring has a fifty-fifty chance of not developing the disease. And most mental illnesses are not thought to be inherited in that way. The risk for developing schizophrenia, manic–depressive illness, or depression increases only to 10 percent for a close relative of someone with the disease, compared to 1 percent in the general population for schizophrenia and manic–depression, and 4 to 7 percent for depression. That still leaves 90 percent of the relatives of mentally ill people without psychiatric problems.

In addition, schizophrenia, depression, and manic-depressive illness can be treated with drug therapy and counseling, or a combination of the two. Although the success of treatment varies with the condition and individual, the situation is far from hopeless for the mentally ill person and his family.

Genetic Counseling for Mental Illness

Some people, including psychiatrists, do not think adoptive parents should know the psychiatric history of their child. There is concern that if the adoptive parents know their child is at risk for mental illness they will be overly concerned about the child's mental health. In hovering over him and worrying about him every time his behavior is unusual, they may create psychological problems where there were none. In addition, since many of these diseases do not appear in childhood, cannot be predicted by childhood behavior, and cannot be diagnosed before the symptoms appear, some people question the value of having the psychiatric history.

While not predictive of mental illness, the history can nonetheless be helpful to a mental health professional trying to make a diagnosis. For example, if the adoptee is depressed but not responding to standard treatment for depression, it may be that she is in the depressive phase of manic–depression, which is a different disease than depression. If the psychiatrist treating her knows that one of her parents had manic–depressive illness, her disease might be diagnosed more quickly. But along with the history, adoptees and their parents must have adequate counseling to help them understand what the information means—what the risk is that the child will develop the disorder, how the disease might manifest itself, and possible treatments.

While knowing about the mental health of the adoptee's biologic family may not be helpful now in predicting mental illness in the adoptee, in the future it may be critical to have this information early in a person's life. Research into the causes, methods of transmission, and early diagnosis of mental illness is continuing. While psychiatrists cannot now predict who will develop schizophrenia or manic–depression, it may not be long before we know what kinds of childhood behavior are precursors of mental illness in adulthood. There may soon be metabolic tests or other diagnostic tools, such as the PET scanner that measures brain metabolism, that can be used to determine whether the person has inherited a tendency to a condition long before symptoms appear. In the meantime, knowledge of psychiatric problems in a person's biologic family can help parents or the adoptee intervene sooner than they might otherwise if there appears to be a psychiatric problem. The adoptee should not be rushed to a psychiatrist every time he loses a friend, acts aggressive, or withdraws just because his birthparents had some mental illness. But the adoptive parents who are troubled by ongoing interpersonal problems their child seems to be having might pass off such behavior as typical of adolescence or a phase that the child will outgrow unless they know that their child has a greater risk of developing a psychiatric disturbance. Schizophrenia, depression and manic–depressive illness are all treatable mental illnesses, although they vary in the degree to which they are treatable. Treatment for dementias may be developed in the future. As with all diseases, the earlier mental illnesses are diagnosed, the easier they are to treat.

THE PSYCHOSOCIAL HISTORY

In addition to physical and psychiatric histories of the adoptee's birth family, adoptive parents and adoptees should know about the incidence of alcoholism and antisocial behavior in the birth family, as there are indications that these may be influenced by genetics as well as the environment.

Alcoholism

There is clearly a genetic factor at work in the development of some kinds of alcoholism, particularly among males. There is also evidence that an alcoholic environment contributes to alcoholism, although the connection seems to be stronger for males than for females.

Not every form of alcoholism can be explained by genetics; for example, alcoholism is sometimes secondary to other psychiatric disturbances. And there are likely to be other environmental factors involved than just alcoholism in the home. It's difficult to identify environmental factors in studies of adoptive families because most families are stable and have similar levels of education and income. But the studies that have found a high rate of alcoholism among adoptees whose close biologic relatives were alcoholics indicate that adoptees from an alcoholic background are at greater risk for developing the problem themselves.

Researchers looking for an explanation of how the tendency to inherit alcoholism may be expressed are studying adverse reactions to alcohol in which intoxication occurs after ingesting a small amount of alcohol; greater tolerance for alcohol that would enable a person to drink large quantities of alcohol; differences in the way alcohol affects the psyche, perhaps making some people feel better when they drink than other people do; differences in the metabolism of alcohol; and inherited differences in personality that would make some people more likely to drink excessively.

Before someone can become an alcoholic they must be exposed to alcohol, and usually they have warnings that their alcohol consumption is becoming excessive before they actually become alcoholic. One of the explanations for the lower rate of alcoholism among the female offspring of alcoholics is that males are exposed to alcohol consumption more than females, and it is more socially acceptable for a man to drink excessively than it is for a woman. Adoptive parents who know their child has biologic relatives who are alcoholics can reduce the chance of their child becoming an alcoholic by educating him about responsible alcohol consumption. Parents cannot keep their adolescents away from alcohol, but they can inform them about the dangers of alcoholism and the increased risk they may have of developing the problem. Adolescents can be instructed in ways to minimize the effects of alcohol—not drinking on an empty stomach, or adding ice to a drink to dilute it at a party where people are expected to keep their glasses full. They can also be taught how to avoid situations in which alcohol consumption is likely to be expected, or how to avoid drinking at all if in those situations, for example, by requesting a club soda with a twist of lime. Most teenagers experiment with alcohol use, and parents of children at risk for alcoholism may want to allow their teenager to drink a beer at home so he doesn't have to experiment away from home where excessive alcohol consumption would be more likely. Parents who discover that their adolescent is intoxicated sometimes ignore the incident, believing that the accompanying nausea and hangover are adequate punishment or will teach the child the necessary lesson. That is often an appropriate response; but if the adolescent is at risk for alcoholism, the parents have to take a more direct approach.

Alcohol consumption is not the only early sign of alcoholism. Some studies have found that behavior such as truancy, being in trouble at school or with the law, associating with gangs or companions that the parents find undesirable, aggressive behavior, and hyperactivity is greater in children who later become alcoholics. Most parents are concerned if their children skip school or hang around with children who get into trouble a lot and would probably take steps to change the child's behavior. If the child also has biologic relatives who suffer from alcoholism, parents should recognize that the behavior may be an early indication of potential alcoholism and not only take steps to change the child's behavior, but to educate him about alcohol abuse.

Antisocial Personality and Behavior

People with antisocial personalities engage in activities that bring them into conflict with society. In children, the behaviors include theft, incorrigibility, truancy, staying away from home overnight, aggression, impulsiveness, and lying for reasons other than to avoid punishment. Adults with antisocial personalities may be criminals, vagrants, alcoholics or drug addicts, and have difficulty holding a job, maintaining a marital relationship, or having a normal sex life. Once called "psychopaths," people with antisocial personalities are predominantly male and usually display antisocial behavior before the age of twelve.

Studies have found that adoptees with antisocial personalities are more likely to have biologic relatives with antisocial personalities than adoptive relatives, indicating that genetics may predispose a person, particularly a male, to antisocial behavior.

None of the researchers who are studying the heritability of antisocial behavior are excluding the likelihood that environmental factors are also at work. Some environmental factors that have been connected to the development of antisocial behavior are exposure to a psychiatrically disturbed member of the adoptive family, alcoholism, and low socioeconomic status. Again, it is difficult to isolate the environmental factors that may influence antisocial behavior by studying adoptive families because the social factors in adoptive homes do not vary greatly. Researchers suggest that the environmental factors that lead to antisocial behavior may be most influential when there is a genetic factor present that predisposes the person to such behavior. In other words, children with a genetic factor for antisocial behavior may respond to certain stimuli in the environment by acting in ways that society does not condone.

Because symptoms of antisocial personality show up early in the child, parents can intervene by discouraging their child from associating with disreputable people, being consistent and firm in discipline, and providing the child with clear, enforced limits. This is consistent with good parenting and is more likely to be found in healthy adoptive families than in families where one or more parents have antisocial personalities. But the parents who know their child is at risk for developing an antisocial personality may react to symptoms of deliquent behavior by also seeking counseling. Without the child's psychosocial history, parents may be inclined to wait for the child to outgrow the problem, or be unaware of the serious symptoms.

GENETIC COUNSELING FOR THE ADOPTIVE FAMILY

While information about mental illness or chronic physical illness in the adoptee's family can be disturbing, it also can help in making an early diagnosis or preventing or minimizing a disease. But information is not helpful unless it is accurate, complete, and up-to-date. Even if they were willing to do so, most social workers, lawyers, and even physicians are not qualified to obtain the kind of history of the birthparents that is needed. There is more involved than just asking the birthparents if there is any mental illness in the family. Ask a fifteen-year-old girl if anyone in her family has ever been depressed and she will be likely to answer affirmatively. But that doesn't mean there is anyone in her family who has been diagnosed as having depression, as psychiatrists use the term; nor does it differentiate between depression and the depressive phase of manic–depressive illness. An alcoholic is not likely to admit his problem to himself, much less a social worker. The first requirement of a genetic counseling program is that there be accurate diagnoses. Adoption agencies that want to provide genetic information will need the assistance of a geneticist, a psychiatrist, or both. Geneticists also have to be available to explain the diseases and the risks of disease to the adoptive family. It isn't enough to provide information; parents need help interpreting that information.

Obtaining a complete history of the adoptee is an ongoing process. Most of the psychiatric problems and many physical diseases that are inherited do not develop until after adolescence. The teenage parents placing their child for adoption may not have shown signs of schizophrenia or heart disease. The agency that decides to do genetic counseling will have to maintain contact with the birthparents to continue to obtain information about the adoptee's genetic heritage.

The International Soundex Reunion Registry* is trying to meet the need birth families and adoptive families have for updated medical and psychiatric information. ISRR has a genetic evaluation guidance committee that reviews information or requests for information from adoptees and birthparents. If the information is determined to be genetic or familial in nature, ISRR contacts the agency that handled the adoption and requests that the adoptive family or birth family be notifed. Compliance is voluntary.

Part III

The Adoptee Grows Up

Chapter 7

Sexuality and the Adoptive Family

When sex and adoption questions overlap, as they frequently do, even normally open parents can feel unprepared. In adoptive families, subjects such as illegitimacy, infertility, and incest may be more than hypothetical situations. Discussions of such subjects may reflect on real people in their lives or actual experiences, making the talks more difficult. Even simple questions such as "Why can't sisters marry their brothers?" become more involved when the sister asking the question is not biologically related to her brother.

PUBERTY

Much of sex education is geared to preparing children for the onset of puberty. Parents often "time" their discussions to ensure their children will understand body changes, menstruation and nocturnal seminal emissions before they happen.

Anticipating the Onset of Puberty

Anticipating puberty is easier if one knows when the child's birthparents matured. However, because puberty is influenced by environmental factors such as diet, exercise, and general health, a child who is in a dramatically different environment than her birthparents may mature at a different rate. Experts believe girls begin menstruating when they reach a certain body weight. Genetics certainly influence an adolescent's growth, but nutrition plays an equally important role.

Generally, girls will enter puberty around age eleven, although it can be as early as nine; boys enter puberty about two years later. Parents may want to anticipate their child entering puberty earlier rather than later and be sure their child is prepared. If the child hasn't entered puberty by age eighteen, a physician should be consulted.

Knowing when to expect a child to enter puberty is more difficult when the exact age of the child is unknown. Children adopted at an older age from a foreign country may not have an exact birth date. In such a case, instead of the child's chronological age helping to determine when puberty will begin, the onset of puberty will be awaited as a means of setting chronological age. (See Chapter 10 for a more detailed discussion of the child whose age is unknown.)

Even a child whose chronological age is known may reach puberty years before her classmates because she is older. Children who are developmentally delayed, who have fallen behind in their schoolwork while they were adjusting to their new family, or who have not attended school because of the circumstances of their life in a foreign country may have a chronological age incongruous with their academic or developmental age.

Children must be prepared when their bodies start to change or they may become quite frightened. Parents should always take the lead in helping their children understand sex and not depend on the school's sex education program, especially when the school's program is geared to the grade level rather than individual age. Parents may want to discreetly notify the teacher when the child begins to mature sexually—a third grade teacher may not think of menstrual cramps when a girl complains of abdominal pain. Teachers and parents should be prepared to help their child deal with the inevitable teasing that is the burden of the first person in the class to develop sexually—snapping the bra straps of the only girl in class with breasts large enough to warrant wearing a bra, for example.

Sexual Jealousy Among Siblings

Siblings who are not related genetically may mature sexually at different ages. The result can be a fourteen-year-old who needs to shave long before his sixteen-year-old brother.

Shirley is an adoptive mother with several children, including three girls: ten, twelve, and twelve. Because the twelve-year-olds had such difficulties in their previous homes, they fell behind in their schoolwork. All three girls are in the fifth grade. However, the ten-year-old is physically more developed than her older sisters. In fact, one of the twelve-year-olds is so petite that she is frequently mistaken for an eight-year-old. She is understandably jealous of her better endowed, older-looking sister.

One reason children are so sensitive about entering puberty is because adults and other children treat sexually mature children differently. Sexually mature children are considered more attractive and are expected to behave in a more adult-like manner. It can be frustrating when a twelve-year-old sees that she is not only mistaken for an eight-year-old, but is treated like one as well, while her younger sister is treated as more responsible simply because she looks older.

Shirley has tried to minimize the competition created by incongruous development in her three fifth-graders by seeing that they are in different classrooms at school. She also stresses individuality at home and encourages the three girls to have different friends and pursue different activities.

Sexual Self-Image

Girls look to their mothers in developing a sexual identity as much, if not more, than boys look to their fathers. However, physical characteristics are connected to a sense of "masculinity," while emotional or behavioral characteristics are associated with "femininity." A man is big and strong with hair on his chest. A woman is nurturing. Therefore, it may be more important to a boy to look like his father than it is to a girl to resemble her mother.

At a 1984 adoption conference, a panel of male adoptees talked about the difficulty some adolescent boys have developing a sexual self-image because they are physically so different from their adoptive fathers. One said he couldn't identify with his father because he was taller than his father and didn't have his father's impressive low voice.

If the boy is slightly built while the father is tall and muscular and has a deep voice, the boy may have a particularly difficult time thinking of himself as "a man." If the opposite is true—if the son outweighs his father by fifty pounds and towers over him—the son may question the father's credentials as a sexual role model.

Of course, it sometimes happens that boys in biologic homes grow up bearing little resemblance to their fathers. However, when that happens, the parents often have an explanation, such as: "Your Uncle Jerry was a real beanpole at your age." The important point, however, is that the adopted boy may believe that he wouldn't be having the same difficulty if he were living with his biologic father. Adoptive parents should encourage their sons to have role models other than their parents. A scout leader, coach, teacher, or choir director may become important to a boy who is seeking a particular man to identify with.

The adoptive father's sexuality also may come into question if the parents adopted because of infertility. Masculinity often is closely tied to the ability to procreate; even if the mother is infertile while the father is not, his "failure" to produce offspring may reflect on his sexuality. Again, the stereotyped role of a man is physical—siring a child; while the stereotyped role of the female is nurturing—raising a child.

Another male adoptee was athletic, while his adoptive father was not. The son was pleased that his father attended his football team's practices and games regularly. But he wondered if he wasn't expected to compensate for his father's lack of athletic ability. In his own mind, he saw his father's infertility and lack of athletic ability as related—both indicated a lack of masculinity.

Male and female roles are changing in our society. A man's masculinity is no longer brought into question if he plays a nurturing role with his children. Men are more likely to show their emotions and discuss their feelings. As the roles for men expand and parents focus on supporting the child as an individual, there should be less emphasis on resemblance between father and son to indicate manhood.

TEENAGE PREGNANCY

There are no statistics on the number of adoptees who become pregnant outside marriage. However, some experts such as Reuben Pannor, a social worker who has specialized in working with adolescent adoptees and birthparents, think adolescent adoptees are vulnerable to an unwanted pregnancy. While boys as well as girls may engage in early sexual activity, parents are more concerned about their daughters because of the double standard and the fear of pregnancy.

Some teenage adoptees become pregnant to identify with their birthmothers. However, Pannor believes most teenage pregnancies among adoptees are not attempts to reenact their own birth. Many pregnancies are the result of excessive parental pressure on children not to behave like their birthparents. Adoptive parents are particularly sensitive to the possibility that their daughter, who may be trying out her sexuality by wearing tight jeans, will end up with an unplanned pregnancy like her birthmother.

Most parents believe that somebody else's teenagers are making up the statistics on sexually active adolescents. However, adoptive parents of a child born to teenage parents know that their child's birthparents were sexually active as adolescents. Because they associate their child with her birthparents, adoptive parents are more likely to consider their child sexually active. The situation is similar to families in which parents become suspicious of the younger daughters after an older sister gets pregnant as a teenager.

Parents who think, "like mother, like daughter," may become excessively strict about dating. This subtly conveys to the adolescent that her parents don't think she can be trusted because she is adopted. And while some teenagers may become pregnant by rebelling against the strict rules that have been imposed, others may be simply living up to their parents' worst fear.

Carol said her adoptive parents' excessive strictness about dating resulted from fear that she would become pregnant out-of-wedlock just like her birthmother. At age twenty, she did. She had an excellent relationship with her father until she started dating, when he expressed dislike for most of the boys she dated. He insisted on a strict curfew, once opening the door and pulling her inside because she was fifteen minutes late. Her parents never said anything to imply that they were afraid she would get pregnant, but Carol understood that she wasn't trusted. Years later, she realized they didn't trust her because they feared she would be "like her birthmother."

The best way to avoid unplanned pregnancy is for our children to have complete, accurate information about sexual development, intercourse, and contraception. The more knowledgeable the teenager is, the less likely she is to act irresponsibly about sex.

DISCUSSING SEXUAL VALUES

Adoptive parents of children born to unmarried parents need to explain that situation in a nonjudgmental way, so that neither the birthparents nor child born out-of-wedlock is portrayed as "bad." However, parents still need to communicate their own moral values—that they do not want their child to have sexual intercourse as a teenager, or that she should take precautions against pregnancy. Some adoptive parents are so flustered by this dilemma that they respond by lying to the child about her birthparents' marital state. Children usually see through lies, which only serve to inhibit the communication and trust between parent and child.

It is better to handle the situation honestly and matter-of-factly. Parents should explain that it is easy to get in over one's head in a sexual relationship; that girls as well as boys have sexual desires that can lead to unplanned intercourse. They can add that the birthparents may not have used birth control because they didn't know about it or didn't expect to need it.

Parents can say that while the birthparents were not being sexually responsible, they were not bad people as a result. Teenagers can be encouraged to see how they can benefit from the experience of their birthparents when making their own sexual decisions.

Discussing the Pregnant Woman's Options

Infertile parents may have a particular problem discussing options available to someone with an unplanned pregnancy. Knowing how difficult it was for them to get pregnant, they may be resentful of those who get pregnant without trying or while using birth control. Those who spent years waiting for an available baby to adopt may be opposed to abortion as a result.

Educators Constance Hoenk Shapiro and Betsy Crane Seeber point out the need for parents to understand how their infertility is affecting their views on the options available to women with an unplanned pregnancy. We cannot rid ourselves of our prejudices just by willing them away, but we can communicate to our children that this is our opinion because of a particular experience and provide them with other sources of information on the subject. For example, we can say: "We waited five years for you because so many women who didn't plan to get pregnant got an abortion rather than making plans for adoption. That made us angry, and we're still angry at women who have abortions. However, you may want to get some other opinions about abortions."

Adoptees themselves may have strong feelings about abortion, recognizing that their birthmothers may have come close to choosing that option for them. In addition, they may feel such a need for a genetic connection to someone that they could not consider abortion. One thirty-eight-year-old adoptee was distraught that her biologic daughter had an abortion. To her, it was cutting off a branch of the family tree that had just been established. Adoptees who feel strongly against abortion need information about completely effective ways to avoid pregnancy, including abstinence.

Changing Sexual Ideas

Jan was bathing her four-year-old son when he referred to his penis as his "nasty." Most likely, he was "caught" masturbating in some previous family by an adult who said, "Don't do that. That's nasty."

Children who are adopted after living in previous homes may have different values, attitudes and terminology about sex than the rest of their adoptive family.

They may know only slang expressions for body parts and sexual functions. Or, they may have been in sexually permissive homes and been exposed to sexual stimuli from a very early age. They may have been sexually abused, or their relationships with adults may have had some kind of sexual overtone.

A good social history, supplied by the social worker or foster parent, will go a long way toward helping the adoptive parents understand their child's attitudes and behavior. But this information is not always known or made available.

One sign that a child has been sexually abused is inappropriate sexual play. All children have a healthy interest in each other's bodies, evidenced by "playing doctor." However, when a child displays knowledge of sexual activity rather than simple curiosity—for example, when a five-year-old knows about oral sex—that should be a warning that she may have had first-hand experience with an adult.

In the home, parents should gradually introduce an appropriate vocabulary for body parts and body functions, while taking care not to criticize the child for using the only words he knows. Parents can say, "The adult word for that is _____. That's the word we use in our house."

Parents may need to take the lead in initiating discussions about sex. Children who have had early exposure to sexual stimuli may think they know the subject thoroughly, or may be confused about what they have seen or heard. Parents can seize appropriate opportunities to discuss sex, matter-of-factly questioning a child about her knowledge and gently correcting any misconceptions. (An abused child's resistance to physical contact is discussed in Chapter 11.)

THE INCEST TABOO

At some point in every family, dad suddenly notices that his adolescent daughter is not a girl any more, but a rapidly developing woman. One day it feels perfectly natural for the daughter to sit on her father's lap. The next day her coy, cute behavior with daddy seems decidedly inappropriate.

The same situation applies to mothers and sons. One day it is acceptable for the teenage boy to walk from his bedroom to the bathroom in the nude. The next day, his mother is uncomfortable looking at her naked son and reminds him to wear a bathrobe.

Flirtatious Behavior

All parents have to deal with their child's sexual attractiveness. However, innocent flirtatious behavior between a child and the parent of the opposite sex can lead to tension in the adoptive family if either parent's behavior brings into question the incest taboo.

We have a taboo against incest in our culture partly because of the risk of birth defects in children produced by an incestuous relationship. (See Chapter 6.) The adoptive parents may wonder whether the incest taboo will hold when the biologic reasons for it are not present. The incidence of incest in biologic families indicates that adoptive parents are not necessarily at any greater risk than biologic parents to engage in incest. Perhaps the more effective taboo is that adults do not have sex with children. While statistics on the sexual abuse of children indicate that this taboo is not as strong as it should be, it is a taboo that is equally valid in an adoptive or biologic family.

One way to diffuse sexual tension is for a couple to discuss it. (It's more difficult for a wife to have an extramarital affair after she's told her husband that she finds a particular man exciting, for example.) It is difficult to discuss incest. Often the father is embarrassed to admit that he finds his daughter attractive. The mother is ashamed of her suspicions. A husband and wife should discuss their feelings about the situation with each other; bringing the issue out in the open relieves the tension and reinforces the fact that their feelings are normal and not dangerous.

Although the adolescent often is aware of the tension between husband and wife, the issue should not be discussed with her. She already is self-conscious about her sexual development; there's no need to plant in her mind the idea that she might have incestuous feelings for her father. When the air is cleared between the parents, the child will feel better too.

Parents shouldn't worry that they are on the verge of incest just because they receive pleasure from physical contact with their children. Because of the incest taboo, we sometimes think that any pleasure we receive from touching our children is wrong and abnormal. Yet mothers who breast-feed report that there is a strong component of physical pleasure from the experience. It is not the same as the physical pleasure a woman receives from breast stimulation by her sex partner, but it is pleasurable in a physical and therefore sensual way.

Parents in candid conversations say they receive physical pleasure from hugging their children or other kinds of nonsexual touching. This is not abnormal, deviant, or unusual. It does not mean that the parent wants to have a sexual experience with the child. Adoptive parents should not be concerned that they are having these feelings because they are not biologically related to their children.

Seductive Behavior

Flirtatious behavior by a teenager toward a parent usually is unconscious, innocent, and relatively easy to deal with. Sometimes, however, the behavior becomes openly seductive. The teenage daughter rubs up against her father. The adolescent boy makes a suggestive remark to his mother.

The teenager may not be aware of what she is doing or why. The child who has lived in other homes may have only seen people relate to each other sexually. She may be trying to get close to her parent but not know appropriate ways for a child to express affection to an adult.

Parents can make a point to be more openly affectionate to each other in the presence of the child, showing her that the parent already has a romantic partner. They can also gently direct the child to more appropriate displays of affection, while reassuring her that they want her love. They can say, for example, "We love you and we're glad you want to hug and kiss us. But in our family we kiss each other with our mouths closed."

Sometimes, however, the seductive behavior is deliberate. The child who has been sexually abused may want to know if the parent's love is unconditional, that she has not been adopted for her body.

Family therapist Jack Frank believes deliberately seductive behavior by teenagers is usually not an attempt at sexual seduction but at the seduction of authority. The child is trying to cause problems between the parents as a way of gaining control. In addition, if the parents are busy fighting with each other, they are less likely to fight with the child.

Keeping the lines of communication open between husband and wife can help diffuse such situations. However, a family in which a child is deliberately seductive, whether because she was sexually abused or because she is trying to cause problems between the parents, needs professional help.

Sexual Behavior Among Siblings

Parents who wonder about the incest taboo between parent and child may also wonder whether it holds with siblings. Parents who would consider "playing doctor" to be normal in a biologic family might become alarmed to find adoptive brothers and sisters in some stage of sexual exploration.

The seriousness of the situation depends on the social histories of the children. An older child who has been in the child welfare system for more than a year may have been sexually abused. Parents should not assume that because there is no mention of sexual abuse in the child's history that this has not been the case. They should trust their own instincts, should they observe behavior that makes them suspicious.

Children who have been sexually abused sometimes make sexual advances to their siblings. Parents who know or suspect that the adoptee was sexually abused should give the other children in the family some guidance in handling sexual overtures. While parents today are more cognizant of the need to warn their children what to do if an adult tries to touch them inappropriately, we do not indicate to our children that an inappropriate sexual suggestion could come from another child. There is no need to stigmatize one child by indicating that he is likely, because of his history, to make a sexual overture. Children can simply be told that sometimes other children want to touch them in a way that makes them feel uncomfortable, that this is not appropriate, and that they won't get in trouble for telling about it. Parents who suspect a problem with inappropriate sexual activity may require an "open door" policy during play while periodically checking on their children's activities.

Adoptive parents of older children repeatedly report that they were not informed about their child's sexual history. This reluctance to pass on negative parts of a child's past results from fear that no one will adopt the child. This attitude is changing due to pressure from parents who say they are willing to take on serious problems, if only they know about them in advance. Social workers who know that a child has been sexually abused or has abused other children in the past must pass this information along to the families; this way parents can get the necessary therapy for the child and protect other children in the family from possible abuse.

On the other hand, in a family where the children were raised together from infancy and have had a healthy sexual upbringing, the children are at no greater risk for incestuous sexual behavior than they would be in a biologic home. As in a biologic home, parents should not tempt fate by having their school-age or adolescent children of different sexes share sleeping quarters.

However, an "open door" policy whenever the brothers and sisters are alone together is usually unnecessary.

THE RE-EMERGENCE OF INFERTILITY ISSUES

Couples today are encouraged to grieve for the biologic children they will never have before they adopt a child—and most do. But feelings of loss associated with infertility may crop up again. This doesn't mean the parents didn't complete their grief process prior to adoption; only that their feelings of infertility were resolved in a particular context and now must be resolved in a new context. Shapiro and Seeber say that when parents see their children entering puberty and presumably becoming fertile, they may have to deal with their infertility again. These feelings may be complicated if the mother enters menopause at the same time the children reach puberty.

In addition, children adopted by infertile parents may have misconceptions about infertility that are tied to their view of sexuality.

Children's View of Infertility

Infertile parents may need to show affection to each other in appropriate ways in front of their children to let them know that infertility does not imply a lack of a sexual relationship. While showing affection is healthy in any family, it may be more necessary in the adoptive home. Most children can't imagine their parents having sexual intercourse, but assume they must have had intercourse the minimum number of times necessary to produce the children in the family. When there are no biologic children in the home, adopted children have difficulty imagining that their parents ever had sex.

Adoptees are also aware that their infertile mother was never pregnant or never delivered a baby. When they are pregnant themselves, they are sometimes unsure whether pregnancy is a sensitive issue for their mothers. Adoptive mothers should let their grown children know that they do not mind talking about pregnancy and that they can share in their excitement. As one adoptee said, "I wish my mother had said, 'I'm really glad you're pregnant,' instead of just being glad."

Yet an adoptive mother should also be aware that her daughter may need information or stories from women experienced with birth to alleviate her concern about her upcoming delivery—something that daughters traditionally turn to their mothers for. Like the adolescent boy who needs male role models other than his adoptive father, the pregnant adoptee may need permission to turn to other women for information or reassurance. It may be hard for a mother to accept that her daughter is turning to her mother-in-law more during her pregnancy than to her mother, for example. Yet, the daughter needs to know that her mother understands that she needs something only another woman who has been pregnant can provide.

Couples who adopted after a history of miscarriages, stillbirths or other complications of pregnancy need to be especially careful to keep their anxieties about pregnancy to themselves. No pregnant woman needs to hear about someone else's difficult pregnancy. Nor are women who are experiencing normal pregnancies likely to benefit from the overprotective attitudes of fearful parents.

Parent's View of Infertility

Sometimes the uneasiness adoptees feel about their parents' infertility is the result of messages from the parents. Parents who have difficulty resolving whatever infertility issues have re-emerged may have a harder time talking about sex and reproduction with their children. They may also be uncomfortable discussing why they were unable to conceive or carry a child. It is important to many adoptees to know exactly why their parents adopted, including the specifics about their infertility and the treatment they sought for it.

We should anticipate our children's questions about sex, reproduction, and infertility so we can feel at ease talking about those subjects, and not give our children the impression that these topics are off-limits.

Parents who have not resolved all their infertility issues may be jealous or resentful of their children's entry into fertility. Children need to have this change in their status from child to fertile man or woman accepted by their parents—especially by the parent of the opposite sex. By accepting the adolescent's emerging adulthood, the parents also affirm the adolescent's emerging sexuality.

The parent who refuses to buy a bra for the daughter who is self-conscious about breast development, or who doesn't respect the developing adolescent's need for privacy concerning his body, may be displaying an inability to come to terms with the child's fertility.

On the other hand, parents who have never given up on the idea of conceiving a child may go too far in associating sexual development with procreation. They may have difficulty communicating to their sons and daughters that intercourse can be engaged in for pleasure as well as to produce children. The child needs to have a healthy sexual self-image that is not related to his or her ability to produce offspring.

PREPARING FOR POSITIVE DISCUSSIONS ABOUT SEX

Parents who are unable to work out infertility issues alone should contact Resolve, Inc.,* a national organization that provides information and support to infertile persons. Its members are sensitive, caring, and nonjudgmental.

Parents can become more open about discussing sex with their children by discussing the subject with each other or with their friends. We can approach good friends with children older than ours about the experiences they had discussing sex with their children, ask them how they overcame their inhibitions, and what kinds of questions their children had. In addition to receiving information, parents can benefit from the experience of talking about sex with someone other than an intimate partner.

A university or continuing education course in human sexuality is another way to become more informed about sex and more comfortable with open discussion of it.

Books such as *The Family Book about Sexuality*, by Mary S. Calderone, M.D., and Eric W. Johnson (New York: Harper and Row, 1981), and *What's Happening to Me?* by Peter Mayle (Secaucus, N.J.: Lyle Stuart, 1975) are also helpful.

Chapter 8

The Adolescent Adoptee

The job of the adolescent is to become an adult—to discover what makes him an unique individual, distinct from his family and friends. It is also a time to finish childhood. At times, this conflict between wanting to be grown up and wanting to be a child causes turbulence in the family.

When the adolescent is adopted, self-discovery may be complicated by a lack of information about his birth family. But for parents, this may be a time when they can appreciate one of the characteristics of the adoptive family—the diversity of personalities, interests, and abilities in their sons and daughters.

Some conflict between parents and their adolescents is normal, but we as parents can keep conflict from becoming crisis by understanding the differences between adoption issues and adolescent behavior, and by giving our sons and daughters confidence that they will be able to handle the challenges of adult life.

GROWING INDEPENDENCE

Adolescents become aware that the values they were raised with are not universal; everyone does not share the political, religious, economic, or social beliefs of their family. Adolescents often try on some views of other people to test whether these values make more sense than the ones they have grown up with.

Whether it is rebellion or a testing of the parents' value system, the effect is much the same—parents question if they have had any influence on their child's values.

For the adoptive parent, this question can have an additional dimension. Not being the child's biologic parents, we are more aware that much of what we provide to a child is the environment of our home and our value system. Adoptive parents may believe, for example, that passing on the value of reading is more important than passing on their intelligence. In this atmosphere, open rejection of the parents' beliefs can be interpreted as a rejection of the parents themselves.

It is helpful to think back to our own adolescence and early adulthood and the many ways we vowed we would not be like our parents. In some ways we are different, but most of us are amazed at how much like our parents we have become, particularly with respect to childrearing. Adolescents test their parents' views and ultimately replace some of them with beliefs of their own. But the foundation of their value system is the one they were raised with.

Using Adoption as a Weapon

If the adopted adolescent senses that the parent is particularly vulnerable to references to his birthparents, he may try to exploit that feeling during conflicts with the parent. For example, the teenager who is rebelling against his parents' 11 p.m. curfew may say, "I wish I lived with my real mother; she'd let me stay out later." If we are threatened by comparisons to the birthparents we may not see that the teenager does not really want different parents. Making parents feel they must compensate for some past hurt is a typical ploy of teenagers to get their own way. Other adolescents might say, "I didn't ask to move to this town," or "It's not my fault you and dad are divorced." These teenagers aren't interested in discussing adoption, reasons the family moved, or reasons for divorce; they are trying to exploit the vulnerability of the parent. We should not allow these taunts to distract us from the real issue, which is whether the child can stay out late, take the car, or otherwise win the argument. We can say, "If you'd like to talk about your birthmother another time, we can, but right now we're talking about what time you're coming home, and it will be before 11 o'clock or there will be consequences."

No matter how easy it may be to separate adoption issues from adolescent issues in the abstract, it is always a jolt to be told, "You're doing that because you don't love me enough." It is particularly difficult for adoptive parents; we have to deal with society's doubt that love between people related by adoption is the same as that between people related biologically. An immediate reaction is for parents to reassure the adolescent of their love, either by giving in to his demand or by discussing how much they do love him. Either way, the teenager wins. He either gets what he wants, or he succeeds in distracting his parents from the matter at hand. It's difficult, but necessary, for us to pull back and say, "I love you a lot, but you still can't go on the camping trip." Otherwise, the adolescent will realize that this method of manipulation through guilt works and will use it again.

Rebellion as an Adoption Issue

Adolescence can be a difficult time for parents and teenagers. Although most parents recognize occasional turbulence as normal, parents and teenagers often look for simple explanations for the problems they are having in the hope of finding simple solutions, and try to fix blame for the problems. One spouse may blame the other for some imagined parenting failure, or a single parent may think divorce was responsible for the adolescent's rebellion. Adoption provides some easy targets for blame during adolescence. Adoptive parents and adoptees may blame genetics for their conflicts, thinking they would understand each other better if their personalities were more alike. Parents may think "My own child wouldn't act this way," while teenagers engage in fantasies about how much more sympathetic their birthparents would be. In his study of Scottish adoptees, John Triseliotis found that the greater the conflict between parents and adoptee, the more likely the adoptee was to blame adoption. It provided them with an easy explanation for their difficulties.

Occasionally, in looking for an extreme way to rebel against his parents, the adolescent adoptee may imitate a birthparent's behavior. This is especially likely to happen if the adoptive parents have indicated that they disapprove of the birthparents. Parents must talk about the birthparents in positive terms and particularly avoid negative comparisons between the adoptee and his birthparents. In the heat of an argument, adoptive parents have been known to yell, "You're no better than your birthfather." Though parents regret the comment later and try to apologize for it, such a statement can negate all the positive statements the adoptive parents have made about the birthparents as their child was growing up.

The Teenager's Growing Independence

Even though the teenager is growing more independent, and should be encouraged to be independent, this is not a time for parents to ease up on discipline. Adolescents need and want firm limits, even though they may complain about them. Being independent is often a scary prospect, and teenagers can be secretly happy to fall back on parental rules. "I can't go to a drive-in movie unless there's another couple with us," a teenager may tell her date, communicating that she thinks such a rule is parental stupidity. But inside, she may be relieved that she won't be alone with a date in a car.

Those adoptive parents who still question their right to parent the adoptee, or fear that discipline will result in the adolescent's withdrawal of love, are likely to have difficulty setting firm, consistent limits. Fitzhugh Dodson's book *How to Discipline with Love* (New York: New American Library, 1978), as well as Thomas Gordon's book *P.E.T.: Parent Effectiveness Training* (New York: Peter H. Wyden, Inc., 1970), can help parents develop a consistent pattern of effective discipline.

Parents also need to give their children opportunities to develop skills such as decision-making and self-reliance that will help them meet the challenges of adulthood. Part-time after-school jobs and full-time summer work not only give teenagers opportunities to earn money, but also give them the confidence in their ability to function well independently.

Adolescents also benefit from participating in activities with an element of risk, such as downhill skiing. Teens who can get thrills in ways that are socially acceptable, and which can be controlled by proper training and equipment, may not feel a need to get thrills by driving a car too fast. It may be frightening for us to allow our teenager to stay home alone while we go away for the weekend. We may worry that he'll eat nothing but potato chips and have wild parties. But according to Claudia Jewett, the adolescent who knows his parents have confidence in his ability to take care of himself—and who learns to take care of himself—will develop more self-reliance than the teenager whose parents communicate to him in various ways: "You cannot be trusted to make responsible decisions or take care of your basic needs." Sometimes the adolescent who seems least able to handle such an experience is the one who needs it the most.

In addition, we should remember that we are the child's parents and not his social worker or therapist—an easy role for adoptive parents to fall into if we become too psychologically sophisticated. This confuses the child. Parents should react emotionally at times. After all, the child needs someone to rebel against. If parents are completely accepting of each new teenage fad, the teenager may have to escalate his rebellion until he finds something that gets a reaction from his parents. Rob thought he would be understanding when his teenage son came home and said he wanted to wear a gold earring in one pierced ear. "That's interesting, why do you want to do that?" Rob said. But he was unable to maintain his composure indefinitely, and ultimately screamed: "No son of mine is wearing an earring to high school." He was embarrassed that he hadn't been more tolerant, but his response was appropriate for a parent. Rob's wife carefully steered their son into a new hairstyle, and that change apparently served his need to look more like his friends, without his wearing a pierced earring.

While there are some seriously troubled teenagers who need professional counseling (see Chapter 11), therapy is not needed to resolve all parent–adolescent conflict. Nevertheless, group sessions offered in some communities by adoption agencies, organizations, or therapists may be helpful for parents and their adopted teenagers. These give families an opportunity to identify their feelings and gain an understanding of the ways they are influenced by adoption. The teen-oriented novel *Who Is David? The Story of an Adopted Adolescent and His Friends*,* by Evelyn Nerlove, discusses how one family was helped by such group sessions. Communities may also have workshops for parents of adolescents sponsored by churches, schools, or the continuing education departments of universities on particular methods of discipline, such as P.E.T. (Parent Effectiveness Training), or on raising adolescents.

Adolescence is a time of change, and some families accommodate change more smoothly than others. While it sometimes appears that our teenagers are rejecting our values, we can rely on the solid foundation laid down during the preteen years to carry our sons and daughters through this time. We can also feel confident that if our relationship with our adolescent has been good, and we have maintained a positive attitude toward adoption, whatever tension there is at this time will be short-lived.

HANDLING CRISES IN ADOLESCENCE

Conflict between parent and adolescent is normal, but occasionally it escalates into such serious problems that parents do not think they are capable of handling the situation at home. Those who work with troubled teenagers are concerned about the unexpected numbers of adolescent adoptees who are in residential treatment centers, foster care, or other alternatives to living with their families. While problems are often expected when an older child with a history of trauma or multiple foster families is adopted, it is suprising to find parents who adopted newborns saying years later that the adoption is "not working out."

No one knows exactly how many infant adoptions are "disrupting" more than ten years later; certainly disruptions are the exception. Nor does anyone know why they disrupt, although researchers at the University of Texas, headed by Ruth McRoy, are looking into the problem, as is therapist Claudia Jewett. Perhaps people who sought a "problem-free" infant adoption are less able to cope when there are problems, or perhaps their experience with adoption made them aware of alternatives, such as foster care, that other parents might not consider to be an option for a troubled youth. Perhaps there was a failure to attach, or maybe the pressure on parents and child to realize high expectations sometimes causes a breakdown in the family system. We can only hope that a greater awareness of how adoption affects parents and children will reduce the number of problems that develop in adolescence. When problems do occur, however, options are available to help deal with them before they result in an alienated family or a "disrupted" adoption.

Preparing to Leave Home

Family therapist and adoptive parent Claudia Jewett has been looking at the ways adolescents leave home for clues to how parents can avoid and deal with crises. The suggestions in this section are based on her observations.

In most families, adolescents leave home at age eighteen. After finishing high school, adolescents are expected to go to college, get a job, join the armed forces, get married, or otherwise take responsibility for themselves and the rest of their lives. High school students are expected to know what they want to do after graduation, perhaps even what they want to do for the rest of their lives. And sometimes the conflict between parent and adolescent centers on these issues. Parents may not like their teenager's choice of companions—people who might lead their child to choose a course other than the one the parents think is desirable. They want their adolescent to work hard at school so he can get his diploma or get into college. Parents fear their teenager's "lazy" habits, failure to take care of his possessions, or inability to handle money will not change in time for his entrance to adulthood.

It can be a scary time for parents as well as adolescents, although teenagers may project an apathetic attitude. Both parents and teenager would like adolescence to be over quickly, so that they can all be reassured she will make it on her own. The more unsure the adolescent is that she will be able to make it as an adult, the more likely she is to precipitate adulthood by leaving home early—running away, getting married, or orchestrating a crisis that leads to her removal from the home. Jewett suggests a number of ways we can reduce the possibility of this happening:

— Emphasize areas in which the child is competent. Parents sometimes consider adolescence a time for remedial work, emphasizing the need to gain or improve skills that are inadequate. For example, parents may be concerned that the adolescent cannot budget her money. In communicating the need to improve in that area, they are saying: "I don't think you'll make it as an adult because you can't handle your money." But we need to remember that adolescents aren't adults and they aren't supposed to have all the adult skills they will need. Instead of focusing on areas in which the adolescent is inadequate, we should emphasize—to ourselves and to our teenager—the skills she does have. For example, she may have gained a reputation as a valuable employee at her part-time job.

— Encourage the adolescent to have experiences that will give him and his parents confidence in his ability to handle the responsibilities of adulthood. The person who has been away at camp, traveled by himself on a bus, held a job, or otherwise tried on adult roles is going to be more able to visualize himself on his own as an adult. The less able the adolescent is to handle these kinds of experiences, the more he needs them.

— Give the adolescent opportunities to handle his own mistakes. Instead of rushing in with solutions, we should ask the child how he plans to deal with the problem. If he doesn't know, we can suggest how we are willing to help him, but leave the choice of accepting the help up to the adolescent. Sitting in court one day were three eighteen-year-olds who had been caught buying beer with false identification. Only one had brought his parent along to pay his fine. The other two indicated they would be able to pay their fines themselves and clearly had no intention of notifying their parents of the arrests unless they had to by virtue of a jail sentence. They had done a stupid thing by misrepresenting their age to buy beer, but they were willing to take responsibility for it.

— Remember, the adolescent may have a plan and timetable for leaving home that differs from ours. Parents who plan for their teenage to go to college after graduation may not be open to his plan to get a job after high school. Rather than initiate a confrontation, he may drop out of high school, virtually eliminating the possibility of going to college. We should think about how we left home and how and when we expect our sons and daughters to leave home. Conflict is eased dramatically when the child chooses to leave home in the same way and at the same time that his parents did. Part of being able to accept the way the child wants to leave home involves accepting differences, including different values. The family may value a college education highly. Can they accept someone without that degree as successful?

— Keep in mind that the adolescent who has been made to feel that he was "rescued" from a disadvantaged circumstance by being adopted is being made to feel helpless. Someone who feels like a helpless victim is not going to feel capable of handling the responsibilities of adulthood.

— Show children that being an adult is enjoyable. Sometimes parents become so overwhelmed by the conflicts of adolescence that the marital relationship suffers. We must remember that we are models for our children. If we are not taking care of ourselves, having fun, and enjoying life, the adolescent may decide being an adult is not a desirable goal.

For the adolescent adoptee, preparing to leave home may remind him that he was involuntarily separated from his first home and birthparents. He may need some time away from his adoptive home so that he can come back and say, "You decided to adopt me eighteen years ago, now I choose to come back to this home." Claudia Jewett is finding that many adoptees who leave home precipitously in adolescence and have a chance to gain confidence in their ability to function in the adult world are returning home eighteen to thirty-six months later to "claim" their adoptive family. They need, she believes, a chance to experience other lifestyles—what might have been had they not been adopted—and gain confidence in adult responsibilities. To get this, they may need more freedom and responsibility, not the increased restriction and protection of a residential treatment center.

When adolescents do leave home suddenly or in a way that parents do not view as desirable, parents should remember that leaving home doesn't mean leaving the family. Some adjustment in our thinking may be necessary; we may think a "family" lives together, and if we're not together, we must not be a family. Parents should leave the door open to their adolescent. This doesn't mean that an adolescent's return home can't be contingent on acceptance of certain rules, for example, in his agreeing not to use drugs in the home. But parents should make it clear that the teenager is still a member of the family and will be welcomed home when they can all make the adjustments necessary for living together.

ESTABLISHING AN IDENTITY

One adoptee's father, uncles, and grandfather graduated from Princeton University and expected him to attend their alma mater. As the only one in his family who was artistic, he chose to go to an art school instead. He was not simply rebelling against family tradition, he was trying to show himself and his family that he was an individual with talents to develop that were different from those of the rest of the family.

Identification with Parents

Students of the psychoanalyst Erik Erikson believe that one of the keys to the development of identity in adolescents is their understanding of how they are different from their parents. In other words, one way to understand the ways in which we are unique is to look at the people we are most like and compare how we are the same and how we are different.

Applying this theory to adoptees has some built-in difficulties. The adoptee has to discover how he is similar to and different from not one but two sets of parents. The artistic child born into a family that is not artistic might look back a few more generations to see if there is evidence of the talent there. Finding none, he might accept his ability as unique to him. The artistic child in the adoptive family may wonder whether his talent is unique or derived from his biological family.

Unfortunately, most adoptees do not have enough information about their birth families to know the ways they might be the same or different. One reason adolescent adoptees are curious about their birthparents is they are trying to discover how they themselves are unique. It's a difficult concept to grasp for those of us who grew up being told, "You freckle easily, just like the rest of the McCarthys," or "Your mother could play the piano beautifully, too."

The transracial or transcultural adolescent adoptee not only has two sets of parents, but dual ethnic backgrounds to consider in developing his sense of "self." The black child raised by white parents in a white community or the Filipino child raised as an American must discover to what extent they have adopted the culture of white Americans and to what extent they retain their ethnic heritage.

This sounds traumatic. Some people believe adopted adolescents have difficulty integrating their diffuse pasts into solid identities. Without a firm sense of who they are and how they are different from significant people in their lives, adoptees may have low self-esteem and difficulty forming lasting relationships or selecting careers.

Others have postulated that the number of adoptees with identity conflicts is small, but appears to be large if researchers look only at those adoptees in therapy. In one study of fifty adopted and forty-one non-adopted adolescents selected from the general population, no evidence was found that being adopted had adversely affected their identity formation. Studies of black adolescents in white homes and Korean children in American families showed they had self-concepts comparable to those in the control groups.

The problem with studies of adoptive families selected from the general population is that only those families who are not having major conflicts may agree to participate. Families having serious problems may not want to be scrutinized by researchers.

So despite these studies, the question of whether adoptees have more difficulty developing a positive identify or self-concept during adolescence remains unanswered. At the very least, it appears the adoptee has some additional tasks in the formation of her self-concept—she has more people to identify with and more people to separate herself from. She may not have as much information about the people she needs to identify with as other adolescents do. While these seem to be major hurdles for some adolescents, others appear able to develop positive self-concepts despite them. Being adopted can get in the way of identity formation, but it doesn't have to. The adolescent who has a good relationship with her parents, gets along well with friends and siblings, trusts other people, is able to be independent, has a positive sexual identity, and can set goals and achieve them, is going to develop a positive self-concept whether or not she is adopted. The adopted teenager may go about forming her identity in a slightly different way, or she may need to reflect on her sense of self more or somewhat differently, but generally the adoptee emerges from adolescence ready to tackle adulthood.

Discussing Adoption Issues

Because the adopted adolescent does have some additional factors to consider in the development of his self-concept, it is important for adoptive parents to continue their willingness to discuss adoption issues. Researchers have found that open communication about adoption issues enhances the positive self-concepts of adolescent adoptees, particularly, as discussed in Chapter 4, when the adoptive parents are open from the very beginning of their relationship with the adoptee.

Adoptive parents may have to take the lead in talking about adoption issues. While some adolescents do ask questions about their birthparents or otherwise indicate an interest, others refrain, thinking their adoptive parents will be hurt by their interest in their biologic family. Some adolescents may even resist talking about adoption when the parents bring up the subject. This doesn't necessarily indicate a lack of interest, but perhaps a reluctance to think about issues that are sometimes painful.

Teenagers are interested in knowing why they were placed for adoption and what their history was prior to joining the family. But these questions are not always expressed directly. The teenager who says, "I want to find my birthmother" may not really want to meet her, but may be indicating he'd like some answers that only his birthmother can provide.

It is essential that we present information about the birthparents empathetically at this time. The adolescent adoptee often thinks unkindly of his birthparents and their decision to place him for adoption. He may think only a "bad" person would place a child for adoption. In my visits to high schools to talk about adoption I am always impressed by the predominant feeling among adolescents that people who "get caught" by getting pregnant have an obligation to "take their punishment" by raising the baby. It is as though premarital sexual behavior is acceptable if the woman is willing to raise a baby; but if she "gives away" the result of her sexual activity, she is promiscuous.

The adolescent may also be seeing for the first time some inconsistencies between the positive things the adoptive parents are saying about his birthparents and his own feelings about being adopted. He feels rejected, but is told it takes a lot of love for a birthmother to place her baby for adoption; he sees his birthmother's decision as selfish, but is told that she made her decision with her child's interests in mind. Rather than discussing the adoptee's personal situation, we might want to discuss adoption in more general terms, talking about the alternatives that are available to women who get pregnant and the grief process that birthparents go through. It is important to communicate that birthparents do resolve their grief so that the adoptee doesn't believe the birthparent is still mourning for him. One excellent book that describes the decision-making process that birthmothers go through before placing a child for adoption is Suzanne Arms' *To Love and Let Go**.

An adoptee may be angry at his birthmother during adolescence for her decision to place him for adoption. He may make statements such as, "I'd never allow my baby to be placed for adoption." This does not mean he doesn't like his adoptive home or parents. More likely it reflects his feelings of rejection and confusion, as well as the possibly accurate assessment that adolescence might have been easier to deal with if he didn't have adoption issues to contend with.

Searching for Birthparents

In the vast majority of cases, adolescents want information about their pasts, but not necessarily a meeting with their birthparents. They are looking for information about where they came from to integrate into their sense of who they are. A reunion isn't necessary at this time, nor is it advisable.

Sometimes adoptees think their parents are deliberately withholding information about their birthparents. If parents have information that has not been shared with the adoptee—such as a letter from a birthmother explaining her reasons for placing the child, or the original birth certificate—it should be shared during adolescence. Parents may want to document efforts they have made to obtain more information about the child's origins, and share with the child copies of letters they sent as well as replies received. If more information is needed, we should volunteer to return to the adoption agency or other intermediary with the adoptee to request it. The adoptee can also be told he can leave information with the adoption agency that can be given to the birthparents if and when they request it.

Some adoption agencies offer "homeland tours" for foreign-born adoptees and their families. The adoptee has an opportunity to see her country of origin, visit the orphanage she spent time in or other significant places, and perhaps even talk to officials at the agency that placed her. Though foreign travel is expensive, allowing an adolescent to take a homeland tour, or sharing the experience with her, can be an important way parents can let their adolescent know that they recognize how important it is for her to have contact with her past.

By taking action rather than just talking about adoption issues, we demonstrate our understanding of the importance of information to her and our willingness to help her obtain it. Even if much information is not found, it is important for the adoptee to realize that it is not the adoptive parents who are standing in the way of her search.

Most adoptees are not seeking face-to-face meetings with the birthparents, although some adolescents express a desire to observe the birthparents undetected. One teenage boy faked car problems near the remote rural home of his birthmother. On the pretext of seeking help at her farmhouse, he was able to observe her without revealing his identity. However, some adoptees seem to want reunions. If the adoptee does express a desire to meet the birthparents, it could be he still is looking for more information.

Many adoption experts who support the idea of adult adoptees searching for their birth families do not think such meetings are advisable while the adoptee is an adolescent. Searching for birthparents is often a highly emotional experience and adolescents already have enough emotional ups and downs to deal with.

Searching can also be time-consuming and interfere with an adolescent's schoolwork. Adolescents may treat a reunion with the birthparents almost frivolously, afraid to show how they really feel. In addition, it is confusing for an adoptee to form a new relationship with a parent figure at a time when his life task is to break away from parents. Nevertheless, adoptive parents who refuse to allow their teenager to search may have to deal with a rebellious adolescent who finds something forbidden more desirable. We should acknowledge the need for information, help the adoptee find what information is available, and promise to support him in his search at a more appropriate time. (Chapter 9 discusses contact between minor children and birthparents.)

RELATIONSHIPS WITH PEERS

In moving into adulthood, adolescents are moving away from their parents and depending more on relationships with their peers. It is important for them to be accepted by people their own age and to be like their peers.

As with other stages of life, adoption adds another dimension to this aspect of adolescence. The adoptee wants to be like her friends, but may think being adopted makes her different. The child who enjoyed the reactions she got when she answered the question, "Are you Irish?" with, "Who knows? I'm adopted," may suddenly be reluctant to place herself in the spotlight. Given a biology class assignment to trace the genetic origins of the color of her eyes, she may fail to turn in the homework rather than point out to the teacher why she is having difficulty with the assignment.

Parents may need to be more tolerant of the ways the adoptee compensates for feeling different by conforming to her peers. More than some other adolescents, she may need to dress like her friends and wear her hair the same way.

Dating

The emerging sexuality of adolescents draws them into close relationships with members of the opposite sex. But dating can pose particular problems for the adoptee. Many adoptees worry that they might be dating biologic relatives, although the chances of this are extremely remote. The transracially placed child, who grew up feeling accepted by white parents and white friends, may discover that transracial dating isn't acceptable to some people—including some people who had accepted him as a friend. At the same time, having grown up in a white culture, the adoptee may not identify with people of his own race or ethnic background.

In addition, the teenager's increasing awareness of his own sexuality can add to the curiosity he may already have about his origins and the relationship between his birthparents.

As soon as children enter school, parents learn they cannot provide a protective environment for them forever. They will be exposed to people with racial prejudices and there will be painful times for the transracially adopted teenager. Parents can't make all the hurts disappear. They can, however, prepare the adoptee for the inevitable encounters with prejudice and provide an atmosphere in which the adolescent is able to talk about his concerns. Sometimes, despite the willingness of the parents to discuss issues that are troubling their teenager, the adolescent does not want to talk to them. He may be trying to spare his parents the pain of knowing, for example, that he is experiencing racial prejudice. He may instead turn to the parent of a friend, a coach, teacher, or other adult. While it may be upsetting that he would take someone else into his confidence, parents should be pleased that he is at least discussing what is troubling him with someone.

An End to Some Adoption Activities

Families who have been active in adoption organizations often find that their adolescent children are less interested in going to potlucks or other activities with other adoptive families. Most likely, this is an outgrowth of teenagers wanting to choose their own friends and has nothing to do with adoption. With younger children, similarity in age is practically the only requirement for an afternoon of play. Adolescents have more complicated companionship needs. Parents should respect their adolescent's wishes or work out a mutually agreeable compromise if, for example, he no longer wants to spend the weekend camping with members of the local adoption support group.

Some teenagers may be uncomfortable celebrating their adoption anniversary, either because they have not sorted out their feelings about adoption, or because they think such celebrations are childish. One adoptive father was surprised to discover that his adult son had revived the celebration, after affecting indifference to it during adolescence.

Chapter 9

Contact with Biologic Relatives

As open adoptions replace traditional closed-record adoptions, as the adoption of older children increases, and as reunions between adult adoptees and their birthparents become more commonplace, the amount of contact between birthparents, adoptees, and adoptive parents is increasing. Sometimes the contact is planned; other times it is unexpected. Sometimes the birthparents are viewed as threats, and sometimes they are welcomed into the family circle. But whether or not the contact is looked on as desirable, it is often awkward. How do we address one another? What do we do if we don't like each other? Everyone has an opinion on whether adoptees and adoptive families should communicate directly with each other by mail, telephone, or in person. But when it appears our son or daughter will have contact with a birthparent, we should know what our role should be and how we can help our son or daughter at this important time.

CONTACT WITH MINOR CHILDREN

In most cases, contact between minor children and their birthparents is initiated by the birthparents, not the adoptive parents. In the case of foster parent adoption, the birthparents may know how to contact the adoptive parents. Occasionally contact comes in the form of a letter or telephone call from a birthparent who has been searching for her child. But while contact with the birthparents may not have been initiated by the adoptive parents, adoptive parents are in a position to decide whether to allow contact and determine how much contact is desirable.

Some prospective adoptive parents discover that so many birthmothers want to meet their children's adoptive parents that their chances of adopting a baby are much greater if they agree to an open adoption. Others are embracing open adoptions rather than just going along with them and are searching for their child's birthparents while the adoptee is still young. But they, too, must determine the limits of the contact.

Contact with birthparents and other biologic relatives is not the same as information about them. It is a distinct advantage for the adoptee to have as much information as possible about her genetic, medical and social histories, and about the reasons she was placed for adoption. However, the desirability of an ongoing relationship between the young adoptee and her biologic relatives is still highly controversial.

Before becoming involved in direct contact with birthparents, we should know the advantages and disadvantages of such contact; the different ways to have contact, such as a single meeting, a series of visits, gifts, telephone calls, or letters; and our role in setting the rules for that contact.

Advantages of Contact

Direct contact with birthparents is an efficient way for adoptees and their adoptive parents to obtain credible and up-to-date answers to questions they have about the adoptee's origins. Certainly there are other ways to obtain information about what the birthparents were like, how much education they had, what diseases run in the family, and why they were unable to care for the child themselves. The adoption agency or other neutral party can pass this information on to the adoptive family and keep the birthparents informed about the adoptee's progress. Some agencies are experimenting with open adoptions in which the adoptive parents and birthparents agree on the level of contact they would like to have, and the agency agrees to serve indefinitely as an intermediary, passing letters and photographs as well as information back and forth. It would be ideal if agencies would be willing to pass developmental updates as well as important medical information from the adoptive family to the birth family and vice versa, and more agencies are becoming involved in this. But when attempts at communication through a neutral party fail, some adoptees, birthparents, and adoptive parents may choose to get the information they want directly from one another. An advantage of direct communication is that it is believable. An adoptee may resist information from her adoptive parents or the agency, but may be more accepting when she hears it from her birthparents. Of course, birthparents are human and may not be reliable sources of information about an emotional event, especially years after the child was placed for adoption. Guilt, subsequent experiences with the other birthparent, later parenting success, contact with other birthparents, and society's changing views of unmarried pregnant women may color their perceptions of their decision to place their children for adoption. But generally, birthparents are credible sources of information.

Contact with the birthparents may help the adoptive parents understand the adoptee better or help the child through some crisis. Jaimie and her husband have been struggling to raise two sisters who were adopted at the ages of seven and nine. Jaimie thinks that just because the girls' birthmother is unable to raise them does not mean that she has no insight into them. She'd like to be able to bounce parenting ideas off of the birthmother sometimes. Jaimie is an unusual adoptive parent in this regard. But other adoptive parents have wondered whether contact with the birthparents might put a stop to certain fantasies that are getting in the way of their child's normal development. And some adoptive parents think inappropriate behavior that seems to mimic what the child thinks her birthparent is like will stop once the adoptee meets the birthparent.

Other adoptive parents have found that while the birthparents were unable to care for the child, there are some other members of the child's biologic family, such as grandparents, who can make valuable contributions to the child's upbringing.

Finally, recognizing that their child might someday want more information about her birthparents, and perhaps even a meeting, some adoptive parents have searched for them. Most people believe the sooner the search for the birthparents begins, the more likely it will be successful. And by searching when the child is young, adoptive parents hope to spare the child years of searching that could interfere with her adult life.

Disadvantages of Contact

Perhaps the biggest fear adoptive parents have concerning contact between the adoptee and her birthparents is that they will lose their child to the birthparents—either because the child will not love them as much as the birthparents or because the birthparents will abduct the child. This is also the most unrealistic fear. Some adoptive parents who have met their child's birthparents feel much more secure after hearing them explain why they placed the child.

Birthparents have related how, having met the adoptive parents, they have been able to let go of the child, secure in the knowledge that she is with capable, loving parents.

Perhaps a more realistic worry is that the child will have divided loyalties, be confused about who her parents really are, and feel insecure about her home arrangement. As discussed in Chapter 4, some psychoanalysts think the preschool-age child should not be told she is adopted because she cannot make sense out of having two sets of parents. This confusion may be greater if the child is expected to relate to both sets of parents. In addition, children younger than eleven or twelve have difficulty comprehending the judicial system well enough to understand that their adoptive placement is permanent. If they are spending some time with their adoptive parents and some time with a birthparent, they may not be clear on which home is permanent. Adoptive parents legitimately worry about the amount of stress it will place on their child and on the entire family to accommodate not just the knowledge of, but the presence of, another parent. In some cases the child may use the situation to play one set of parents against the other, manipulating them to gain advantages, either material or emotional.

Some adoptive parents also worry that contact will somehow be harmful to their child—that their child will be exposed to a negative influence or develop a negative self-image if the birthparent is an alcoholic, sexually promiscuous, or abusive. Some of these worries are realistic; not all birthparents or biologic relatives are capable of acting in the best interest of their child—that's why the child is being raised by adoptive parents. But sometimes the adoptive parents fear the birthparents simply because they don't know one another.

Deciding What's Best

When the adoptee is under eighteen and living at home, it is up to the adoptive parents to decide whether she will be able to have direct contact with her birthparents. They have to sift through all the possible advantages and disadvantages to decide whether their child will be well served by having a relationship with her birth family, or whether the overall effect would be detrimental. We have to look at the possible advantages and disadvantages and see which ones pertain to our situation. Is it possible to get reliable information without having contact? Will our fears of the effect of direct contact inhibit our ability to parent the child? Is there some factual basis, such as a criminal record, for believing that contact with the birthparent would be harmful?

It may be desirable for the adoptive parents to meet directly with the birth-parents themselves before deciding whether the adoptee should have contact. Through direct communication, the adoptive parents can learn how the birth-parents view their decision to place the child for adoption, why they are interested in having contact, what kind of relationship they hope to have with the child, and the amount of contact they are seeking, as well as get an idea of the level of trust they have for one another and other subtle factors. It is recom-mended that a neutral party, such as a counselor or trained adoption worker, be involved in helping each party communicate their motives and expectations.

If the advantages seem to outweigh the disadvantages, but the adoptive parents are still reluctant, it may be valuable for them to examine why they feel threatened by the prospect of contact with the birthparents. Perhaps they have not developed a full sense of entitlement—a belief that they have a right to act as parents with their child. Perhaps they are denying that there is another set of parents for their child. They may be denying their child's genetic origins, and thereby denying an important part of their child's existence.

Most likely, adoptive parents will be reluctant to have direct contact with their child's birthparents because they simply do not know what to expect from it. They may have had limited contact with adoptive families who have had open adoptions, and even less contact with birthparents. To some degree, they are right in recognizing that they are pioneers in the practice of getting to know their child's birthparents. While open adoptions are not new—historically orphans have been raised by relatives or friends of the birthparents—opening secret adoptions is a new aspect of current adoption practice. There is no research yet to support whether it is a good idea or not—just opinions based on how adoptions have worked in the past and how they might be improved. To become more comfortable with the idea of direct contact with birthparents, adoptive parents may want to find out more about them by reading some of the experiences of birthparents, such as Suzanne Arms' *To Love and Let Go.** Accounts about openness in adoption written by adoptive parents, adoptees, and birthparents, such as those published by the Post Adoption Center for Education and Research* are also helpful. *Dear Birthmother** is the account of Lutheran Social Service of Texas' experiment with open adoptions. And *The Adoption Triangle** by Arthur D. Sorosky, Annette Baran, and Reuben Pannor provides adoptive parents with insight into their own feelings about reunions between adoptees and birthparents, as well as helps them understand the needs and feelings of adoptees and birthparents who search.

Deciding Against Contact

Although there are some distinct advantages to be gained by adoptees and adoptive parents in meeting the child's birthparents, it is not always a good idea for a particular family, or at a particular time in a child's life. Adolescence, in particular, is a tumultuous time in a child's life when he is trying to understand who he is in relation to two sets of parents. Information about his heritage can be very helpful; contact may be disruptive. Or the adoptive parents may decide that the adoptee or the birthparent expects something from the relationship that is unrealistic.

Joe, for example, a thirty-six-year-old birthfather who recently made contact with his fifteen-year-old daughter, hopes he can develop a good relationship with her because her adoptive parents, in their fifties, are "more like grand-parents" to her and don't understand her. To hear Joe talk, he had been against the decision to place the girl for adoption, but as a father had little to say about her fate—although he had signed the placement papers. It is easy to imagine the effect it would have on a teenage girl who was having the normal amount of parent–adolescent conflict to suddenly have a young, attractive man enter her life who is willing to side with her against her "out-of-touch" parents. Those adoptive parents would be justified in feeling threatened by Joe's presence in their daughter's life. It is not the right time for her or the right role for Joe.

Setting Rules for Contact

Adoptive parents who decide that some contact between their child and her birthparents is advantageous need not feel powerless to set the limits of the rela-tionship or later rescind the right for their child and her birthparents to have contact. Adoptive parents who feel they have a right and responsibility to make other important decisions for their child's welfare seem to sometimes decide they have no right to make any decisions when it comes to their child's birthparents. When we allow our child's birthparents into our lives we are not giving the other parents equal rights to parent the child. We are not initiating "joint custody" of the child. Nor have the birthparents become part of our family. There is no obligation, for example, to allow the child to spend holidays or vacations with the birthparents; neither must the birthparents be invited to stay in our home when they visit our child. In fact, I am surprised to read so many accounts of reunions, even involving minor children, which relate how the adoptee spent the next holiday or birthday with her birthmother. Adoptive parents do not have to feel guilty that they have been celebrating the child's birthday and other holidays with her. They do not have to compensate the birthparents for what they have missed in the growth and development of the child.

If the adoption is to be open from the beginning, the parties involved are often less rushed and less intense about the contact than they are if a meeting is to take place after years of secrecy. The parties usually have a few months even before the child is born to work out the degree of openness that is agreeable to both parties. If an intermediary experienced with open adoptions is handling the direct placement, he can and should provide counseling or guidance to the parties in developing a plan that is agreeable to everyone involved. In fact, no one should act as an intermediary in the placement of a child if he is not able to provide such counseling (or refer the parties to someone who can provide adequate counseling) or not willing to continue acting as an intermediary throughout the life of the adoptee.

Time for counseling and working out a mutually agreeable plan for contact is desirable even when contact with the birthparents is not expected. Too often, though, the party seeking the contact is impatient. Having finally found the other party, they are eager for the initial meeting. So many autobiographical stories of searches relate how the individual made contact by telephone or letter, promising to let the other person have some time to think about the new situation, only to call or write and say: "Ready or not, here I come." This is when the adoptive parents have to be firm, either with their child or the birthparents, and insist that a meeting not take place until everyone is ready, and until they have had an opportunity to meet with a neutral party who can serve as an intermediary. Adoption workers who have substantial experience with open adoptions emphasize that contact between adoptees and birthparents can be disastrous unless the parties first have a chance to understand their roles, clarify their motives and expectations, and develop mutually acceptable rules and plans for the contact. For example, Joe, the birthfather discussed earlier in this chapter, blamed his daughter's birthmother for the decision to place their child for adoption. He needs to understand that, like his daughter's adoptive parents, he must discuss the birthmother empathetically rather than criticizing her or her decision. Most importantly, all parties have to understand what it means when birthparents transfer parental rights to the adoptive parents at the time of placement, and understand that the transfer of those rights is not altered by the reappearance of the birthparents. It is particularly helpful for the adoptee to have the clarification of roles come through a neutral party. If either the birthparents or the adoptive parents try to outline the roles they will play to her, she may see them as being influenced by their vested interest in the situation.

In working out a plan for contact, the adoptive parents, birthparents, and adoptee need to agree on how much contact they will have, the types of contact, the method for contact, and the procedure for changing the agreement. Here again, a neutral intermediary can help find a solution that is acceptable to everyone. It's hard for the adoptive parents to know what is in the best interest of their child when they are feeling confused and somewhat threatened by the idea of contact. Left on their own, adoptive parents might overcompensate for their own resistant feelings, allowing more contact than they think is actually desirable; or they may react to a personality clash with the birthparents by denying contact that is quite reasonable.

A neutral party can also see that communication does not break down between the birthparents and adoptive parents due to cultural differences. It is highly likely that the birthparents and adoptive parents will have different socioeconomic backgrounds, different levels of education, or be of different races. This can all hinder communication.

An ongoing role by the intermediary can be helpful in controlling the timing of contact between the adoptive family and the birthparents. For example, a phone call from the birthparent asking if the adoptee can go away with the birthparent for the weekend can complicate family life if it comes when the adoptee is "grounded" and angry about her punishment. The adoptee may try to use the birthparent's invitation to gain her "freedom," accusing her adoptive parents of being strict just because they don't want her to be with her birthparent. Such a situation would be diffused if the request from the birthparent came through a neutral party who could then inform the birthparent that the adoptee cannot go and set up another time for the outing.

When Contact is Disruptive

What should the adoptive parents do when they have agreed to contact but the birthparent is not following the rules they agreed to, when the child seems unhappy each time she has contact with the birthparent, or when the birthparent becomes threatening? The first step is to determine the extent of the disruption. Is it merely annoying that the birthparent calls twice each month instead of once, or is the extra phone call interfering with family life? Who is upset—the child or the parents? Is there a real risk of danger from the birthparent? If an intermediary has been involved in the contact between the families from the beginning, it is easy to allow that neutral party to help sort out the problem. For example, parents may observe that following a visit or call from their child's birthparent, she is withdrawn or even cries. They may want to cut off contact as a result. A counselor can help them determine if the child is being harmed by the contact, or experiencing some grief or sadness. Parents don't want their child to be unhappy, but sadness is part of the human experience. It may not be appropriate to cut off contact in an attempt to keep their child's life artificially happy.

The neutral party can also help enforce the rules or analyze whether the rules need to be altered. If the birthparent refuses to abide by the rules or continues to be threatening, the adoptive parents can and should threaten to break off all contact with her. A threat is usually enough to ensure cooperation, but if she still doesn't comply, the adoptive parents should implement that threat, getting an unlisted telephone number, refusing to pass along mail, or even getting a court order prohibiting future contact. The birthparents have no legal right to contact, even though they may be caring people. The adoptive parents may need outside help to sort out what kind of contact and how much contact is appropriate. But they have the right and obligation to protect their child's welfare.

When Interest in Contact Wanes

At the start of an open adoption, those involved are usually enthusiastic and curious. Once the initial questions are answered, though, interest may wane. It is not unusual for the birthmother involved in a direct placement to communicate frequently with the adoptive parents during the year after the placement when she is grieving for her child. Often, after about a year, she has had her curiosity and concerns about the adoptive family satisfied; she recognizes that even with an open adoption, she cannot follow the daily progress of her child, but must get on with her life. It is not unusual for her to back off from contact with the adoptive family as she gets her life in order. After a few years, when her new life is established, she may increase the amount of contact she has with the adoptive family as she tries to integrate that experience with her current life. The adoptive family should not interpret a temporary lack of interest as the birthparent's attempt to break contact. They should think of her as they would a good friend who has moved away. Sometimes they write and call frequently; sometimes they communicate only through a yearly Christmas card. Very few of us would stop sending Christmas greetings to a friend because we expected to get three letters from her during the year and didn't receive them.

There's a difference between waning interest and a desire to change the rules for contact. The birthparent may decide she cannot manage occasional contact and want to prohibit the adoptee from calling. That's a time for renegotiation of the rules, and an intermediary may need to be involved.

Sometimes a child expects more contact with her birthparents than they are interested in. The adoptive parents can communicate this to the birthparents, but since they can't force them to have more contact than they want to have, their role may be to comfort the adoptee and try to help her express her feelings of grief and rejection. This may be awkward for the adoptive parents if they feel in competition with the birthparents for the child's affection—something like the wife comforting her husband who has just been rejected by the "other woman." The adoptee needs reassurance that the lack of interest by the birthparents is their problem, and does not reflect on the adoptee's value as a person.

Sometimes the adoptee is not interested in maintaining contact with the birthparent or doesn't follow through on the interest he has. It may be hard for him to write to someone that he only sees once a year, for example. The adoptive parents and the birthparents should not expect a minor child to take responsibility for maintaining contact. The agreement outlining how much and what kind of contact was made by adults, and should be carried out by the adults involved. The child needs to understand that contract, but it isn't up to him to live up to it. For example, the adoptive parents should let the child know that it is all right for him to send a birthday card to his birthmother, but they shouldn't nag at him to send one. It should be the child's choice, within the limits of the agreement. If he doesn't choose to do so, it's up to the adoptive parents to communicate with the birthparent. The situation is not much different than that of a child and his grandparents. Often the child who lives a great distance from his grandparents and doesn't know them very well can't remember to send them birthday cards or a school picture. Rather than nagging the child, most parents just sign the child's name and enclose the photograph. And just as they don't interpret a child's lack of interest in the grandparents as a sign that they should cut off all contact between grandchild and grandparents, adoptive parents shouldn't decide against open adoption just because the child does not maintain enthusiasm about it. It's best to let the child determine how active a role he wants in having contact with the birthparent, but the adoptive parents should maintain the relationship so that it's there when the adoptee is ready to take a more active part in it.

CONTACT WITH THE ADULT ADOPTEE

The adult adoptee is able to make her own decisions about whether to have contact with her birthparents. She does not have to consult her adoptive parents or get their permission. Nevertheless, the feelings of the adoptive parents are important to most adoptees who consider searching for their birth-parents. Many adoptees delay searching until after the deaths of their adoptive parents, so concerned are they not to hurt their adoptive parents. Others just do not tell their adoptive parents that they are trying to meet their birthparents.

In some respects, a meeting between the birthparents and the adoptee can be more threatening to us after our son or daughter reaches adulthood than it is when he or she was a child. We often view ourselves as nurturers. Once our son or daughter leaves home, we may be concerned about our future relationship. If the grown child no longer needs nurturing, is there a need for us? If there is no blood tie, will our son or daughter come home? If the adoptee begins his adult life by searching for his birthparents, these fears can be even greater.

Why Adoptees Search

It isn't unusual for adoptive parents to wonder why their child wants to find his birthparents, particularly if there is no medical emergency requiring infor-mation from the birthparents. We wonder if the adoptee has been dissatisfied with his life all along, or if he doesn't really love us. We wonder if the desire to search reflects a psychological problem. We wonder if we have failed him—told him too soon or too late that he was adopted, or not explained his adoption in the right way.

Research studies have tried to discover why some adoptees search for their birthparents and have come up with a variety of results. Some have found adoptees who search to have psychological problems. Others have concluded that the desire to find the birthparents is normal and understandable.

We simply don't know why some adoptees search and others don't, mainly because it is hard to get a good representative sample of adoptees who are searching and a control group of those who aren't. Researchers end up studying people who have replied to an advertisement or letter, perhaps because they want to be studied. It's difficult to draw generalizations from such self-selected populations.

What we do know is that a desire for information about their genetic and social origins is not unusual in adoptees, nor does it reflect abnormal adjust-ment to adoption. Many adoptees who are searching for their birthparents are not looking for a father or mother, but for information. For some reason, they have decided that the best way to obtain the information is to talk directly to the birthparents. For a few adoptees, the development of a relationship with their birthparents is the goal of the search. One study of adoptees who were searching for their birthparents found that those who were most satisfied with their life and had received generally positive information about their birth-parents were looking for information only, while those who were dissatisfied with their life and had received negative or no information about their adoption wanted a relationship. That theory makes sense, but adoptive parents of an adoptee who develops a relationship with her birthparents should not conclude that the adoptee is dissatisfied with her life. I suspect some adoptees are not looking for a relationship with their birthparents, but after investing years of their time and energy into finding them, cannot simply gather the information they came for and walk away again. We should not feel we have somehow failed our son or daughter if he or she wants to meet the birthparents, par-ticularly if we seem otherwise to have a good relationship.

An adoptee is most likely to search for her birthparents after a significant life event such as marriage, divorce, or the death of an adoptive parent. The birth of a child is frequently mentioned as an event that forces an adoptee to think about her genetic makeup and what she might be passing on to her children. Pregnancy and childbirth cause a woman to wonder about her birthmother's experience. Questions from her physician may point out to her the importance of knowing whether her family has a history of early labor or twins. In addition, adoptees say how profoundly aware they are of meeting someone for the first time to whom they are genetically connected when they have their first child. That often causes them to think about meeting other biologically related people. Losses, such as divorce or death, may cause the adoptee to seek out as many sources of comfort as possible. And at some point, the adoptee's awareness of her own advancing age reminds her that if she delays her search, her birth-parents may die before she finds them.

A general sense of dissatisfaction with life may also prompt an adoptee to search for her birthparents. We all have periods in our life when it seems something is missing. We sometimes look for a simple answer to our dissatis-faction—a new job, new spouse, another child, or move to a new city. The adoptee may focus on her absent birthparents as the cause of her dis-satisfaction. I received a letter from a prisoner who was inquiring about how to undertake a search because he thought meeting his birthparents might somehow explain why he couldn't stay out of trouble with the law.

Most adoptees who search are looking for information about the cir-cumstances of their adoption, including the reasons they were placed for adop-tion. It's easy to see why they would prefer to get these answers directly from the birthparents—information can be obtained from a written history, but direct communication is needed to learn the emotions and subtle pressures involved in decision-making. Adoptees also want to know what their birthparents and other biologic relatives are like. Again, a written history can give educational levels, relate marks of achievement, and even describe a person. But a person's personality is much more quickly ascertained in a face-to-face meeting. Often adoptees want to see what the birthparents look like and see if they share any physical characteristics. Most of us would want to know these same things if we had the opportunity to meet our sons' and daughters' birthparents.

Supporting the Search

When we are faced with the prospect of our grown son's or daughter's searching for his or her birthparents, we can choose whether or not to support the search, but we can't prevent the adoptee from searching. If we do not support the search, our son or daughter may postpone it until we die or until the adoptee thinks it can be delayed no longer. Or, the adoptee may proceed with the search without telling us. By expressing disapproval of the search, we may keep the adoptee from searching, but probably won't keep her from wanting to search. The adoptee may be resentful and angry at us for frustrating her search, which may be a greater threat to our relationship than a reunion with birthparents.

Discouraging an adoptee from searching may have even more serious results. Many adoptees search for their birthparents to put to rest the identity issues that have been plaguing them since adolescence. Some are able to resolve the identity questions without a meeting with the birthparents, but adoptees who need or think they need a reunion with the birthparents may be unable to proceed with their lives until those issues are settled. They may have difficulty forming relationships or selecting occupations until they resolve their identity questions.

We shouldn't assume our sons and daughters know how we feel about a search, neither should we wait for the adoptee to ask us how we feel. If the topic has not been specifically discussed in the home, many adoptees assume their adoptive parents will be disappointed or angry if they search. This is a subject that needs to be discussed; we should be the ones to initiate that discussion. We should be honest about our feelings, but also open to the feelings of the adoptee.

The first level of support from the adoptive parents is permission—letting the adoptee know it is all right with them if she decides to search. Related to this is the sharing of any information the adoptive parents have about the birthparents or the adoption. It is hypocritical for us to say it's okay with us if the adoptee searches, but withhold information that could assist her in that search.

The extent to which the adoptive parents get involved in the search beyond that is up to them and the adoptee. The adoptee may be delighted to have her parents attend workshops sponsored by adoptee search groups with her, or even help her look through telephone directories for people with her birth-parent's name. Or, she may prefer to search alone or with the help of other adoptees. If the search is successful, the adoptive parents, adoptee, and birth-parents are faced with the question of whether the birthparents and adoptive parents will meet. Just because we have supported the idea of searching doesn't mean we are ready for a face-to-face meeting. One does not necessarily lead to the other. Genevieve is a woman in her seventies who recognized that her adopted daughter's kidney condition required that she find her birthmother. She talks candidly about her daughter's meetings with her birthmother, and in no way appears threatened by the other mother in her daughter's life. But she has resisted meeting her herself. She's not quite sure what she would say to her, and fears a meeting would be too emotional.

Dealing With the Lengthy Search

In most states, adult adoptees still cannot open their sealed adoption records on request. Yet many adoptees have found their birthparents. They are using standard genealogical techniques of tracing relatives through birth, marriage, and divorce records; through telephone directories; and are sometimes sneak-ing looks at adoption files or sealed birth records. Keeping adoption records sealed is not keeping birthparents and adoptees apart. It is just dragging out the search process. Certainly some adoptees get discouraged by this and abandon their search. Many, though, get angry because they believe they have a right to information about their origins. I have seen the pain that these adoptees are in when kept from information they want and often need because the adoption and legal systems are trying to "protect" them. They feel they are being treated like children even though they are adults. They spend years tracking down the most obscure clues and spend large sums of money on private investigators and long distance telephone calls. Sometimes careers and relationships are sub-ordinated to the search, which becomes a full-time job.

Seeing their child involved in a lengthy search is likely to be more troubling to adoptive parents than any possible threat finding the birthparents could pose. Adoptive parents sometimes respond to their son's or daughter's pain by taking a more active part in the search—testifying in court for the opening of the adoptee's records, calling the adoption agency or intermediary they worked with, or even trying to change legislation to make searching easier. Others respond by trying to encourage the adoptee to give up what seems to be a hopeless search and get on with her life, although in most cases, they probably would not be successful. There are times in every parent's life when we see our children doing something that we think will only cause them more suffering. Often, there is little we can do but stand by, let them do what they have to do, and be there to pick up the pieces. It's probably one of the most difficult aspects of being a parent.

Effect of Finding the Birthparents

Searching for birthparents is not a rejection of the adoptive parents. Nor do the vast majority of adoptees replace their adoptive parents with their birthparents after they are found. Sorosky, Baran and Pannor report in *The Adoption Triangle** that when the adoptee's relationship with the adoptive parents is good, finding the birthparents strengthens it. When the relationship is poor, the adoptee is often able to see it from a new perspective. For example, the adoptee who has fantasized that her life would have been much better if she had been kept by her birthmother might find that her birthmother was an alcoholic and realize that her life would have been much different than she imagined.

Adoptees often fear that when they find the birthparents they will find out something negative, such as that they are in prison or in a mental hospital. They also fear another rejection by the birthparents. Adoptive parents may share these concerns. Adoptee search organizations or a counselor can help an adoptee recognize her expectations of the birthparents and the possibility that the reunion with the birthparents will be somehow unsatisfactory. Whatever the outcome of the reunion, we can be available to comfort the adoptee and do what we can to help her accept what she has found.

In general, the purpose of finding the birthparents is to get answers to questions and to integrate the divergent parts of the adoptee's life into a whole. Even when the information received from the birthparents is negative, or when the birthparents reject a reunion, the adoptee is likely to emerge from the search in better shape than she started. This is not to say that adoptees who search are better adjusted than those who don't. But people who have a need, identify it, and take action to fill that need are likely to feel better than they would if they denied that they had that need.

Part IV

Special Issues in Adoption

Chapter 10

Growing Up in the Minority Family

A few years ago, a television commercial showed a Korean girl as valedictorian of her high school graduation class, reminiscing about her life with her adoptive parents. The advertisement captured the hope of parents who adopt transracially—that despite our differences, we will grow and thrive as a family. The great majority of transracial and intercountry adoptions have been highly successful for parents as well as children. Studies of such placements have found that families generally form strong attachments, and adoptees develop good self-images. Problems that do arise are more often due to the age of the child at the time of adoption or previous trauma than to differences in racial or ethnic backgrounds. Still, raising a child of a different race or ethnic background has some unique aspects that must be considered along with the issues that all adoptive families share. Some of these are discussed in other chapters: the reaction of relatives to transracial and intercountry adoption in Chapter 2, the difficulty both infants and older children have in adjusting to new foods and customs in Chapter 2, why attachment may take longer for infants and mothers who are racially different in Chapter 3, and identity issues for adolescents in Chapter 8. In addition, the minority adoptive family shares many of the adoption issues of other adoptive families, such as concern over a lack of medical history and how to talk to children about being adopted.

BECOMING A MINORITY FAMILY

When we adopt children of a different race or ethnic background we become minority families, a fact more obvious as children grow up, begin dating and have children of their own. Racial and ethnic issues do not end when we decide we can accept and love a child who is racially or culturally different. Most of us recognize that we will encounter both outright racism as well as subtle prejudice. The first is easy to recognize; the second may not be, especially in ourselves.

Dealing with Our Own Prejudice

One form of prejudice among parents of minority children is an attitude that they have "rescued" a child from what would have been a disadvantaged life—given a homeless child a home; a malnourished child an abundant diet; an impoverished child middle-class advantages. All adoptive parents are vulnerable to feeling that they have rescued their child by adoption, but it may be easier to resist falling into this trap when adopting a healthy white baby because parents know that their infant would not have waited long for another family. But when adopting a child who has lived on the streets, who has been neglected, or who was otherwise disadvantaged, parents can believe the child's life would have been much worse had he not been adopted. In many cases, it's true. But sometimes there is underlying racism or nationalism in that belief. We may think being raised in the United States, in a traditional Judeo-Christian religion, or in a middle-class white family is automatically better than being raised in Colombia, being raised Buddhist, or being raised in a working class black family.

Children do not benefit by being cast as victims in need of rescue. In the first place, a victim is only a victim until he is removed from his life-threatening predicament. Once removed, he does not continue to need to be saved; he is no longer helpless. More importantly, being cast as a victim implies that the child owes his parents something for saving him—a debt he can never repay and that he may come one day to resent, since he did not choose to be saved by these parents.

It is not enough for parents to be tolerant of the differences between themselves and their child, they need to be tolerant of all racial differences. The family who refrains from jokes about Asians after adopting a Korean child but continues to tell Polish jokes is saying they do see some ethnic groups as inferior to others. Allowing some racial slurs—even though they do not refer to the child's race or ethnic background—tells the child that racial, religious or ethnic differences do matter and that non-whites, non-Americans, or people of other religions are inferior.

As children grow up, parents should consider whether their expectations are in any way tied to the child's race or ethnic background. Do we expect our Asian daughter to be a whiz at math? Do we think our tall black son is more likely to enjoy basketball than our tall white son? We have all been bombarded with racial and ethnic stereotypes throughout our lives, and though parents generally do not adopt transracially or transculturally unless they reject these stereotypes, they may be more influenced by society than they think. The conscious rejection of stereotypes is an ongoing task.

Dealing with the Prejudice of Outsiders

We often become aware that our child will encounter prejudice when the child goes to school for the first time and is clearly a minority in the classroom. Before children enter school, parents can, to some extent, structure their environment so they are not exposed to prejudice. Once a child is in school, however, parents cannot protect him from misinformed people.

Most transracially adopted children encounter prejudice in the form of teasing, comments, or insults. A few experience more violent racism or nationalism. And the teasing and insults can come both from white children who view minorities as inferior, and from members of the child's own ethnic group, who view the child living with a white family as disloyal to his race or ethnic group. One boy decided to go to a racially integrated high school because he was teased about being the only black in his junior high school. But having been raised in a white neighborhood by white parents, he was taunted by the other blacks at the high school for not "dressing black" or "acting black." He became embarrassed to be seen with his parents. It was not until he was successful on the football team that he felt accepted by his peers. A Mexican girl found that every time Central America was discussed in her history class, her teacher expected her to be more knowledgeable than the other students. Although she wasn't being insulted, she quite rightly thought she was being singled out because of her ethnic background. Not only did she feel conspicuous, she felt disloyal because she did not know more about her country of birth.

Children know parents will be hurt when their children are teased because of race or ethnic background, so they do not always share these incidents with their parents. Consequently, it is important for us to prepare our minority children when they are young to deal with prejudice. While we may be tempted to let minor incidents pass in the hope that our child didn't notice, these incidents can be useful ways to initiate discussions of prejudice and teach children how to handle similar situations in the future. When a child pointed to Sally's Asian son in the grocery store and said, "Why aren't his eyes open all the way?" Sally responded by explaining that they were open, but that his eyes were shaped differently. Later, she brought up the incident with her son, saying, "It seemed that your feelings were hurt when that boy asked about your eyes." Sally let her son know that it was okay for him to feel sad or angry, reassured him that his eyes were fine, explained that the problem was due to ignorance, and let him talk about how he could handle the problem next time.

Talks about prejudice do not have to focus on the teasing a particular child may encounter. It can be discussed in general terms, which may be easier for both parents and child. Books and television shows in which characters encounter difficulty because of their race or ethnic background can be excellent ways to initiate discussions of the ways prejudice can surface.

While private talks are helpful, parents should not refrain from dealing immediately and directly with someone who teases or insults a child on the basis of his race or ethnic background. For example, overhearing one of our child's playmates saying "Eenie, meenie, miney, moe, catch a nigger by the toe," we can say, "Do you know what 'nigger' means? It's a word that isn't very nice that some people use to describe black people. We don't use it in our house."

While parents should not blow an incident out of proportion, they should handle it in the presence of the minority child so that he knows he can count on his parents for support.

Even if a racial slur is not directed at the minority child, parents should not let it pass.

Dealing with Prejudice in the Family

Parents of minority children are sometimes surprised to hear their own children talking about themselves or other minorities in derogatory terms. Having diligently maintained an atmosphere of tolerance for other people's differences, parents forget that stereotypes and prejudice are pervasive in our society and children will be exposed to them outside of the home. While letting our child know that such attitudes are unacceptable, we should not feel we have somehow failed if our child makes a racist remark.

Parents should decide if it is all right for minority children to refer to themselves in pejorative terms, for example, for the Hispanic children to call each other "spic." There is a belief that making fun of ourselves is acceptable, such as, "It's okay for me to tell a Polish joke—I'm Polish." Nevertheless, those kinds of comments subtly denigrate the person or the ethnic group. Even when made with the "permission" of those involved, racial, ethnic, and religious slurs imply that "niggers" or "dumb Polacks" do exist.

Sibling Issues

Some experts say parents who adopt transracially or transculturally should do so more than once—especially if there are children born into the family or the same race as the parents. It may be difficult enough for the minority child to deal with the ways he is different from the majority of society without being the only member of his family to be black, Hispanic, or Asian.

Although the attachment is often slower to develop when the new child is older at the time of placement than when he joins the family in infancy, differences in race or ethnic background do not prevent adoptive siblings from feeling like brothers and sisters. In fact, children often feel protective of their minority brothers and sisters. Though there may be the usual amount of scrapping at home, the siblings in the family often present a united front at school or with their friends, not tolerating any verbal or physical attacks on one member of the family, especially if there are racial overtones to them.

Children who would otherwise not stand out in a crowd have to become accustomed to the visibility of the multi-racial family. Naturally, sometimes children like the additional attention, and sometimes, particularly during adolescence, they prefer not to be so obvious. Siblings have to explain to their friends why they have a brother or sister of a different race, or why they are showing affection to this person of a different ethnic background. Alex, who is ten, sometimes denies that he's related to his nine-year-old sister, born in Chile. It's not that he's ashamed of her, but he sometimes tires of the long explanation that automatically follows when he says they are related. *Is That Your Sister?** by Sherry Bunin and Catherine Bunin, is a children's book that addresses this particular issue.

Because siblings of minority children are often thrust into the role of educating their peers on adoption, we should be sure they understand what adoption means and why we have chosen to adopt a child of a different race. We should also discuss with our children how much information about their siblings it is appropriate to share with people outside the family.

One clear benefit of having minority children in a white family is that the white children are exposed to racial and cultural differences that broaden their outlook on life. As a natural outgrowth of this, sociologist Rita Simon found they seem to overcome the idea of white superiority.

DEVELOPING A SENSE OF RACIAL IDENTITY

Historically, minority children have had a difficult time developing positive images about their own races, but recent research has found better self-images among non-white children than there were twenty years ago. Faced everywhere with evidence that white people have advantages that people of color do not have, it is easy for minority children to think of themselves as inferior. This appears to be changing, due to the emphasis on racial and ethnic pride that began with the civil rights movement of the 1960s and continued through the 1970s after the book and television special *Roots* reminded us of the importance of origins.

As parents raising children of a different race we have an obligation to let our children know what race or ethnic group they are members of and help them develop positive attitudes about being members of those groups.

Physical Differences

Children as young as three or four are conscious that they belong to a group distinguished from other groups by physical differences. Somewhere between four and seven years of age, they become aware that more than physical characteristics distinguish the races—there are attitudes and expectations associated with people of different color. Children acquire their racial attitudes as preschoolers, generally through observation and indirect messages—they see the kinds of jobs people of different races have, and neighborhoods they live in. They overhear conversations and learn there are social implications to membership in different races. They read books, hear their friends talking, watch television and observe their parents' interaction with people of different colors.

The first difference children notice is skin color. When reading a multi-racial picture book to her three-year-old Asian son, Marge asked the boy if he saw any children who looked like him. She was surprised when he pointed to a picture of a black boy instead of an Asian boy. But children are aware of slight differences in skin color before they are aware of the differences in eye shape or hair color. Awareness of those other differences comes later, although the exact age is not known. The inheritance of physical characteristics is a fairly advanced concept for children, with many not understanding it until their high school biology course. Consequently, while young children are aware of the physical differences between themselves and their adoptive parents, they may not realize this is evidence of their adoption.

Discussions of the child's physical differences should be held when the child brings up the subject. Parents should not try to develop racial awareness in their child by pointing out his differences or those of other people, such as saying, "Do you see that woman in the sari? She's from India, too. See how she has brown skin like you?" But if the child notices the woman and remarks that she must be from India, parents can ask, "What clues did you have that she is from India?"

Parents should, however, take the opportunity to make positive comments about the child's physical features whenever it is appropriate. These don't have to be made in racial terms. A mother can comment on how nice and thick her child's hair is while she is combing it, or how nice a particular shirt looks with the child's coloring.

It isn't unusual for transracially adopted children to sometimes wish they were the same color as their parents. Most likely this is not a rejection of their racial identity, but a desire to be like the people around them. They don't want to be a different race; they simply don't want to stand out.

Children occasionally express a dislike for their skin color or other racial characteristic. While this is normal, parents should take the opportunity to let the child know they like that feature. The child may just be dissatisfied with a physical characteristic of himself, but he may be wondering if his parents would love him more if he looked like them. The child needs reassurance that he is valued as he is. If a child is persistently dissatisfied with his racial features, though, he may be having difficulty with self-esteem or with his racial identity.

Parents of Asian children, in particular, need to remember their children are physically quite different from the majority of the population and need to reassure them they are attractive. While this is also true of other minority children, the increased racial awareness of blacks in the United States has resulted in attractive role models portrayed in magazines, television shows, and movies. Latin American children often appear similar to whites. But the Asian child's features are obviously different, yet he does not have the "heroes" the black child has to help him feel good about his racial identity—he is not going to find many Asians depicted on posters of movie stars, rock singers, and television actors.

Awareness of Racial and Ethnic Heritage

Racial identity is more than skin deep, of course. Minority children raised by white parents sometimes think of themselves as white, despite their skin color. It is this attitude that people critical of transracial adoptions are concerned about. Parents of minority children have an obligation to see that their children develop a sense of racial or ethnic heritage so that they are not deprived of an important aspect of who they are.

Parents are more likely to encourage the development of racial identity in their minority children when the differences between themselves and their child are striking, when they think there is a greater likelihood of the child encountering prejudice, and when they are adopting out of "preference" rather than infertility—infertile parents being more inclined to minimize rather than embrace the differences between themselves and their children. For these reasons, and perhaps because white parents who adopt black children have been those most criticized by opponents of transracial adoptions, parents of black children apparently are more aware of the need to encourage a sense of racial identity. In one study, transracially placed black children were less likely to be ashamed of their ethnic group than Colombian and Korean children.

Parents who do not encourage their child to develop a sense of their heritage sometimes say that if they had biologic children, they wouldn't "push" an awareness of their ethnic heritage, so why should they do so for an adopted child? What they forget is the child being raised within her culture—with parents of the same ethnic heritage, in a community of similar background—will develop a positive sense of ethnic identity naturally. But the child who is "different" and knows she is different needs to know that her differences do not make her inferior. The best way to do that is to make an effort to show her that her cultural and racial origins are valuable.

Parents are often enthusiastic about developing a sense of ethnic heritage shortly after the child's placement, but interest tends to diminish as time goes on. This is probably due in part to a heightened awareness of their differences at the time of placement. As attachment and a family feeling grows, differences are noticed less. But it is important to continue to encourage the child's awareness of her background. Although one study found that racial identity is often unrelated to the quality of adjustment among transracially placed adoptees, a critical task for the adolescent is to integrate his dual heritage into his sense of "self."

An awareness of racial or ethnic heritage is accomplished in several ways, including:

— Contact with other people of the same race or ethnic group;
— Assimilation of aspects of the child's culture into the home, such as foods, language, customs, and traditions;
— Exposure to racial and ethnic features through dolls and books;
— Exposure to information about different races and ethnic groups through books, television, films, and cultural exhibits;
— Discussion in the home of different customs and traditions.

While all these are important and valuable, children develop a positive sense of ethnic identity not only by being exposed to cultural roots, but by having their parents show that their heritage is valued. Consequently, while living in a racially integrated community is valuable, it may be more important for parents to read and discuss ethnic history and significant people of the child's culture. Allowing a Korean child to take taekwon-do lessons may be more valuable than taking him to an taekwon-do exhibition because it does more than expose him to culture, it gives him permission to embrace it.

Whatever families do to expand their cultural horizons must come from a sincere interest in the customs and traditions of other people and not out of a sense of duty for it to effectively demonstrate to the minority child that his heritage is valuable. In addition, awareness of the child's culture and customs should be a routine part of family life rather than a special event. For example, making certain Indian foods part of the family's regular mealtime fare does more to show how valuable and accepted that aspect of the child's culture is than having a special "Indian meal" once a year and avoiding curry the rest of the time. More than one adoptive family has driven many miles to an international food festival only to have their foreign-born children opt for the hamburger booth.

Parents will want to communicate not only that the child's heritage is important, but that all cultures are valuable. Instead of buying white dolls for white children, Korean dolls for Korean children, and black dolls for black children, all children should have dolls of various ethnic backgrounds. Folk tales of the child's country of origin should be available, but so should stories from other countries. Families should try foods typical of various cultures, not just of their child's native country. Awareness and acceptance of ethnic diversity should be a way of life in the minority family. In addition to those resources listed in Chapter 2 about customs in other countries, there are cookbooks, dolls, holiday ornaments, and other materials that expand a family's cultural awareness. Many of these are advertised or ordered through OURS*.

The goal is for minority children to be proud of their heritage, even though they are likely to identify primarily with the culture of the people who raised them. There is no need for them to choose between their dual heritages—indeed that would be impossible. Minority children raised by parents of a different ethnic background are going to have a different sense of racial identity than they would had they been raised in a racially homogenous family. They are a minority within a minority, with their own unique culture.

INTERCOUNTRY ADOPTIONS

Parents of a child adopted from a foreign country have some nationality issues to consider along with racial and ethnic ones. The child needs to become a citizen of the United States, and may have to learn a new language along with new customs. He may also have medical conditions uncommon in this country. (See Appendix for information on birth certificates and naturalization for children born abroad.)

Learning New Customs

When a child older than the age of three is adopted from a foreign country, parents are discouraged from trying to "Americanize" their child as quickly as possible. While it may seem to be in the child's best interest, what is communicated is that his past is something that should be discarded because it isn't worthwhile. Parents should not fear their child will be stigmatized if he isn't Americanized quickly—he will quickly abandon his language and customs on his own. The grief he is experiencing for the loss of his country and culture, and the loss of being similar to those around him will paradoxically motivate him to assimilate his new culture.

The first stage of the grief process is denial. The transracial adoptee denies he's different from those around him by hiding those differences. Eventually, says psychologist H. Sook Wilkinson, he will experience a re-awakening of his ethnic heritage, acknowledge it, and seek out people of the same background with whom he can identify. Ultimately he will accept his ethnic background.

Children move through these stages at different rates. And the foreign-born child adopted as an infant may go through them when she is old enough to understand that her racial or ethnic background sets her apart from others. It is going to be difficult for a child to perceive her ethnic background as positive when in the denial phase, and she is unlikely to want to associate with people of her race or ethnic background. Parents should remember that her lack of interest in her ethnic heritage is temporary and try to preserve as much as possible of the child's cultural background so that when she is ready to embrace it, it is there. For example, they can save any mementos of her country, even though she may say she doesn't want them any more.

Bilingualism

Children who are speaking their native language when they arrive in the adoptive home should be encouraged to speak their language, or at least should not be discouraged from speaking it. The child who is pressured to speak only English may not be able to express his feelings during the critical adjustment period because his grasp of the language is too limited. In addition, he may feel that his cultural past is not valued.

Since most of us cannot provide our children with adequate opportunities to speak their first language, all but those adopted after the age of nine or ten are likely to forget it. That is not going to be detrimental to the child as long as he is allowed to use his first language for as long as it is helpful to him.

There are educational as well as psychological benefits to allowing a child to use his first language while he learns English. Researchers have found that bilingualism enhances a person's intellectual and educational abilities because it increases opportunities to use and analyze language. Obviously, there is more to learning a language than learning words and grammar; there are concepts involved. For example, the difference between 'on' and 'over' is subtle, but the two-year-old just learning to talk does not get the concepts confused. She learns the difference in those concepts before she learns to talk. If she is forced to suppress her first language, she also suppresses much of the conceptual basis developed before she learned to talk. On the other hand, if she is allowed to use her native language, her early language skills can be used to process concepts unclear to her in English. This does not diminish her capacity to learn or use English, but enhances it, although parents should not expect great jumps in academic achievement as a result. The child who continues to use her native tongue may take longer to learn English, but she will have a greater awareness of language, increased capacity for creative thought, and greater conceptual development.

Of course, the child's ability to transfer language skills from his first language to English is dependent on the quality of his early language development. The child who had poor language skills in his first language is not going to have much to draw on conceptually.

It is not easy for parents to communicate with a child who speaks a different language, particularly when the child is scared and confused by his new surroundings. Bilingual dictionaries, language tapes, introductory word books such as those used by toddlers just learning to talk, and interpreters are all used to bridge the communication gap. We should keep in mind that communication problems we are having are as much due to our lack of ability in the child's language as to the child's lack of skill in ours. The child should not feel responsible for misunderstandings due to language differences.

MEDICAL CONSIDERATIONS WITH FOREIGN-BORN CHILDREN

Children from foreign countries may have parasites, skin diseases or venereal disease, or have been exposed to tuberculosis, measles, or other diseases. Most physicians are familiar with these medical conditions, but parents may want to suggest that their children be tested for some of them immediately. In addition to the medical conditions the children come with, children from foreign countries may be susceptible to other diseases or medical conditions long after their adjustment period is over, and some of these are not familiar to many physicians in the United States.

Immediate Medical Attention

A child from a foreign country should be examined by a physician shortly after her arrival so that her overall medical condition as well as developmental condition can be assessed. This initial examination should include a test for parasites such as roundworms, pinworms and tapeworms. Because some varieties of parasites take several months to reach the adult stage, the child showing symptoms of parasites, such as diarrhea, should be checked again, even though the initial stool sample showed no signs of parasites.

Agencies placing children from India also recommend that a stool culture for salmonella be obtained. Even though the child is not showing signs of the bacterial infection, she can be a carrier of the disease.

If the child has not been immunized against measles, mumps, rubella, diphtheria, polio, and pertussis, parents will want to arrange for those immunizations. Table 1 outlines the schedule recommended by the American Academy of Pediatrics for immunizing children who were not immunized in early infancy. A tuberculin skin test should be given before immunization against measles as the measles vaccine can temporarily depress tuberculin skin sensitivity. If the tine test is positive, it may be due to preventative treatment programs in the child's country of birth, and a chest X-ray should be taken to rule out active or inactive disease.

Children also should be screened for venereal disease and checked for lice and scabies. A complete blood count to rule out anemia and a urine analysis should also be done.

Table 1

Recommended Immunization Schedules
for Infants and Children Not initially Immunized at
Usual Recommended Times in Early Infancy

First visit	DTP #1, OPV #1, Tuberculin test (PPD)
1 Month after first visit	MMR
2 Month after first visit	DTP #2, OPV #2
3 Month after first visit	(DTP #3)
4 Month after first visit	DTP #3 (OPV #3)
10-16 Months after last dose	DTP #4, OPV #3 or OPV #4
Preschool	DTP #5, OPV #4 or OPV #5
14-16-year-old	Td

DTP = Diphtheria and tetanus toxoids with pertussis vaccine.
OPV = Oral, attenuated poliovirus vaccine.
Tuberculin test = Mantoux (intradermal PPD) preferred.
MMR = Live measles, mumps, and rubella viruses in a combined vaccine.
Td = Adult tetanus toxoid (full dose) and diptheria toxoid (reduced dose) in combination.

Reprinted with permission from *Report of the Committee on Infectious Diseases*, 1982 edition.

The Malnourished Child

Some children from foreign countries are malnourished or undernourished when they arrive in their adoptive homes. Most studies have connected malnutrition with retarded mental development, but the children in these studies remained in deprived situations. One study found when malnourished children receive adequate nutrition and stimulation early enough, the effect of malnutrition on a child's growth and intellectual development may be reversed.

Pediatrician Myron Winick, an authority on the effects of malnutrition on mental development, studied malnourished and undernourished Korean children who were adopted by the age of three and found that their growth and intellectual development four to thirteen years later was normal. Malnourished children adopted after the age of three did, however, have achievement levels below norms for children in the United States.

While the effect of malnutrition seems to be reversible if the child's environment is enriched soon enough, the change may not be immediate. Pediatricians in Latin America who studied the effect of an enriched diet and proper stimulation on malnourished infants adopted before the age of two did not see the dramatic improvement in the children after one year that was seen in the Korean children after several years. They suggest it may take longer than one year for the effects of adequate nutrition to be seen.

Parents whose child has been undernourished, malnourished, or understimulated should expect to see a significant weight gain immediately after he arrives in his adoptive home, reflecting the more adequate nutrition and care. Eventually, the child's growth will stabilize in a normal pattern.

Measuring Growth of a Foreign-born Child

Tom and Lucy took their daughter, who arrived from India at three months of age, to the physician for her 12-month check-up. The physician was concerned that she was still only in the fifth percentile for weight. Yet she was eating well and seemed healthy. Tom and Lucy suggested that perhaps it was not appropriate to compare her against a growth chart designed for North American children. Perhaps on a growth chart for Indians, she would be average.

It isn't necessary to measure a child from a foreign country against a growth chart developed for people in that country to determine whether that child is growing adequately. But it is also unreasonable to expect the child to achieve the same standards for height and weight as North American Caucasians.

An infant's size is determined by *in utero* conditions and postnatal factors such as diet, exposure to infection, and stimulation, but the effect of genetics on a child's size is not seen until the infant is about nine months old and does not dominate until the child is two years of age. In other words, differences in the size of babies younger than two years of age are due to prenatal and postnatal environmental factors. Consequently, all babies can be evaluated using the same growth chart. If an infant is unusually small, it is not because his mother and father were small, but because conditions for the child *in utero* or immediately after birth were not optimal. If a six-year-old is small, though, it can be because his parents were small.

Even after the age of two, it may not be appropriate to evaluate a foreign-born child against a growth chart developed for his race or country if the child has been living in North America and eating a North American diet. Growth charts reflect not only constitutional factors for a group but environmental factors for that country. If people in the country typically have inadequate nutrition and high exposure to disease, expectations for their growth will be lower than if they were receiving adequate nutrition and health care. A child born to Indian parents, therefore, may have a predisposition to be small, but if he is raised in the United States where there is proper immunization, use of antibiotics to treat infection, and a nutritionally sound diet, he is likely to be larger than he would have been had he remained in a Third World country.

Parents and physicians should not be as concerned about where the child falls on the grid for height and weight as long as his growth remains consistent, and the child's height is proportionate to his weight.

The Child of Unknown Age

In her practical guideline, *Parenting the Ageless Child,* * Joyce Kaser relates how a child development clinic gave her son a thorough examination before saying he was about eight years old. Their pediatrician, orthodontist and dentist, however, fixed his age at somewhere between eleven and thirteen. Shortly after the evaluation, the boy reached puberty.

A child adopted at an older age may not have a record of his exact date of birth. Parents may assume that fixing an exact age for a child is relatively simple, given today's sophisticated medical diagnostic techniques. In fact, assessing a child's age is more complex than examining his teeth or taking an X-ray of his wrist. The process may take several evaluations by different specialists. Even then, there may be conflicting results. The best the specialists may be able to come up with could be a three- to five-year age range. Factors such as nutrition, emotional health, and illness can all influence dental, musculoskeletal and sexual development. It can be extremely difficult to assess the age of a child if the heights and weights of his birthparents are not known; if the child has emotional problems stemming from abandonment, separation or trauma; if the child had poor nutrition or inadequate dental care; and if the child's formal education was nonexistent, sporadic, or interrupted.

Age assessment should include: measurements of height, weight, head and chest circumference; developmental screening; bone age evaluation; dental assessment; and genital examination with estimation of testicular size in males and assessment of sexual maturity in children older than five years. It may be necessary to follow the child's development over time to establish patterns of growth. Parents of a child with an undetermined age are understandably anxious to establish a precise age as quickly as possible. However, the process may take a long time, may not be conclusive, and may be very expensive. Parents should remember that other aspects of a child's adjustment, such as attachment and the correction of immediate medical problems, are more important than knowing exactly how old the child is.

A child whose age cannot be precisely determined faces some unique situations. The child should be placed in a grade at school appropriate for his academic and emotional levels. But if he has an academic age of eleven and a musculoskeletal age of fourteen, parents and the school may be criticized for allowing him to play sports against other eleven-year-olds—even though they are in the same grade. Emotionally, the same child may prefer to play with nine- or ten-year-olds. Parents of a child with a presumed age will need to get involved with the school system, as well as with groups sponsoring extracurricular activities, to act as an advocate for their child. Ultimately, the parents have to determine what age the child will be considered.

When parents discover that the age on their child's birth certificate is inaccurate, they may want to change it. Birth dates can be legally changed, and new birth certificates issued, but parents should be cautious in changing a date of birth. An initial evaluation of a child's age may not be consistent with assessments made at a future time. And birth dates are used not only to verify a child's age, but to determine when he can vote, buy alcohol, drive, be drafted into military service, retire and collect Social Security. Changing a date of birth is a legal process that varies from state to state, consequently an attorney should be consulted. A birth date can be changed at any time, even after the adoption is finalized, and after the child becomes an adult. Although there is no limit on the number of times a birth date can be changed, common sense dictates that people take the time to think about all the consequences before rushing into court.

Hepatitis B

Because of the prevalence of hepatitis B in certain Asian countries, the U.S. Centers for Disease Control recommends that all Asian children brought to this country for adoption be screened for hepatitis B. Hepatitis B, commonly called serum hepatitis, is a viral infection of the liver. Only a small number of people who contract hepatitis B will show signs of being sick, which include low fever, loss of appetite, jaundice, liver enlargement and malaise.

There is no cure for the disease, but usually the body develops antibodies to fight off the virus. When that happens, the person is no longer contagious and is immune to the disease. People who have had hepatitis B and resolved it are at no greater risk of developing further liver disease. Those who do not develop this immunity become chronic carriers of the disease and can infect others. Carriers also have an increased risk of developing serious liver disease later on, including cirrhosis and hepatic cancer.

Taiwan, Korea, Vietnam, Cambodia, the Philippines, and the parts of India closest to China have the highest incidence of hepatitis B in the world. An estimated 5 to 15 percent of those populations are carriers of the virus, compared to less than 1 percent in the United States. Children who have been exposed to hepatitis B have a much greater chance of becoming carriers than do adults. While an estimated 10 percent of adults with hepatitis B become carriers, 40 to 50 percent of children born to carrier mothers will become chronic carriers. Some hepatitis B carriers seem to be more infectious than others, but generally, the more recently a person has been infected, the more infectious that person is.

A blood test can determine if a person is immune or a carrier of hepatitis B as well as how infectious the carrier is. Because the test only requires that blood be drawn, and is often inexpensive, all Asian-born children should be screened, even if they have been in the country for many years. Efforts are underway to screen children before they arrive in the United States, but that has not been common practice.

If a child already in the home is found to be a carrier, the immediate family should be tested to see if any of them have had the disease or become carriers. Those who are neither immune nor already carriers should receive the hepatitis B vaccine, an effective means of prevention. If the child has not yet arrived and is found to be a carrier, it is probably unnecessary for the immediate family to be screened, given the low incidence of hepatitis B in the United States. They should assume they have not had the disease and be vaccinated. Some health officials recommend being tested after vaccination to make sure the vaccine was effective.

A child with a communicable disease frightens people. Many, including some physicians, are confused about the way hepatitis B is transmitted. In an effort to be safe rather than sorry, they may shun the child. One parent wrote in *OURS* Magazine that physicians learning that her son was a carrier refused to perform elective surgery on him, and that friends have refused to let their children play in the family's yard.

Hepatitis specialists at the Centers for Disease Control say social ostracism is unnecessary for the hepatitis B carrier. The disease is transmitted to another person primarily through the blood, although other bodily secretions can contain the virus. In countries where the disease is endemic, it is commonly spread from mother to child through bleeding at the time of birth. Hepatitis B is not an airborne virus that can be transmitted by coughing or sneezing, and while it may be transmitted through saliva, that probably is an inefficient method. People who live with a hepatitis B carrier or come into intimate contact with him are at risk for contracting the disease, but those who have only casual contact with the person are not likely to be infected. Since the vaccine is somewhat expensive and the risk of contracting the disease from casual contact is small, it is not advisable to vaccinate those outside the immediate family.

Nevertheless, hepatitis B carriers should learn the kinds of activities that might transmit the disease, and until they are mature enough to be responsible for their actions, school personnel and other supervising adults need to be educated about the risks of the disease so they can be alert to behavior that might transmit it.

Young children and retarded children spread the disease by biting, scratching and drooling. Some day-care centers and nursery schools are denying admission to hepatitis B carriers and are legally permitted to do so.

Public schools have not been allowed by the courts to deny a carrier child admission, and rightly so. It isn't necessary for friends, school personnel, and classmates to be concerned about contracting the disease, although schools should be aware of the child's medical condition. Items touched by a carrier do not need to be sterilized, nor is it necessary to prohibit "sleep-overs." But drinking out of a common can of soda or pricking one's finger and intermingling the blood with a friend's to symbolize the depth of the relationship should be avoided with hepatitis carriers. The school-age child will need guidance and supervision to ensure appropriate behavior, but as he becomes mature enough to take responsibility for his interaction with others, it becomes less necessary for others to be informed of his medical condition.

For example, the adolescent will not need to tell his date he is a carrier of hepatitis B before a goodnight kiss. But the sexually active teenager should know he has a disease that can be sexually transmitted. Experts are not sure what to advise carriers about sexual contact. It is possible to transmit the disease through intercourse, although not every spouse of a hepatitis B carrier develops the disease. It probably is advisable for a regular sexual partner to have the screening test or vaccination.

Lactose Intolerance

Though uncommon among white Americans, 90 percentage of Asians, 70 percent of American blacks and Native Americans, and 50 percent of Mexican-Americans develop lactose intolerance by their teens. This means they have an insufficient amount of the enzyme lactase in the lining of the small intestine to break down lactose, the principal carbohydrate in milk. In people with a lactase deficiency, the lactose passes unaltered into the colon attracting water by osmosis. There, bacteria split it into simple sugars that ferment into organic acids and gas. The result is cramps, bloating, diarrhea and abdominal discomfort. Lactose intolerance can be determined by a blood test, stool test or breath test, but is more often diagnosed by removing dairy products from the diet and seeing if the symptoms disappear.

Babies as young as a year old may show signs of lactose intolerance, but it is more common for the symptoms to appear when children are eight to twelve years old and to worsen as the child reaches adolescence.

Many children develop a secondary lactose intolerance following a viral infection of the intestinal tract. The infection has temporarily depleted their available lactase. It may take weeks or even months for the lactase levels to return to normal. Parents should not assume that the child has primary, or genetically determined, lactose intolerance if the symptoms first appear after a gastrointestinal illness. They should temporarily remove dairy products from the diet but reintroduce them later to see if the symptoms persist.

Fortunately, even children with a primary lactose intolerance do not have to give up dairy products entirely. While individuals vary, nutritionists say most children with lactose intolerance can handle up to one cup of milk with each meal. By consuming milk with other foods, the lactose enters the intestine slowly rather than flooding the system with undigestible food. Those foods high in lactose, such as whole milk and buttermilk, may be replaced with foods like yogurt and cheese that have less lactose but adequate amounts of calcium and other nutrients commonly found in dairy products. It is possible to treat milk with a commercial lactase such as LactAid (not to be confused with the breast-feeding device), available without a prescription. The enzyme is added to milk, mixed and refrigerated for twenty-four hours. The disadvantage is that because the lactase breaks down the lactose into simple sugars before the milk is drunk, the milk tastes much sweeter and blood sugar levels increase significantly. In some cities, milk already treated with artificial lactase is available. For those people who cannot tolerate enough milk or dairy products to get an adequate amount of calcium, there are calcium substitutes available. Vitamin D must be given artificially so that the calcium can be absorbed, and parents must take care not to exceed the U.S. recommended daily allowance. Excessive doses of vitamin D can be toxic, and it can cause an excessive absorption of calcium, which can also be toxic.

People whose children appear to be lactose intolerant should consult a physician, nutritionist or dietician to learn the levels of lactose and calcium in various foods.

Trachoma

Although rare in the United States, trachoma is one of the major causes of blindness in the world. It is a chronic infection of the conjunctiva, the mucous membrane that lines the eyelid and exposed surface of the eyeball. It is caused by a virus and complicated by poor nutrition and poor hygiene. In its early stages, trachoma causes redness in the conjunctiva, itching, and some discharge from the eye. If not treated, the conjunctiva and cornea become scarred, which can distort the eyelid and cause vision loss or blindness.

If a child has frequent conjunctivitis or eye irritation, parents should suggest to their physician that the child be checked for trachoma. Because the condition is so rare in the United States, physicians may not think to consider trachoma.

Other Medical Considerations

— Because children in some countries are given antibiotics too frequently, bacterial infections resistant to certain antibiotics may develop. Physicians should culture the site of an infection and test it for sensitivity to a number of antibiotics so that the most effective treatment can be given.

— Infants whose bottles are propped, which may have been the practice in an orphanage, often develop ear infections as a result of milk draining from back of the nose into the eustachian tubes. If not treated promptly, the eardrum may perforate with a possible loss in hearing. Parents who suspect a hearing deficiency in their child should have him tested.

— Poor nutrition or dental hygiene, or a diet high in carbohydrates and low in calcium can result in dental problems in children adopted from foreign countries. Some arrive with bleeding gums, deficient enamel on their teeth, or with many cavities. Parents should be aware of the possibility that their child will need dental work, but save trips to the dentist, other than for emergency treatment, until the child is settled in his new home.

Chapter 11

Serious Behavior Problems

Sometimes serious behavior problems last beyond the typical "testing" phase of the adjustment period and challenge even the most capable and patient parents. These problems may include bedwetting, soiling, temper tantrums, inappropriate sexual behavior, lying, stealing, running away, arson, truancy and other school problems, and inability to form close relationships.

Experts such as therapists and physicians should be consulted for help with specific problems, yet many parents have found effective ways to modify some of their children's behavior and to live with that which they cannot change.

DEALING WITH SERIOUS PROBLEMS

There are many possible explanations for serious behavior problems in children, but experts do not agree on which physical or emotional traumas cause which problems if, indeed, there is a simple cause-and-effect relationship involved. Certainly there are adopted children who have been traumatized, and the list of possible traumas is long: separation from the mother when the child was old enough to have formed a strong attachment; multiple homes and caretakers; failure to grieve for the significant losses; physical, sexual, or emotional abuse; malnutrition and neglect; and failure to experience a permanent, trusting relationship with an adult.

Most children who have been in the child welfare system for more than a year will have experienced more than one kind of emotional or physical trauma. These children will have emotional scars, but not all will react to their early trauma in the same way. Many will demonstrate serious behavior problems, but early deprivation and trauma seem to spur some children to high achievements. Still others develop behavior problems without any apparent history of early trauma or neglect. It is imperative that we as adoptive parents recognize that while early life experiences may help explain a child's behavior problems, they cannot predict them. In particular, we cannot say with certainty that a specific trauma results in a specific behavioral response.

While most of us would like to know why our child is behaving the way she is, knowledge of what happened in the child's past may be only marginally helpful in living with a child who is exhibiting serious, perhaps even dangerous, behavior problems. What is important is that the child change her behavior at least enough to function appropriately in the family and in society.

Much of the behavior that parents find most difficult to deal with can be categorized as:

— Lack of conscience—an inability to tell right from wrong, or to feel remorse or regret when he does something wrong. Often a lack of conscience is the result of the child's failure to make attachments. The child who doesn't care about her parents is not motivated to behave in a way that will please them. Some children fail to develop a sense of conscience because values have never been clearly spelled out, or because they have lived in many places with conflicting values.

— Inability to differentiate and express feelings—the child who has experienced early trauma may not know any other feelings besides pain and the lack of pain. He may not be motivated to improve his behavior because as long as he isn't in pain, he is experiencing the most "happiness" he has come to expect in life. Or a child may have been discouraged from expressing his emotions and so does not know how to express his feelings of anger, fear, grief, or love.

— Failure to attach—failure to develop reciprocal feelings of love and caring with parents and siblings. Lack of caring for other family members is related to a lack of conscience and inability to express feelings.

Children with such problems, along with their parents and perhaps other members of the family, should be seeing a therapist regularly. But parents can use some techniques on their own. If these seem to conflict with the treatment the therapist recommends, parents may want to consider selecting another counselor.

We cannot give our child a conscience—that is a choice the child has to make. But we can show our child why a conscience is important and give her a framework or model for developing her own standards of behavior.

Looking at the Past

The adoptee who has been in several foster or adoptive homes may have behavior problems because she has not completed her grief process. (Helping a child grieve is discussed in Chapter 5.) The child may need to make a life book, or otherwise reconstruct the places she's lived in and the people she's known before she can begin to care enough about her new parents to want to please them.

Adoption specialist Josephine Anderson recommends that a parent sit down with the child a few times a week for about forty-five minutes, holding the child on his lap in such a way that the child cannot flee and is forced to make eye contact. Then the parent should direct the child to think about her past and share her feelings. A mother or father might say, "This is for me. I need to understand you better. There are parts of your life we didn't share, and I feel sad about that. I know you have feelings that also get in the way of our loving each other. I'd like you to tell me about your life before you came to live here." The child is likely to be reluctant to relive her past and try any manipulative technique to avoid it, but the parent should be persistent, acknowledging that the experience is scary, but letting the child know that mom or dad is there to help. The parent should reassure the child that the unpleasant experiences she shares will not be repeated and will not harm their relationship. While the child is sharing her memories, the parent should not react emotionally to them, but can share later in the child's emotional reaction. This "holding technique" ends with physical and verbal expressions of comfort that should help build an attachment between parent and child. This technique can be used with a child as young as two-and-a-half, as long as she has some verbal skills, and with a child as old as ten or eleven years old—as old as fifteen if the child is receptive to being held or two parents are involved in holding the child, Anderson says.

A Sense of Future

Not only do children need a sense of the past, but they need a sense of the future to realize there is more than "living for today." Adoption specialist Barbara Tremitiere says we should talk about future events and plan for them so that our child begins to think in those terms. Discussions of Halloween costumes, summer vacation plans, Christmas celebrations, and other events can begin months in advance. Activities such as 4-H, Junior Achievement, and scouting, in which children work on projects with specific goals in mind, should also be encouraged.

In addition, we should remind our child of past events. We should take pictures of the child and the family engaging in activities, and put them in a permanent album. Children who have lived with many families have never experienced the thrill of looking through a photograph album and seeing the development of the family. A scrapbook, or perhaps the child's life book, can contain mementos of past activities and events.

Talking about the future and reliving the past tells the child that she is a member of the family; the family has a shared history and a future to look forward to.

Physical Contact

Touching is essential to the development of attachment, and attachment is essential to the development of a sense of conscience. Abused children often avoid physical contact at all costs, and while parents may have to proceed slowly with these children, they should not let the child prohibit physical touch. We know we do not intend to hurt the child by touching, so we can proceed slowly, starting with a slight touch on the shoulder and progressing to longer expressions of love. Social worker Linda Katz points out that parents may have to be creative about finding non-threatening ways to touch children who are especially sensitive to physical contact, for example, by brushing a child's hair, or helping a child swing a bat. While these examples may not seem like significant forms of physical contact, touching is so powerful that even casual contact conveys an important message. It may take years for some children to lose their fear of physical contact, but a foundation of trust should be built from the beginning.

One way that child psychiatrist Gerald Nelson recommends for parents to get close to their child and build attachment is the "M&M game," in which the parent sits close to the child, while the child closes his eyes and sticks out his tongue. The parent places an M&M on the child's tongue and asks him to guess its color, pointing out that he won't be able to tell until the M&M melts. While the child is concentrating on the taste of the candy, the parent quietly tells him positive things about himself. Since the child cannot distinguish colors by taste, any color he guesses is "correct," and the child is rewarded with another candy. Parent and child can continue this way for about ten M&Ms. In effect, the child is rewarded for sitting calmly—both with candy and with the good things he hears about himself—and the parent and child have a pleasant, close experience. Even if the child catches on to the game, it can be fun.

Neutral Language

Children with chronic behavior problems have been disciplined so often they no longer listen to people saying they are "bad" or "naughty" or going to be "punished." These emotionally loaded words are also belittling and diminish the child's self-concept, which in turn leads to continued misbehavior. After all, if the child thinks of himself as worthless, he will behave that way.

Neutral terms such as "unacceptable," "inappropriate," "intolerable," or "provocative" may challenge the child to stop and think about what is being said, while not conveying a negative message about the child. Of course, parents must be sure the child understands the words before they are used.

Josephine Anderson recommends parents use a neutral word, agreed upon ahead of time, to "cue" the child that she is starting to behave inappropriately. For example, parent and child could agree that when the parent says the word "cantaloupe," it means the child's behavior is inappropriate, and, if continued, will result in predictable consequences. The word is non-judgmental, doesn't embarrass the child in front of her friends because only the child and parent know what it means, and can keep the situation from escalating. It is important to let the child choose the word, that it be a neutral term, and that the child clearly understand what is meant when it is said. The child can also use the word when she thinks her parents' behavior is starting to provoke her.

Expressing Feelings

Children may have to be taught appropriate ways to express their feelings—a difficult task for parents who were not encouraged as children to express their negatives feelings. Having grown up hearing "Big boys don't cry," or "Don't talk to your mother like that," parents are often unsure how to encourage children with a lot of anger and sadness to appropriately ventilate those emotions.

We should encourage our children to express their anger verbally, but within limits. For example, parents can permit a child to yell at them or a sibling as long as the child does not use vulgar language or personally attack the other person. In other words, the child should be taught to express what he is feeling, not what he thinks of the other person. He can be told that it is all right to want to hit someone, and even to think about it, but it is not permissible to hit someone. He may, however, punch a pillow, slam a tennis ball against a wall, smash empty aluminum cans, chop wood, or otherwise channel his negative feelings into acceptable physical activities.

Many children who are adopted after experiencing physical or emotional trauma do not cry readily, so the problem for parents is letting them know they can express their sadness or grief. One way to help children express themselves is to suggest how they appear to be feeling, for example, by saying, "You look sad. I think it's because. . . " Even if that doesn't result in an emotional release by the child, he will know being sad is all right. Since children are sometimes reluctant to cry in front of other people, Claudia Jewett advises in her book, *Helping Children Cope with Separation and Loss**, that parents suggest to the child crying after he goes to bed or in the shower where no one will hear.

One Minute Scolding

The "one minute scolding" was developed by child psychiatrist Gerald E. Nelson and his colleague Richard Lewak particularly for use with children without consciences and without emotional attachments. The popular disciplinary technique of "time-out," in which the child must leave the social circle until she can behave appropriately, is not always effective with children who have no emotional attachment to their families. These children are already withdrawn from the family emotionally, so physical withdrawal does not represent much change, nor are they motivated to return to the social circle by their emotional commitment. To them, being sent into isolation may be tantamount to rejection or abandonment—experiences that adopted children may be particularly sensitive to. They may infer that whenever they are in trouble, they are abandoned by their parents. Not only does this inhibit attachment, the child learns not to look to others for help when in distress. Nelson recommends that parents who want to use time-out have the child sit on a chair rather than leave the room.

In the one minute scolding, the parent acts immediately to scold the child for her misbehavior. The scolding is done privately, so as not to embarrass the child. The parent makes physical contact with the child, holding her on his lap, holding her arm, or otherwise touching her. For the first thirty seconds, the parent expresses his feelings, taking care to criticize the child's behavior, not the child. The parent should express whatever he is feeling, for example, "I am angry that you talked back to me like that. I want you to respect me. When you talk like that I get so mad I want to slap your face. . ." The child learns not only how the parent is feeling but how he is using self-control to not give in to inappropriate behavior. It is important that the parent's body language be consistent with the way the parent says he feels. It is also important that the parent not be interrupted during this time, either by the child's explanations or by external factors such as the telephone. After thirty seconds—less if crying or other behavior indicates that the child has been affected by the scolding—the parent should take a deep breath, remind himself how much he cares for the child, and change his voice and approach. For the next thirty seconds the parent should remind the child how much he loves her, and explain that he is scolding her because he loves her, and that he will scold her whenever she misbehaves. He should make sure the child knows why she was scolded and that she will be disciplined in the same way if she repeats the behavior. The sessions should end with a hug or other physical expression of affection, and the behavior should not be discussed again or brought up at another scolding time.

The second half of the scolding is often difficult for parents, particularly if they have anger stored up. Although it may feel contrived to express affection at that time, parents would not be angry with a child they didn't care about. The second half-minute also takes advantage of a period of strong feelings to build a positive relationship between parent and child. By using the one minute scolding, parents can modify their child's misbehavior while building attachment.

Natural Consequences

Crucial to the development of a conscience is the understanding that actions have logical and natural consequences. The child without a conscience has little sense of the future and consequently can't see why doing something right now will benefit him later. Teaching a child that there are consequences to his actions requires that the child be allowed to make choices, and this can be difficult for parents. For example, if the child does not take his dirty clothes to the laundry room, they do not get washed, consequently, he doesn't have clean clothes to wear to school. To allow the child to make this choice, parents must be willing to let their child go to school in dirty or wrinkled clothes. Parents must decide what is more important, that their child look clean and neat or that he have the chance to make the choice and take the consequences. In this case, parents may need to remind themselves that looking unkempt affects only the child and refuse to accept responsibility for his appearance—even though there will be some people who think that the boy is untidy because his parents are neglecting their responsibilities. The child's refusal to take care of his dirty clothes may seem like a minor problem compared to his other behavior, such as truancy or drug abuse, but by being forced to accept responsibility for his actions in these small areas, the child learns the idea of accepting consequences for his actions, which he can apply to more important situations.

An excellent example of allowing children to take the consequences of their actions was described in the advice column "Dear Abby." Children who had been suspended from the school bus for misbehavior were required by their parents to walk the several miles to school for the duration of the suspension. The parents followed the children in their car to make sure they went to school and were safe. Though many readers wrote in to criticize the parents, the parents' actions allowed the children to realize that if they did not follow the rules of school bus, they would not be allowed to ride it, and if they could not ride the school bus, they would have to walk to school.

In some cases, the natural consequences of a child's actions may be serious, and parents should let the child know that they are not going to "protect" him from those consequences. For example, parents can say, "We don't want you to take the car without permission because we care about you and want to know where you are going and how you are getting there." Parents should let the child know that they expect him to make the right choice by saying, "We know you wouldn't deliberately cause us concern, so if the car is missing, we will assume it is stolen and report it to the police."

Behavior Diary

It may be helpful for parents to keep a "behavior diary" about their child. Each day, the parents can note actions or events that got out of hand, as well as those actions that were potentially explosive, but kept in control. The time of day and events leading up to the situation can also be recorded. The diary can help parents chart their child's progress, since when the child is in a period of difficult behavior it sometimes seems that she has always behaved that way. It also helps to look back and see that a certain behavior had a definite starting point, and that there have been similar periods in the past. In addition, by keeping track of what led up to the behavior, parents may be able to see patterns. For example, conflict may seem to occur immediately after the child comes home from school. Knowing when behavior is likely to get out of hand can help prevent it. Perhaps the child explodes after school because she is having trouble at school, or perhaps she is hungry then. Identifying the school problem, or sending a snack with her to eat on the way home may prevent or minimize further conflict. Each parent should keep a separate diary, as they often have different interactions with the child, and the child can be encouraged to keep her own record. The diary should be used to chart improvement, and never be used against the child to remind her of past misbehavior.

Parents in Charge

To effectively discipline our children, we must believe in our right to act as our children's parents, though developing this sense of entitlement can be particularly difficult with a child adopted at an older age who has severe behavior problems. Parent and child will not share a history, and the child may remember her birthparents or foster parents and have contact with them. As a result, adoptive parents may feel like outsiders. In addition, the child with behavior problems is likely to have a therapist, a social worker, and perhaps a special education teacher or counselor at school, all of whom have opinions about how the child should be cared for. Parents may feel like a member of a therapeutic or caretaking "team" rather than parents. We must remember that even though the child has had other parents, and has other people who care about her or who play a significant role in her life, we are the only people who can or should act as her parents. Important as professionals are, the social service personnel dealing with the child are not in charge; parents do not have to defer to them. In fact, parents should act as though they are employing them even if they aren't paying the bills. In a very real sense, the helping professionals are working for the family, not vice versa.

While many children have "survivor" skills and give the impression they can take care of themselves, Barbara Tremitiere reminds parents that these children want strong parents so they can act like children. Chances are the child entered the child welfare system because she was in charge rather than her birthparents. The child who has been in control is likely to try to hang onto that control, but down deep she wants to be the child she is, and that means having parents willing to set firm, consistent limits, and follow through to ensure they are not exceeded.

Setting and enforcing limits is not an easy task for parents of children without consciences. Such children are not likely to follow directions for the same reasons other children do—because they like to please their parents, because obeying their parents is the "right" thing to do, or because they fear the consequences of not following the directives. These children do, however, respect someone stronger than they are. Demonstrating who is in charge may seem more authoritarian than many of today's parents would like, but reasoning with a child without a conscience or without an emotional attachment is unlikely to be effective.

Parents who attempt to show they are in charge should select a situation they can have some control over. It also may be wise to take the initial stand on a situation that is not very important to the child, such as hanging up her coat. Then, when authority has been established, more important issues can be settled. Parents show they are in charge by following through on a directive; when the child is told to wash the dishes, the dishes must be washed—and washed well. If they aren't, the child must do them again. Obviously, this situation can turn into a test of wills. It may seem easier to allow a mediocre job to pass for the completion of a chore, but it is important that children learn they cannot manipulate their parents.

A primary goal of a therapist working with families with unruly children should be to help the parents take charge, set limits, and follow through. Developing insight into why problems developed and allowing children to express their feelings are valuable benefits of therapy, but parents who live with children with severe behavior problems need to work out a tolerable living arrangement. Some methods behavior-oriented therapists use to empower parents may be unusual. Parents should find out from other clients whether the techniques are effective before rejecting them.

When setting limits, parents should try to keep the number of rules in the family down to a manageable number. More importantly, they should not make rules they cannot enforce. For example, parents cannot enforce a rule prohibiting the child from using drugs because they cannot be with the child all the time. They can enforce a rule that prohibits the child's use of drugs at home. To do this effectively we need to decide what values are critical in our family, and perhaps let go of some that are desirable, but not critical. In deciding on rules, parents should take into account their personal values, not just what will help maintain order. For example, parents may require that everyone eat dinner together each evening in addition to prohibiting physical violence or alcohol abuse in the home.

Getting Tough

The Toughlove theory, designed to help parents with teenagers who are out of control, says by taking a stand parents precipitate a crisis that must result in some kind of change. And by setting the final limit, the parents—not the child—are in control of the crisis. Some adoptive families have found Toughlove techniques effective, although there is controversy over Toughlove theory and practice among adoption experts.

In practice, parents may decide not to post bail for their child because they think he should learn the natural consequence of breaking the law is being arrested, and being arrested is not a pleasant experience. In some cases the child's behavior becomes so disruptive to the family that it can't be tolerated and parents give the child a choice between changing his behavior and living somewhere else. Usually families make it clear in advance what behavior will not be tolerated, such as physical violence.

Obviously, parents have to be able to accept that the child may not make the change hoped for, resulting in the child moving out until he can make the desired change.

Parents cannot get tough like this by themselves. They need the support of friends, relatives, or other parents in similar circumstances, as well as the cooperation of the social service and law enforcement agencies in the community. Other parents provide advice, help verify that the child is fulfilling her part of an agreement, and provide temporary living arrangements for the child if she decides she is not willing to comply with the rules of her family. Involvement by community institutions provides the clout often necessary to back up a parental decision. For example, a child may be more inclined to work out an agreement with her parents if they meet at a courtroom with a juvenile probation officer present, even though there may be no formal proceeding taking place. In addition, parents are less likely to have their plan inadvertently sabotaged by a helping professional if the professional understands the plan in advance, or be accused of abuse or neglect for their tough approach if the proper authorities are aware of the purposes of their actions.

These are harsh measures, but they are not used because a child is disobedient, they are used because the child's behavior is incompatible with family life. They are fair if the child knows what the consequences will be in advance and makes her own choices. While no parent finds these measures easy, Barbara Tremitiere says adoptive parents may find it particularly difficult to threaten a child with having to move out of the home because they are aware the child has already had to leave one home. Parents shouldn't make the threat unless they are willing to follow through with it. But adoptive parents should recognize they are not telling the child she is not wanted; they are telling her she is wanted, but she must demonstrate her willingness to be in the family by complying with some basic rules. The choice is hers.

The Abused Child

The child who has been abused often will seem to elicit additional abuse, and parents must take great care not to fall into this trap. The child isn't eliciting abuse because he likes it; he is reproducing an anxiety-producing event in the hope that the next time, he will be in control of it. Children who have been sexually abused may be flirtatious or openly seductive, a situation discussed in Chapter 7. The child who has been physically abused may provoke parents to the point where they either strike the child or come very close to hitting him. Besides reproducing the abuse to gain control of it, some children may provoke abuse because it is the only pattern of parent-child interaction they know. Some children may believe, based on their experience, that all parents hit their children and want to find out the limits in this family before abuse occurs. Often, the more the parents resist, the more the child escalates his provocative behavior, in effect negatively reinforcing the parents for their self-control. Said one boy to his adoptive mother after she hit him, "I finally gotcha. I knew I would—it just took you longer than the rest."

Child abuse can be prevented by proper preparation by the adoption agency. Being told the child's history and patterns of behavior can help prepare parents for what to expect. Any parent has the potential to abuse his child. Just because we have never been tempted to abuse other children and have been "approved" as adoptive parents does not preclude the possibility that we will be pushed to the brink of abuse. Parents should analyze their own emotional limits, capacity for anger, and attitudes toward disobedience and rule-breaking so they can anticipate a potentially abusive situation and head it off. If they feel themselves becoming abusive, parents should enlist the services available to abusive parents; that is, they should have some kind of respite child care available and may even want to participate in Parents Anonymous, a self-help group for abusive parents. Parents should also have a social worker or counselor who understands their potentially explosive situation and who is willing to work with them. Ideally, the parents should find out whom they can work with before they need to call that person, having questioned their social worker or therapist ahead of time about her attitudes. Obviously, if the social worker or therapist does not understand the potential for abuse, calling her at a time of crisis could result in the child being removed from the home. Parents will want to be sure that the person they call on for help is as committed to keeping the adoptive family together as she would a biologic family in similar circumstances.

The provocative child is going to be adept at finding the parents' vulnerable points. A recently divorced mother, who cares deeply for her children, was told by her son: "You don't know how to take care of me and you didn't know how to take care of dad." She slapped him; he had found her most sensitive area, and she learned what her emotional limits were.

Adoptive parents who succumb to the temptation for abuse should keep in mind the child has probably escalated her behavior for the purpose of eliciting abuse. There is no defense for child abuse—adults have the responsibility to maintain control of themselves. But a parent should not give up his role just because he equates hitting a child with failure as a parent. If the parent is willing to continue parenting the child, and willing to work with a therapist to prevent further instances of abuse, the abuse incident alone is not sufficient reason to disrupt the adoption. Naturally, the parent will feel guilty. He will probably feel he is "no better" than the birthparents who beat the child. What is critical, however, is that the parent be willing to try to prevent abuse from recurring.

Social worker John Boyne pointed out at a national adoption conference that the child who has been abused may understand the problems an allegation of abuse creates for parents and how to manipulate the child welfare system to make such a report. Some adoptive parents have false claims of child abuse filed against them by a child trying to gain control over his parents or who wants to put distance between himself and the parents he is starting to feel close to, having learned from previous placements that feeling close to someone results in pain when separated from that person. On occasion, adoptive parents will be falsely accused of child abuse by a teacher, medical personnel, or a neighbor who misinterprets the bruises of a hyperactive child or the Mongolian spot that resembles a bruise on Asian and Indian children.

While most child protection workers are fair and want to work with the family, they may not all understand the manipulative child or take into account the child's psychological and social history in investigating the child abuse claim. In addition, child protection workers are trained to believe that children do not lie about abuse—and for the vast majority of children, that is true. But a child who lacks a conscience, does not care about people, has a history of lying and manipulative behavior, and who is sophisticated in the workings of the child welfare system may lie about child abuse.

Adoption and child advocacy groups are encouraging child protection workers to become more informed about adoption and to take into consideration all historical information about the child as well as statements from psychological, educational, and medical resources in investigating a child abuse claim. Adoption specialist Josephine Anderson recommends that parents of children with behavior problems write a statement outlining the child's historical and current behavior patterns and have the document signed by a juvenile court judge, pastor, medical doctor, psychiatrist, psychologist, and social worker. The parent who has a verified statement in hand when a child protection worker begins investigating a claim looks less like a defensive parent and more like a parent who understands and recognizes her child's problems.

The parent who has a false claim of child abuse filed against her, especially by the child, is likely to be devastated, especially if the child has been provocative and the parent has resisted the urge to hurt him. Even if the case against the parent is dismissed, it is likely first to become public, causing embarrassment with friends, relatives and co-workers. Parents having a difficult time with their child may re-evaluate their decision to adopt and wonder if the pain is worth the small difference they seem to be making in the child. Parents will need a firm support system—friends, minister, therapist, social worker, or adoptive parent group—to help them through what will be a traumatic experience.

EFFECT ON THE FAMILY

While serious behavior problems are not limited to those children adopted after infancy, most parents who adopt older children who have been in foster care, residential treatment centers, or other adoptive homes expect their child to have some emotional problems. Agencies today are taking greater care to prepare the child for the move to the adoptive family, and to prepare parents for the kinds of behavior they can expect from the child. Agencies have found that parents are willing to adopt emotionally troubled children as long as they know what to expect, and that many of the difficulties families have faced in the past have been the result of inadequate preparation of the child or the family.

Being prepared helps, but it is not the whole answer. While parents who decide to adopt a child with known behavioral problems have the advantage of realistic expectations both of their child's behavior and of the rewards of parenthood, they are not immune to the effects of that behavior on themselves or the family.

Maintaining a Positive Self-Image

Living with a child with chronic, serious behavior problems is a strain, no matter how much parents understand their child's behavior or how committed they are to raising the child. Furthermore, parents are not completely altruistic in adopting a child—they have their own needs and expectations. Usually people adopt because they want to love a child and feel love in return. The child who does not express affection, whose affection is only superficial, or who seems to demand affection from strangers while rebuffing his parents' emotional overtures, is not meeting the parents' needs. Parents whose child defies parental, community, and school authority because he does not care whether he does right or wrong can cause parents to wonder what effect they are having on the child or will have in the future.

It is not unusual for parents in these circumstances to feel like failures; to feel that they have let down themselves, the agency, and most of all the adopted child. They may be frustrated by the slow progress or lack of progress that their child is making. They may even despair at times of the situation ever improving. Linda Katz says parents do better under these circumstances if they are able to delay gratification—if they don't expect to "get anything back" from their efforts immediately. This is contrary to what most of us expect from raising children. We expect a smile in response to ours, or the "reward" of seeing development proceed as a result of our efforts. It may be years before parents of children with serious behavior problems see any sign that they are having any effect. It may be difficult for parents to realize that the child might be doing far worse in another environment.

Parents often have more difficulty living with a child with serious behavior problems if she is the only child, or if she was adopted as the second child to provide a playmate for a first child. They may have unrealistic expectations of that child, and not enough parenting experience and self-confidence. Parents who adopt a difficult child after raising several other children seem to draw on their previous successes to keep their self-image strong. The parents with one or two children can focus on the child with behavior problems—perhaps overdoing it—while in the large family, the behavior problems are diffused to some extent by the number of children in the family requiring attention.

Parents in the helping professions may be particularly susceptible to feeling like failures. More than one social worker or psychologist has said something like, "I thought I would be the ideal parent for this child. Living with him has helped me do my job better, but my profession hasn't made it easier to live with him." Those in the helping professions should remember they cannot be both therapist and parent to the same child. Nor does the success or failure they experience as a parent reflect on their professional life.

Some parents are most vulnerable when the child's behavior seems directed at them—when the child openly rejects the parents' affection, attacks them physically or verbally, or seems to be deliberately embarrassing them. It is difficult, but important, to remember that the child would be behaving the same way with any new parent; it is not a personal rejection or statement of contempt. While most of us think that a child in an abusive or temporary situation would prefer to be in a permanent home with loving and caring parents, Barbara Tremitiere says children often would prefer what is familiar, even if it means suffering.

Isolation

Parents frequently feel isolated, like they are the only parents having such serious problems. Parents of a child whose behavior has resulted in her being suspended from school or arrested by the police, or has had other public repercussions may be embarrassed and not want to face their friends. Parents who are highly visible in their communities and expected to have children whose behavior is beyond reproach, such as ministers and probation officers, may be particularly susceptible to feeling that their child's behavior has cut them off from their community. Parents need to separate their child's behavior from themselves, not allowing themselves to feel judged for the child's actions.

Adoptive parent support groups can be helpful because people in them are experiencing similar problems. Nevertheless, some parents find it difficult to be open about their problems even with other adoptive parents. Consequently, people who could provide each other with emotional support hold back, each thinking theirs is the only family with such problems. One solution is to form a subgroup of adoptive parents with the criterion for membership being an emotionally troubled child. Such groups have found it helpful to meet apart from the main group, to require attendance at meetings rather than having people come just when they are having a crisis, and to set some rules for confidentiality.

But there are also times when what is needed is a break from parenting. Parents should give themselves a chance to do something successfully, such as their job, church work, or other non-parenting activity. This will not only counteract some of the feelings of failure they may experience as a result of their interaction with their child, it will also give them time away from the child and from parenting.

Strong Emotions

Parents are likely to have conflicting feelings about a difficult child—loving him and wanting him to love them, but sometimes feeling so hurt, angry and frustrated that they want to lash out at him physically or verbally. They may be determined to raise the child, but consider disrupting the adoption. Parents should try to identify exactly what is making them feel uncomfortable—the child's behavior or their own feelings about the child. Linda Katz says many parents are not prepared for the strong, negative feelings their child's behavior will elicit, and what they may want is an end to their unpleasant feelings rather than an end to the relationship with the child. Most of the time they dislike what the child is doing, not the child himself. But sometimes parents may feel that they hate the child. At those times, they can give themselves permission to feel that way, while at the same time setting limits on how long they will feel that way and what the consequences will be, saying, for example, "I'm going to let myself hate her until she goes to bed, but I will not hurt her physically or verbally, and I will not hate her in the morning."

The Role of the Father and Husband

Because the mother tends to be the primary caretaker, much conflict takes place between child and mother. Consequently, she is at greater risk for feeling guilty and like a failure. She sometimes hides these emotions from her husband, not wanting him to know she is a "failure."

The marital relationship may also suffer from the strain of having a child with behavior problems, in part because the family is under a lot of stress, and in part because some children are skilled at playing one parent against the other, having learned that if the parents are arguing with each other, they are not paying attention to the children. Vanessa's son would verbally abuse her and physically attack her when they were alone, but when Vanessa's husband John was there, the boy was calm and pleasant. John thought Vanessa was exaggerating her descriptions of the boy's behavior, and thought she just needed to learn how to handle him as well as he did; after all, even Vanessa agreed the boy wasn't a problem when his father was home. Eventually, through counseling, John learned that his son was being selective and manipulative in his behavior and gave his wife the support she needed.

When there are two parents, the husband needs to do more than provide his wife with emotional support. In a small study, Joyce S. Cohen found that adoptions were less likely to disrupt when the father could provide the wife with relief, giving her time to refresh and rejuvenate herself outside the home while he took over the primary parenting role. When the husband sees his job as merely sustaining the wife emotionally—listening to her express her feelings—he is likely to get worn down by the complaining and may even demand that the source of her problems be eliminated, that is, the child returned to the child welfare system.

Realistic Expectations

Parents who do well at raising children with serious behavior problems are those who can take small bits of progress and see them as major successes. They aren't expecting miracles or drastic changes overnight. They are happy to see any improvement at all, and to know that they, perhaps, made a little difference, or at the very least, kept the child's situation from becoming worse. For example, parents might like their child to quit using drugs completely, but can see progress in the fact that their daughter is no longer prostituting herself to get money to buy drugs.

Parents should celebrate the successes they have. In some cases, it is appropriate to celebrate as a family with a special meal or other pleasant activity. At other times, the parents may want to keep their sense of success private. It would not be appropriate, for example, to have a party honoring the daughter who is no longer selling her sexual favors, but together the parents should somehow take note of the progress and let it revitalize them for future challenges.

Obviously, parents who are expected to find something to feel good about in what is probably a grim situation must have a sense of humor. Perhaps more than anything else, the ability to laugh will help parents through the dark times there are bound to be when raising children with serious behavior problems.

Effect on Siblings

Many of the situations that arise when a child with serious problems joins the family may continue after the adjustment period. Parents should be prepared to continue to deal with the issue of fairness—that they have different standards for different children—as well as be aware that other children in the home may be embarrassed by the behavior of the child, particularly at school. Siblings may continue to be the object of inappropriate sexual overtures, and parents should take care to protect them. (These issues are discussed in Chapters 2 and 7.)

Siblings should be given permission to express their feelings about the child with behavior problems. A sensitive child will recognize that her parents are having a difficult time and may think if she complains about the child's behavior, she is adding to her parents' burden. One mother reported that her son burst into tears one day, saying about his sibling, "I've tried and tried to like him but I just can't." He clearly felt he had let his parents down by not doing his job—liking his sibling. The mother reassured him there were days when she didn't like the boy either, and let him know his feelings were both normal and acceptable.

Like their parents, brothers and sisters of the child with serious behavior problems may need respite—a place to go when the situation at home becomes too difficult. A relative, friend, or parents of one of the child's friends could be enlisted to keep the child overnight or for a weekend when he or she needs a break from turmoil at home.

In addition, the siblings may be involved in counseling. Many therapists believe it wise to include all family members in counseling, even though there may be one child in particular having problems, not only because that child's problems affect the entire family, but because it is less stigmatizing to the child with problems if everyone is in therapy. Rather than the child being isolated as "the problem," the problem is the family not functioning smoothly.

Living with a sibling who has serious behavior problems often contributes to the maturity of the other children, especially those born into the family. They learn tolerance, compassion, and how to interact with people with different values and attitudes. Though the experience is sometimes painful, the children are much less isolated from the problems of the world than other children and grow as a result.

THE THREAT OF ADOPTION DISRUPTION

Sometimes families and adoptees cannot make the adjustments necessary to continue living together. Technically, when this happens before the adoption is finalized, it is known as disruption; after finalization, as dissolution. But in human terms, whenever it happens it is a disruption for the child and for the family. As we learn more about what causes the breakdown of adoptions and as more agencies provide services to help families in crisis, disruptions and dissolutions should become less common.

Causes of Adoption Disruption

Kathryn Donley, an expert on adoption disruption, believes there are three reasons that adoptions break down:

— Unidentified factors—factors not recognized as critical at the time of the placement, for example, the adoptive parents live on a farm and the adoptee is used to city life. She may not be able to adjust to the different social atmosphere or smaller school.

— Unpredictable life events, such as divorce or the death of a parent, which place additional stress on the family

— Misassessment of the readiness of the child or the family—that is, either the child or the family is not adequately prepared for the adoption, or both. This is probably the primary cause of disruptions.

Although the child with behavior problems is at greater risk for disruption, it is incorrect to assume that the more difficult the child is, the more likely the adoption will end in disruption. Some adoptions of children with extreme behavior problems are succeeding, while the adoptions of children who have less serious problems disrupt. The child must be ready for the adoption—a subjective assessment made by the social worker—and the parents must have the skills and willingness to raise the child who has serious behavior problems.

While the age of the child at the time of placement has been shown to be a factor in some disruptions (older children more likely to disrupt than younger children), Barbara Tremitiere's research suggests the critical factor is the number of places a child has lived in prior to the placement, although there may be a correlation between how old a child is and how many times he has moved from one family to another. If those moves were made because the adoption was disrupted in other families rather than because the next move was planned, he is at greater risk for another disruption.

Disruption often occurs during periods of major change in the child and in the family, such as during the adjustment period, when the child changes schools or the family moves to a new town, or during adolescence.

Stages of Adoption Disruption

Kathryn Donley has identified predictable stages families go through when an adoption is disrupting:
— Noticeable family discomfort that does not diminish over time
— Discomfort that markedly increases
— Complaints that are out of proportion. Parents may focus on a particular behavior of the child or may have the general complaint that "everything that child does is wrong."
— A calm period during which conflict is not resolved, but appears to disappear. The family can't explain why things have improved because nothing really has changed.
— Resurfacing of unresolved complaints, resulting in a crisis
— The decision to disrupt the adoption.
Sometimes it is the child who wants to leave, not the parents who want him removed, but the stages are similar.

Families in the early stages of adoption disruption need help because the situation can escalate rapidly. Some families do not call the adoption agency for help until they have already decided there is no choice but to disrupt. Rather than seeking help, they are seeking permission to disrupt, saying, in effect, "Look how bad this situation is. There is no solution but disruption." And if they have not had help until that point, their conclusion probably is accurate. Many times, though, a different solution could have been found had the family sought help earlier. Ideally, families should be able to look to their social worker for help in resolving conflicts. But not all social workers are trained to work with families that are in crisis, and not all adoption agencies offer adequate post-adoption services. The social worker may panic and remove the child without first trying to keep the family intact, perhaps because of past experiences with families in crisis. Or she may not understand the commitment and attachment in adoptive families and not realize how important it is to try to help the family stay together. Her own ego may become involved if she sees an adoption disruption as a failure of the person who made the placement. All adopting families, particularly those adopting children at high risk for disruption, should find out early the attitude of the social worker towards disruption and the services available through the agency for families in crisis. If the services are not adequate, the family can look for another agency willing to help them if they are in danger of disrupting or find a therapist with experience in this area.

When Adoptions Disrupt

Once a decision has been made to disrupt an adoption, the parents' first task should be to help prepare the child for the move out of the home. The child should know why she is moving, in terms that do not lay the blame on her. For example, parents can say, quite accurately, "We found out that we aren't as patient as we thought we could be, and it scares us that you set fires when you get angry. Perhaps your new parents will be more patient or not as easily scared. Or maybe you'll find a way to express your anger that isn't so scary." She should receive permission from her parents to move on and to love other people. Parents can say, "We care about you and want you to be happy. We'll always remember you, but we hope you will have another family that you can be happy in." She should have an opportunity to say good-bye to other people who are important to her, such as friends or teachers, as well as help explaining to them why she is leaving, again in a way that does not place blame on her. She should take with her photographs of the family and other mementos important to her. She may be hurting so much that she doesn't seem to want any memories of the home or family. If that is the case, the parents should see that her social worker keeps the items for her, because she will need evidence of places she has been and people she has lived with.

While parents might expect to feel relief when the child leaves the home, they are likely to feel grief. In particular, they may feel angry and try to fix blame on someone else—on the agency for not preparing them adequately, on the child for acting the way she did, or perhaps on the therapist who was unable to resolve the crisis. They are also likely to blame themselves, think of the things they should have done, the feelings they might have had, and what could have been "if only. . ." They may feel despondent, that they are failures as parents, failures as human beings. If the grief process is allowed to run its course, they will ultimately reach the acceptance stage, when they can begin to consider another adoption.

If there are other children in the home, parents have to make clear what happened, in such a way that they do not assign blame. Although parents often begin thinking about disruption when they believe the child's behavior is having a detrimental effect on other children in the family, the other children should not feel responsible. Particularly if there are other adopted children in the family, parents will have to reassure them they are not going to have to leave too. Parents may need counseling at this time to help them through their grief, and the other children may need therapy to deal with their fear that staying in the family is contingent on good behavior.

RESOURCES FOR THE FAMILY

Parents adopting a child with behavior problems should not wait for a crisis to develop, but should consider family counseling necessary for the success of the adoption. Other community resources also may be needed to help the child or parents, such as special education services or an adoption support group. If the child has not been adequately prepared for the adoption, for example, if he does not have a life book or other record of his previous placements and significant people, or if he has questions related to where he has been before, that work will have to be done. The social worker, counselor, or adoptive parents can reconstruct the child's past with the cooperation of agencies who have knowledge of the child's history. The family should expect crises in the adoption of a child with behavior problems and line up ahead of time the resources they can draw on at any time of the day or night, such as other families who can take the child for a period of respite, or an emergency number for the therapist.

Working with Professionals

When seeking help from professionals, parents should remember that while the social worker or therapist may give advice, only the parents are responsible for the child and should make the final decisions. This can be particularly difficult before an adoption is finalized because parents may not have a complete sense of entitlement as long as the agency retains a controlling role in the child's life. But it is important for parents to make decisions for the child—first, because even if the child has only lived with them for a short time, they probably know the child better than the professionals; and second, because parents must feel completely in charge to be effective with children who have behavior problems. If the child perceives that the parents do not have the final say in matters concerning her, she may use that to undermine the authority they do have.

Whenever possible, parents should work with therapists and other professionals who understand that adoption adds another dimension to many situations in a person's life and in family life. One complaint of adoptive parents is that professionals do not understand that experiences prior to a child's adoptive placement and the adoption experience itself can affect the child's behavior, both immediately after placement and years later. Professionals with insight into adoptive families are better able to identify when a problem is adoption-related and when it is not, and are unlikely to let misunderstandings or personal prejudices about adoption interfere with the services they are providing. Parents of a child with behavior problems probably related to the number of families she has lived with during her life do not need to feel responsible for all the child's problems.

When parents have no choice but to work with a professional uninformed about adoption, they should keep in mind that they are the experts and educate the professional, keeping him from making decisions based on false assumptions about the adoptive family. Too often, in seeking advice from someone, we defer to the person's authority in all areas; we want that person to solve the problem so we let him be the expert. We must remember we retain some expertise, particularly about our children and families, even though we seek help from someone else. And the professional who is not willing to consider the parents' viewpoint is not worth the parents' time and effort.

Choosing a Therapist

Parents who adopt children with serious behavior problems should select a therapist whose goal is to change behavior, not help the child develop insight, says psychologist James Mahoney. These "task-oriented" or "action-oriented" therapists are likely to be considered unconventional by professionals who practice "talk therapy." Indeed, they may employ unusual techniques because they will do whatever produces results—by going to the family's home for counseling sessions, for example. The children probably will intensely dislike such a therapist during therapy, but when therapy is complete, like him just as intensely; whereas the therapist will be popular with parents during the counseling period because results are apparent within a few months.

Mahoney believes a therapist should have other qualities, such as:
— Accurate empathy—ability to accurately reflect the feelings the client is having
— Unconditional positive regard—ability to find something she likes about the client
— Nonpossessive warmth—enjoyment at being part of the process of improvement, but willing to let go when her job is completed.

Adoptive families seeking a therapist should ask other adoptive families for recommendations and interview the therapists to find out their attitudes toward adoption, their approach to therapy, and experience dealing with children with behavior problems.

Busy parents who have no therapist sensitive to adoption issues in their area might be tempted to use whatever counselors are available rather than drive long distances to see a therapist who has insight into adoption. If these parents live in an area large enough to have several adoptive families needing the services of a therapist, they may be able to entice him to hold "office hours" in their area once a week or once a month. If not, parents should consider the services of a therapist knowledgeable about adoption issues worth the commuting time.

Chapter 12

Special Situations in Adoption

Jim Forderer and Marian Aiken-Forderer met through their mutual interest in adoption. Both were single adoptive parents of physically disabled children, and they shared the challenges of adoptive parents, of single parents, and of parents of disabled children. When their marriage merged them into a family with eleven children, they discovered they had much in common with other large adoptive families. Their particular situation is unique, but there are many families today who do not fit the traditional picture of adoption.

PARENTING THE MENTALLY OR PHYSICALLY DISABLED CHILD

Parents who adopt a child with mental or physical disabilities have much in common with the biologic parents of a child with a similar condition. Additional involvement is required of parents and other family members with a disabled child. Parents must be advocates for the child in the social service system, in the educational system and in the health care system. They must know more than bureaucrats about what state services are mandated for the handicapped, more than teachers about the child's educational needs and abilities, and more than physicians about the child's condition.

It is not surprising, then, that adoptive parents of disabled children are often more involved with organizations that deal with their child's particular condition, such as the United Cerebral Palsy Association or Association for Retarded Citizens, than with adoption organizations, since the disability issues seem more pressing than adoption issues. Nevertheless, there are some differences between being the biologic and being the adoptive parents of disabled children.

Preparation and Expectations

Parents who adopt a child with a known handicap do not have the same reaction to that child's disability as parents who give birth or adopt what they expect to be a healthy child. When a disability is unexpected, parents typically react with shock, denial, anger, and the other stages of grief. They have experienced the loss of the healthy child they expected and respond by trying to find a doctor who can "fix" or cure the child, or by trying to find someone or something to blame for the disability. Biologic parents often feel guilty for somehow causing the child's disability or for bringing him into the world. Parents fear how the child's disability will affect their lifestyle and their future. They will have to modify their expectations of parenthood and the "rewards" they would receive from their children.

Parents who know their child's mental or physical condition prior to adoption have an opportunity to learn what life with the child will be like before agreeing to be his parents. They can investigate community resources ahead of time, consider the effect raising a disabled child will have on other children in the family, and plan for the times that have been found to be critical in the lives of families with disabled children—such as when the child enters school, when the child reaches adolescence, when the child becomes an adult, and when the parents can no longer care for him due to age or infirmity. Without grief or guilt to interfere, these parents can effectively concentrate on the child's needs from the beginning.

There may still be unforeseen aspects of raising a child with a disability, and adoptive parents have to adjust their expectations accordingly, sometimes even going through a minor grief process before accepting the unexpected. Perhaps the medical report on the child was inadequate, or they did not know what questions to ask to get a complete understanding of the child's problem. Jim Forderer points out that parents sometimes are unprepared for conditions that are secondary to the primary handicap, such as body odor or bedsores.

The child with a grim prognosis will often make rapid improvement soon after placement because he is receiving the love, personal attention and treatment he has needed. So the child who had been diagnosed as severely mentally retarded advances to where he can be considered mildly retarded, or the child who was not expected to use his hands learns to feed himself. Observing the effect of love and good quality care, parents may expect the progress to con- tinue until the child is fully able. Ultimately, this unrealistic hope may put them in the same situation as the parents who expected a healthy child, and adoptive parents may have to go through the process of accepting their child's limita- tions.

Developing Attachment

Creative ways to form an attachment to the disabled child need to be found because the usual ways parents and children form attachments may be com- plicated by the child's disability. For example, physical contact may be difficult with a child who is spastic, and eye contact prohibited by a child's visual impairment. The simple satisfaction of feeding a child, which normally con- tributes to attachment, may be overwhelmed by the child's eating problems. The child may not be able to smile, or may smile grotesquely. When the disability is unexpected, attachment can be complicated by the parents' inability to resolve their grief. But adoptive parents who choose to adopt a disabled child often have less difficulty "claiming" such a child.

Some hospitals that specialize in birth defects or in treating the disabled have programs to help parents form attachments to disabled children. Special education programs may offer additional guidance. Many of these programs concentrate on helping parents feel comfortable enough with the child's disability to get close to the child, showing how to hold him and how to develop alternative forms of communication, such as signing. Despite modifications that have to be made to facilitate attachment, families often find living with a dis- abled child provides a common goal, and as each member of the family does his part to achieve that goal, the family is pulled together into a cohesive unit.

Parents sometimes find that their relationship with their disabled child is more intense than their relationships with their fully able children. Intense attachment can reach the point of overdependency for parent and child. An overly solicitous parent should resist feeling she is the only one who can take care of the child and be willing to call on other people to take care of the child, for the parents' sake and the sake of the family.

Acting as the Child's Advocate

Understanding the child's condition is critical to acting in the child's best in- terest. Parents of mentally or physically disabled children are going to be surrounded by experts—physical therapists, physicians, occupational therapists, special education teachers, counselors, and others. In dealing with this management team, parents act as coordinators of services and must remember that each expert sees only his area of specialty. For example, the person who fits the child's wheelchair does not know what the child's school or classroom is like—some modifications may be necessary. Parents of disabled children find they often must be assertive about obtaining the services they need as well as rejecting those they do not need. Parents often become so informed about the various aspects of their child's disability—medical, social, educational, and psychological—that they are truly the experts in his care. Parents should not let their lack of academic credentials keep them from questioning professionals.

Effect on Non-disabled Siblings

Siblings of a disabled child often help care for the child by helping her dress or giving her medications. Frequently the disabled child also depends on the sibling for recreation, particularly if her condition restricts her recreational opportunities. Some siblings resent the additional demands of a disabled brother or sister, while others take them in stride. In general, most siblings of disabled children have a maturity that exceeds their age and learn to be more tolerant of others. One teenage girl reported that as she prepared to attend her first prom, she suddenly realized her mentally retarded sister would never participate in dating and dances, and she was saddened by her awareness.

Parents should make sure other children in the family understand how to care for the disabled child—not only what he needs help with but what he does not need help with. Some siblings become overprotective of their disabled brother or sister and by their help sabotage the independence parents may be trying to foster. Children should also know what their roles are expected to be in the future. The sibling who does not know what the plan is for the disabled child may become concerned about his own future—an adolescent may think he cannot go away to college because he is needed at home, for example.

It is not unusual for the brothers and sisters of a disabled child to feel guilty because they are fully able. They may also feel guilty when they get angry at the child or tease him. It isn't unusual for siblings to be embarrassed by their disabled sibling, particularly as teenagers. Siblings often find they have to explain their disabled sibling's condition to friends more frequently when the disability is mild than when it is clear from the child's appearance that he is disabled.

Nevertheless, children usually rally to their sibling's defense, protecting him from the teasing of other children.

Parents should be sure the demands of raising a disabled child do not blind them to the needs of their other children. While the other children in the family should be involved in caring for the sibling, their responsibilities should not be so great that they are unable to have full lives themselves. Siblings of disabled children need an opportunity to express their feelings, which are likely to be somewhat confusing and contradictory, and some communities have support groups for brothers and sisters of disabled children. Above all, parents should be sure not to neglect children without disabilities because of the time required to care for a disabled child. Because siblings may feel guilty that they are fully able, they may be reluctant to complain about the degree to which they are expected to care for the disabled child, or about the lack of attention they receive from their parents.

THE SINGLE ADOPTIVE PARENT

Single adoptive parents are raising children with as much success as married couples, despite the fact that single applicants have traditionally been restricted to the adoption of special needs children. One reason for their success is that when difficulties arise, single parents have no one to blame for the decision to adopt. Nor do they have conflicts with their spouse over discipline or other parenting decisions. The manipulative child cannot play one parent against the other in single-parent homes, making one-parent homes the placement of choice for certain children. However, single parents do not have a partner to turn to when they are anxious, sick, or otherwise need help. For this reason, it is crucial to have a solid support system. Without adequate support the single adoptive parent can become isolated, frustrated, and ineffective as a parent.

Support Systems

Single adoptive parents meet more resistance from adoption agencies and intermediaries, from relatives, and particularly from friends when they decide to adopt. This is not surprising; while it has become more acceptable in recent years for people to raise children alone, most of the acceptance is directed at those who become single parents unexpectedly—through death, divorce, or unplanned pregnancy. Those who choose to become single parents, either through a planned pregnancy or adoption, often are criticized for taking on an enormous responsibility alone, for raising a child without two parents, or for acting unconventionally. This resistance can be compounded by the friends and relatives who typically have reservations about the adoption of a child with special needs. Yet it is critical that single parents be able to depend on their friends and relatives for support. Sociologists William Feigelman and Arnold R. Silverman found that like married couples, single adoptive parents feel the adjustment period is smoother and attachment develops more quickly when they have support from friends and relatives.

Despite the responsiblity, single persons find it possible to be successful adoptive parents if they have adequate human, financial, and psychological resources. In setting up a support system, parents should examine what they have in common with other single parents, other adoptive parents, and other parents of a child like theirs, since it is likely their child will be disabled, emotionally troubled, or of a different race or ethnic background. Though its primary emphasis is helping single persons overcome the obstacles to adoption, the Committee for Single Adoptive Parents and its publication *The Handbook for Single Adoptive Parents,** edited by Hope Marindin, are useful resources.

Financial Resources

Single parents need a job or supervisor flexible enough to allow them to deal with the inevitable crises of parenthood. In addition, they need a health insurance policy that will allow them to add a child.

Both for the obvious practical reasons as well as for peace of mind, single parents should have disability insurance or an emergency fund so they can continue to provide for themselves and their children should they become temporarily or permanently disabled, as well as adequate life insurance to provide for the child in case of the parent's death. (See Appendixes for information on childrearing leave, insurance, and wills.)

These considerations are not much different from those a biologic parent should have. They are, however, more critical for the single adoptive parent, for in many cases single parents adopt children with special needs requiring additional medical expenses, therapy, and special education or day-care arrangements. In addition, the demands of raising a child with medical or emotional problems increase the likelihood that a parent will need to take time off from work for appointments with professionals or to care for a medical or behavioral crisis.

Emotional and Human Resources

Like many of us who have adopted, single parents often feel they must be "superparents." Having decided to become parents despite the obstacles and resistance they meet, and often having adopted a child with special needs, they may have difficulty acknowledging their feelings of discontent or failure. While an adoptive parents support group is helpful in providing needed help, single parents often find more assistance from a single parents group, such as Parents Without Partners, whose members can understand the particular difficulties of raising a child alone.

But single parents need more than emotional support. They need human resources, such as satisfactory child care (which can be difficult to find for a disabled child or one with behavior problems), and friends or relatives close by who can provide emergency child care and other kinds of physical assistance, particularly with a disabled child. One adoptive mother said she didn't need someone to commiserate with her nearly as much as she needed someone who could help get her children with cerebral palsy dressed each morning.

Taking Care of One's Self

During the home study, adoption workers often question a single applicant about the effect a child will have on her social life. In general, the social worker is more concerned about this than the parent. Fully committed to raising children, the single parent is attracted to people with similar values who can understand the parent's decision to adopt or to adopt a child with special needs. In fact, the single parent often is so committed to her role that she may not take enough time for herself. Single parents are usually working parents and are therefore subject to the same demands all of us who hold jobs share as we try to compensate for the time we are at work by spending our free time with our children. And after overcoming the difficulties facing single adoptive applicants, it may be hard for the single parent to admit there are times when she wants to be away from her child. For the first year after Mary Ellen adopted her son, she insisted he be included in all social activities, taking the attitude that she didn't want to spend time with anyone who didn't want the child along. Eventually she realized it was important for her to take time by herself and time with her friends without her child, and that it was important for the child to learn she had an adult social life as well as an adult work life.

Attitudes of Others

Single adoptive parents receive conflicting messages from people outside their support systems, alternately being told how wonderful they are for taking on such a big responsibility and being given unsolicited advice on how to raise a child. Adoptive fathers in particular may be treated as incompetent care-givers, while at the same time being extolled as models for other men. One single father said teachers sent notes home from school with his children with condescending pieces of advice.

Single adoptive parents sometimes have difficulty convincing the professionals caring for their children that some of their children's behavior problems may be the result of trauma or experiences prior to the adoption. Professionals may ignore evidence demonstrating that the child's behavior problems were present prior to his placement and focus on the lack of a second parent in the home as the cause of the child's problems.

There is little we can do about people with such attitudes except try to differentiate between when they are a nuisance and when they are actually interfering with the child's well-being. For example, a teacher who blames a child's behavior problems on his single-parent home needs to be educated about the child's history; a therapist with the same attitude should be replaced with one who is more sensitive to adoption issues. But when attitudes of others are merely annoying, we should ignore them and call in our support system of people who care and understand.

Single Through Divorce or Death

Not all single adoptive parents applied for adoption as single parents. Some have become single since the adoption through divorce or death.

We don't know if adopted children have more difficulty dealing with grief after the death of a parent or after the parents divorce than do non-adopted children. Some experts say death and divorce are so traumatic to a child that all he can do is deal with the immediate loss—he simply doesn't have the energy to connect the loss of his adoptive parent with the previous loss of his birth-parents. But we do know young children are concrete thinkers who believe they are the center of the universe. They think if something happens, they caused it. One boy thought the reason his adoptive father didn't send child support was because the boy wasn't his father's biologic child. Parents who are divorcing are suffering themselves, but they must remember to allow their child to grieve too, and consider that the child's grief may be affected by his past losses.

Cassandra and Bob told their child, as most divorcing parents do, that while they were no longer living together, they would still be the child's parents. "You can divorce a husband or a wife, but you can't divorce a child," they said. The parents realized immediately how hollow those words might sound to a child whose connection to her birthparents has, in fact, been legally terminated. Fortunately, their child seemed to accept the explanation. Perhaps she needed to be reassured and was willing to accept the explanation, ignoring the holes in logic; or she may not have made the connection between the two legal proceedings. But parents may need to reassure their child that divorce does not affect adoption.

In some cases, the non-custodial parent does not have contact with the child after the divorce. Under such circumstances the adoptee is most likely to feel that if he were the parent's biologic child, the parent would stay in touch. The parent with custody should make it clear to the child that the other parent is not living up to his responsibilities; that it is the adult's problem, not the child's.

Divorce usually is not precipitated by an adoption unless there already were marital problems. In most cases, if it comes to a choice between marriage and child, a couple will disrupt the adoption rather than divorce. But whatever actually causes the divorce, some parents may associate their conflicts with stress connected to adoption and blame the child for the divorce. Obviously, a parent with these feelings needs counseling because children should not feel responsible for their parents' marital problems.

A common reaction to divorce in an adoptive home may be guilt. Parents who believe a stable marriage was a prerequisite to their approval as adoptive parents may feel they obtained a child under false pretenses. If the child was born to an unmarried woman, the feeling of obligation to provide a two-parent home may be a particular burden. As a result, the parents' sense of entitlement may be shaken, and they may doubt their suitability as parents. But it is critical that parents overcome guilt and retain a strong sense of entitlement so that they can continue to be effective as parents during a difficult time.

THE VERY LARGE FAMILY

The logistics of the large adoptive family are staggering—washing dirty clothes, preparing meals, finding ways to distinguish one toothbrush from twelve others. And the majority of large adoptive families are integrating children considered to have special needs—older children, many with behavior problems; children of different racial backgrounds; and children with mental or physical disabilities. Often parents have biologic children as well. It is hardly surprising that some people do not understand the motives of those who adopt many children. In fact, parents of large adoptive families probably do not have different motives for adopting, but they do have different expectations from those with small families. They can take great joy and satisfaction in little successes—in knowing they have made some difference in a child's life.

Maintaining Order

Some large families are highly structured, well organized, and efficient. Others rely on flexibility. How people respond to the problems of cooking, cleaning, laundry, and shopping depends on their own organizational style. Among large adoptive families surveyed by Barbara Tremitiere, nearly half the parents had come from families with five or more children and very likely drew on their own childhood experiences for help in working out the logistics of the large family. Some parents use work charts to assign chores, while others say they can't afford the repair bills if their children use the washing machine or dishwasher. Most parents of large families find it helpful to have contact with similar families, not only for emotional support, but for ideas on solving daily household maintenance problems.

One mother of twenty-one children cautions parents not to be so concerned with maintaining order in the family that they fail to notice when some aspect of the household is functioning smoothly. When many people are living together, any one aspect that is out of order can have a cascading effect on the rest of the household. Consequently, there is a temptation to focus on what needs to be "fixed." Parents need to reflect often on what is working well.

Maintaining Individuality

It is not necessary for every child to have the same things or participate in the same activities. Indeed, it isn't fair, for example, to deny ballet lessons to one talented child just because the family cannot afford special lessons for all the children. Neither does everyone have to participate in Boy Scouts just because it's easier for parents to transport five children to the same place than five different places.

Getting outsiders to understand this is a major task. Parents should let friends and relatives know they are not required to invite all the children in the family swimming just because they are inviting some. One mother was delighted when her friend returned from a trip with thoughtful gifts for two of her seventeen children. Had the friend felt compelled to buy souvenirs for all seventeen, it is likely she wouldn't have bought anyone anything. As it was, two of the children received gifts this time; the others would receive something from someone else another time. Of course, young children in particular do not look at the large picture, but see only their sibling receiving a treat they didn't get. Parents can deal with envious feelings by validating natural reactions, saying, for example, "I know it doesn't seem fair to you," or, "It would be nice if we all had received new shirts. Amy is really lucky. I can see why you might feel jealous, but we shouldn't deny Amy the fun of getting a new shirt just because we all didn't get them."

With many children in a family, it is possible that there will be more than one child of the same age. When this happens, parents should treat them, and encourage others to treat them, as the unique people they are. Depending on their backgrounds, the children may not be performing academically at the same grade level. As a result, children of different ages may be in the same grade, or an older child may be in a grade below that of a younger child. These situations require a great deal of tact. If at all possible, siblings should not be in the same classroom; there is enough competition at home. The children in the family should understand why one child is in a grade below that appropriate for his age in a way that doesn't place the blame on the child. For example, parents can say, "In some of the other places George lived, the parents didn't know how to make sure George went to school every day, so he didn't do all the work he should have last year. Now he is getting another chance at doing well in the fifth grade and we want to help him as much as we can." Parents should make it clear that teasing a child because he is repeating a grade is not tolerated.

Depending on circumstances, some children in the family may have more knowledge of their birthparents than others, and perhaps more contact with them. The jealousy this evokes may be difficult to deal with. Parents should attend to each child's desire for information, providing him with as many details about his birthparents as is appropriate, and allow him to express his feelings of sadness or anger when his siblings have more information.

In an effort to give each child enough attention, privacy, and special treats, some adoptive families have been able to enlist the aid of individuals who act as "godparents" or honorary aunts and uncles to their children. This way each child has a special person who may take him out for dinner occasionally, provide a place where he can go when the family is overwhelming, or even provide money for special activities that would otherwise be unaffordable with so many children. This solves the problem of a friend or relative who wants to be involved with the family, but thinks she can't manage all the children and doesn't want to "play favorites." By letting them know it is all right to be a special friend to a particular child, the honorary aunts and uncles are able to have the active involvement they want, at a level they can handle; the child benefits from the individual attention; and the parents can get time away from the family.

The diversity of the large adoptive family is one of its greatest strengths. While parents sometimes wonder if they are being fair to other children in the family—especially to their biologic children—by adopting large numbers of children who require additional care, they often find it an enriching experience for their children as well as for themselves. Children who might otherwise be sheltered learn about different values and experiences.

Family Subgroups

While members of a large family generally develop strong attachments, children naturally like some siblings more than others and often divide themselves into natural subgroups. Parents should not expect the children in the family to like one another equally—there are bound to be preferences and personality conflicts. Indeed, one advantage of living with many children from different backgrounds is that children learn how to get along with people they do not always like.

Parents should not try to break up subgroups in an attempt to better integrate the family. As one experienced mother put it, raising the large adoptive family is not like *The Sound of Music*—the children are not going to sing together in harmony. But when parents observe a member of one subgroup going to the aid of someone in another group, or the children acting as a unit in defense of the family, they know that underneath the daily routines, arguments, and jealousies, they have a family.

The Sibling Group

While not every family who adopts a sibling group is classified as a large family, small families sometimes become large ones with the placement of a group of three or four siblings. How this affects the family depends to some extent on whether the siblings have been together prior to their adoptive placement. If they have been in separate foster homes, they will need to get to know one another and develop a sense of biological identity as well as become integrated into the adoptive family. If the children do not have life books, they can be started as a way to show the threads of their shared lives, and perhaps explain why they have not always been together.

Siblings who have lived together in previous families may feel particularly close to one another because of the loss or trauma they have shared. This attachment can help them during the adjustment period; even though they have experienced losses, they have a sense of continuity from having lived together.

Parents should respect that the siblings have biologic ties to one another as well as emotional ties to the rest of the family. Their relationship to their adoptive siblings is not the same as their relationship to one another because they share a history with their biologic siblings that they do not share with the rest of the family. Respecting this does not mean endorsing the idea that the biologic relationship is better than the adoptive relationship; it just recognizes that those children share something the rest of the family will never be part of.

Sometimes children are more receptive to disquieting information about their pasts when it is provided by a sibling rather than by a parent or other adult. Older siblings who remember the circumstances in their biologic family or foster families may be able to verify the parents' explanation of why they were placed for adoption.

Recognizing their biologic heritage will help the sibling group with some of the identity questions they may have as adolescents. By observing the ways they are alike and different from their biologic siblings, they may be able to develop a better sense of their genetic heritage than other adoptees.

Maintaining Normalcy

The large adoptive family, particularly if it includes disabled children and children of different races, is highly visible in the community. Children often are embarrassed by this, particularly when they reach adolescence. Parents should remember that the reaction they get to being a large family is often different from the reaction the children get. Parents are complimented for their courage, tenacity, and altruism, whereas the children may gain a group reputation based on the actions of the child with the worst behavior. The parents are known by name, while the children are asked, "Now, which one are you?" In one family, the children complained that whenever they went to a restaurant, a large table was set for them making them stand out. The parents allowed the children to enter the restaurant in groups, be seated at tables set for four to six people, and be given a limit on how much to spend. One father found himself resisting an obvious solution to the growing size of his family—the purchase of a bus. As long as the family could travel together by van he did not feel conspicuous.

Children sometimes feel less unusual when they have contact with other large adoptive families. But parents should remember that unless the children from both families happen to be close friends, the children are likely to prefer friendships of their own making.

Financial Considerations

Raising a large family is expensive, and though there are subsidies for many special needs children, subsidies don't cover all the costs involved in raising them. Families do not have to be rich to raise a large family, but they do have to be good money managers. Families will have different ideas about allowances, what kinds of expenses children should pay for with income from part-time jobs, and other financial questions. But parents should not become so preoccupied with staying within their budget that the children become financially insecure. Barbara Tremitiere found children in large adoptive families remarkably aware of the financial strains on the family. While it is healthy for children to have a sense of economic reality, children should not worry about whether there is enough money to last the month.

Some parents find it is important to spend money on an occasional extravagance as a way of maintaining a sense of normalcy. Taking the family to a circus, fair, or other special event may cost close to one hundred dollars, but parents sometimes feel their children should not miss out on normal childhood activities just because their parents decided to adopt eighteen children. Family conferences, which many people believe are essential in the large family, can be used to decide whether an activity or purchase is important and what sacrifices the family is willing to make to accommodate it.

Sarah, a mother of sixteen, was frustrated by the number of boxes of unwearable used clothing that people dropped at her house. While she was grateful to those people who made useful contributions to the family, she felt some were making themselves feel good about giving to a "needy family," while she had to wash, mend, and dispose of tattered, dirty garments. She also was concerned about her children "looking like orphans." Sarah finally decided not to accept used clothing from any but a few friends who were thoughtful enough to pass along only wearable clothing. Other families are concerned about the emotional implications of wearing hand-me-downs—children might feel they have to wear cast-off clothing because they are "cast-off" children—and try not to depend on second-hand clothes.

A free copy of "Because We Care So Much," a newsletter for adoptive families with five or more children, is available from Tressler-Lutheran Service Associates, 25 W. Springettsbury Ave., York, Penn. 17403.

THE FAMILY WITH BIOLOGIC AND ADOPTED CHILDREN

Parents with both adopted and biologic children want their children to know that the manner in which each joined the family has no bearing on their parents' love for them. They forget society frequently gives children another message—that biologic relatedness does matter. This can confuse both the adoptee and the child born into the family.

Effect on the Child Born into the Family

In trying to give their adopted children a sense of full membership in the family, adoptive parents frequently emphasize the value of emotional relationships over genetic relationships. We tell our children that parenthood is more than giving birth, it is raising the child. In trying to make our adopted children feel that not being born into the family is all right, we may inadvertantly encourage the belief that being adopted is better than being born into the family.

This is obviously going to provide some conflict for the child who is born into the family, particularly when he sees that not everyone shares this view. The message from society is that the adoptive relationship is tentative, and the genetic tie matters.

In trying to resolve the confusion that naturally results from these conflicting messages, the biologic child may conclude that origins and blood relationships do matter, but not in his family because there is something wrong with him. He may think that if other people value blood lines but his parents don't, it must be because he has somehow failed to fulfill his role.

Parents should take great care not to denigrate one form of relationship to validate another. Slogans such as "Adoption Means Love," which frequently appear on bumper stickers, buttons, and T-shirts in adoptive families, imply that love is not a motivation in other ways of forming families.

One way in particular that parents sometimes devalue their biologic child is by avoiding discussion of his birth for fear that if they communicate the excitement felt when their child was born, the adoptee will feel less important. As a result, the biologic child feels less important. Parents should speak honestly about the emotions connected with the arrival of each of their children—biologic and adopted.

Post-adoption Pregnancy

Five percent of people with untreated infertility problems will conceive after adopting—this same percentage applies to those infertile couples who do not adopt. Yet the myth persists that one sure way to get pregnant is to adopt. Some people assume that a supposedly infertile couple who conceives after adopting regrets not having tried a little longer to achieve a pregnancy before turning to adoption. One of those with that assumption may be the adoptee.

Gail and her husband had a three-year-old adopted daughter and were getting ready to apply for a second adoption when Gail discovered she was pregnant. "See," she was told by more than one person, "you didn't have to adopt after all." Adoptive parents who are expecting the birth of a child should anticipate some insensitive remarks and have a close friend, perhaps another infertile adoptive parent, who can share their outrage.

It is more difficult to deal with the issue when the adopted child is the one questioning whether the parents still want him, or wondering if they only wanted him because they didn't think they could have a child any other way. The adoptee may not verbalize this question, but adoptive parents should assume it is there and reassure the child that he is an integral part of the family. When telling him about his adoption, parents could say, "We tried for many years to have a baby and we didn't want to wait to be parents anymore," implying, quite correctly, that the motivation to adopt was a desire to be a parent at that time, not a failure to conceive. But while the adoptee may have doubts from time to time, the parents' sincere love for him will be the best reassurance.

Since a pregnancy usually will arouse curiosity in a child, the child who has not been told where babies come from and how adoption is different from being born into a family is likely to ask the appropriate questions when a new baby is on the way. Parents who explain that a baby is growing inside mommy should expect the adoptee to ask, "Did I grow inside you, too?" Janice Koch's book, *Our Baby: A Birth and Adoption Story,** is a helpful way to explain how all children grow inside their mothers, but some then join another family through adoption.

If possible, the adoptee should learn about conception and how adoption differs from being born into a family before he learns about the new baby that is being expected. While not crucial, it probably will help him feel better about his status in the family if he does not hear about adoption first as something that sets him apart from his sibling.

While the issue may be more apparent in the family with both biologic and adopted children, all children adopted by infertile couples may at some point think that their parents would have preferred to conceive. Parents should reassure the adoptee that while adoption may have been a second choice, it was not a second-best choice.

Appendixes

Appendix A: Childrearing Leave and Adoption Benefits

Many adoption agencies are backing away from established policies prohibiting an adoptive mother from working, requiring instead that prospective parents show an appropriate child care plan. This change reflects the recognition that some women want both a career and a family, and that in many families, two paychecks are necessary to support the family.

While some adoptive mothers (or fathers) do leave their jobs to care for their child full-time, many are requesting that their employers give them a short leave of absence comparable to the maternity leave granted pregnant women. Some employers comply. Others have resisted giving an adoptive parent a paid leave of absence, but have been willing to allow a leave without pay. Still others have refused leave to adoptive parents. Carole Fezar of Ambridge, Pennsylvania was denied unpaid maternity leave by her employer of eighteen years. Fezar's union contract provided for a six-month unpaid maternity leave, but Fezar was told that was for pregnant women. An arbitrator ruled in her favor and she received a six-month maternity leave without pay, with an option to renew the leave for an additional six months, and a guarantee that her job would be waiting for her when she returned.

Legally, employers covered by Title VII of the Civil Rights Act of 1964 must treat the time women are unable to work because of giving birth exactly like any other temporary disability. An employer does not have to provide maternity leave if the employer does not provide disability benefits for any other type of health condition.

Consequently, because there is no physical disability for an adoptive parent, employers are not required to provide the same coverage provided following a pregnancy. Employers can provide "childrearing leave" that enables a parent to remain home with a child for an extended period of time. By federal law, employers having this type of leave policy must provide it to men and women, and should have it available to any parent, regardless of the circumstances by which they became parents.

The Double-Bind

We are understandably angry when we discover we are not entitled to the same maternity benefits we would have received had our child been born to us. Many employers will pay for up to six weeks of maternity leave, even though it usually takes no more than two weeks to heal any trauma to a woman's body caused by a vaginal delivery. The remainder of the maternity leave is needed because women are tired from caring for a newborn and want to spend time with the baby—requirements that adoptive parents share. Those who adopt older children point out their need to spend time getting to know their child, to get him established in a new school, and to be there as he grieves for the people he is separated from and adjusts to his new family.

Some adoptive parents have been criticized for wanting a maternity leave rather than quitting their jobs. Because there are so many couples waiting for babies, some people question whether the few that are available should be placed in families where both parents intend to work. One adoptive mother was told that a mother had just given up a child into her care, and she should feel lucky just to have a baby. Another mother was told, "Instead of worrying about leave, you should be thrilled just to have her." These kinds of comments reflect a double standard. Adoptive mothers have the same right to choose a career and a family as any other mother. Just because a woman wants to be a mother so much that she is willing to wait years for the placement of an infant doesn't mean she wants to be a mother exclusively. No woman is less committed to being a parent because she also wants to work.

Requesting Childrearing Leave

In the majority of cases, adopting parents will be able to take an unpaid leave of absence when their child arrives, although the length of time allowed may vary. If they want more unpaid leave or want to be paid during their time off, parents should read their contracts, employee handbooks, or other written policy statements to see if childrearing leave for adoptive parents is specifically spelled out. One teacher found that her union contract provided for three paid days of leave for adoptive parents; but in most cases, adoption will not be specifically addressed. If that is the case, adopting parents should look for references to childrearing leave, usually mentioned in regard to biologic fathers. Any childrearing leave, as distinct from maternity leave, must be provided for adoptive parents as well as biologic parents. If no childrearing leave is provided, prospective parents will have to negotiate for the benefits they want. They can start by finding out what precedents there are for employees who have not been pregnant to take paid time off to care for a new child. If there are none, they will be breaking new ground and are likely to be more successful if the request is made quietly. For example, if an employee goes to the personnel department, union representative, or attorney for the company and asks for an official policy on childrearing leave for adopting parents, the employer is likely to make a decision based on the minimum amount the law requires so as not to set a precedent. But if the request is handled between the employee and her supervisor, personal factors—such as how long the employee has worked for the employer and how valuable she is to the company—are more likely to be taken into consideration.

Even if the childrearing leave is spelled out, the employer has the freedom to provide more, so adopting parents may still want to negotiate for the same maternity benefits that biologic mothers are entitled to. Sometimes employers are sensitive to the needs of people who are adopting. The attorney for a large public employer was asked by a supervisor whether an adopting mother could use her accumulated sick leave when her child arrived, as a pregnant woman would be allowed to do. The attorney said that the employer was not required to let her use her sick leave, but told the supervisor to approve the request. The attorney thought the request was reasonable, though not required by law, and that there were not enough adopting parents to make it a costly precedent.

Adoptive parents should encourage their employers to develop benefits for employees who will need extensive infertility treatment and for those who adopt children. Some employers have begun to offer adoption benefits that parallel maternity benefits, usually providing some funds for medical, legal, and transportation expenses after the adoption is finalized. Since only 4 percent of women adopt, there is not much pressure on employers to provide benefits. Unions are unlikely to negotiate hard for benefits that affect such a small percentage of their membership. However, all employees can benefit from the "smorgasbord" approach to employee benefits that some companies now offer. This allows employees to pick and choose the benefits they are most likely to want or need. For example, a working woman who is covered by the health insurance offered by her husband's employer may decline that benefit in favor of more vacation time. Adoptive parents could reject pregnancy coverage on their health insurance, choosing instead a paid childrearing leave. "The Adoption Benefits Plans: Corporate Response to a Changing Society," is a booklet describing adoption benefits plans that have been implemented by some corporations. It is available from the National Adoption Exchange, 1218 Chestnut St., Philadelphia, Penn. 19107.

Appendix B: Health Insurance

Most family insurance policies are required to cover infants from the time of birth, including any congenital abnormalities the child might have. However, when a child joins a family by adoption, the child's health is subject to more scrutiny. Insurance companies may try to exclude from their coverage any pre-existing conditions (those present in the child before he was added to the policy), or may resist covering the child until he is legally adopted, usually several months after placement. Since insurance policies vary from state to state and from group to group, and usually don't mention adoption at all, it is wise to question the insurance provider specifically about coverage of adopted children and to get the answers in writing.

Health Insurance for Infants

When Clark called his insurance company to ask if his daughter would be covered by his insurance policy for all conditions at the time of placement, he was asked: "Are you adopting a baby?" Since he and his wife were expecting a child under the age of one, he replied that they were. He was told there would be no problem; she would be covered for all pre-existing conditions from the time she arrived at their home. When they tried to enroll her, though, they were sent a copy of a health statement for their physician to fill out. Any pre-existing conditions that showed up during that examination would not be covered. When Clark questioned the insurance company about this discrepancy, he was told that the policy covered the adoption of a "newborn." A seven-month-old baby had to have a health statement before being enrolled on the policy.

Insurance coverage of newborns usually is the same whether the infant is adopted or born into the family. Parents should find out how soon after birth the baby must be placed in their home and enrolled on their policy to qualify as a newborn. One insurance provider, for example, requires that a baby be enrolled within thirty days of birth to be considered a newborn.

Health Insurance for Older Babies and Children

If the child being adopted is not a newborn, parents should find out:

— Whether the child can be added to the policy at the time of placement or only at the time of the adoption's finalization

— If the policy will cover any pre-existing conditions the child may have

— Whether all pre-existing conditions will be covered or just those diagnosed after the child is added to the policy

— If there is a waiting period after the child is added to the policy before treatment for pre-existing conditions will be covered

— Whether such a waiting period applies to all conditions, even when the need for medical treatment is known in advance.

Some insurance companies will only cover a child on the policy of a legal guardian. In most cases, the adoptive parents are not the legal guardians until the adoption is finalized. Insurance companies may want to see proof that parents have agreed to be legally and financially responsible for the child before they agree to cover the child from the time of placement.

Parents whose child is not automatically enrolled on their health insurance policy at the time of placement also need to know whether the policy will cover any pre-existing conditions the child might have. For example, Jim and Martha received information from the adoption agency about a child with an "innocent" heart murmur. Their insurance provider agreed to cover the child except for any heart-related problems that might arise. After consultations with the agency and Jim and Martha's family physician, the insurance company understood that the heart murmur did not represent any health risk to the infant and agreed to cover her for all conditions. Many more children today are being adopted with serious health problems or conditions that require surgery, such as cleft palate. Whether treatment for all health problems will be covered, or just those that develop or are diagnosed after the child is added to the policy, is information parents should have.

Sometimes an inherited or congenital condition is considered a pre-existing condition even though symptoms of the condition do not appear until years later. Insurance companies may cover only those diseases or conditions that were contracted after the child was enrolled on the policy.

Even if the insurance company covers treatment for pre-existing conditions, it may require a waiting period. This means, for example, that parents who adopt a child with kidney disease will be able to have all his medical care related to his kidneys taken care of after a waiting period of perhaps ninety days. Treatment needed within that time, such as an immediate kidney transplant, would not be covered. If there is a waiting period, parents should find out if all conditions are covered after it is up, including those for which medical treatment is predictable. For example, parents of a child who needs surgery for a heart problem should find out if an operation performed after the waiting period will be covered, even though they knew when the child was placed with them that he would need that surgery.

Clearly, the problems of health insurance coverage are complex and will vary from one policy to the next, and from one state to another. Adoptive parents should check directly with their insurance company or with the benefits officer at their place of employment for clarification of their plan and get that clarification in writing.

Appendix C: Wills and Life Insurance

Despite the recent trend for states to pass laws making it easier for an adopted person to inherit from her adoptive family and more difficult to inherit from her birthparents, families should be explicit about the inheritance and beneficiary rights of adoptees in the family. In the past, if a person who placed a child for adoption died leaving no will or a will that did not distinguish between that child and children she later bore, the courts frequently recognized that the child placed for adoption had a claim to her estate. Increasingly, though, states have passed legislation cutting off an adoptee's right to inherit from her birth family in the absence of a will clearly stating that as the deceased person's intent. The new statutes reflect society's greater acceptance of adoption and its diminished emphasis on a blood relationship for inheritance. They support the concept that the adoption process legally replaces the person's birth family with her adoptive family.

Even though most states now treat adoptees as heirs of their adoptive relatives, attorneys recommend that the families of adoptees be clear in their wills and life insurance policies by stating that adopted persons are to be treated as heirs. They can say: "When I use the term 'child,' 'issue,' or 'lineal descendent,' it is meant to include adopted persons," or ". . .persons adopted before the age of twenty-one." This ensures that there will be no problem about the inheritance should the relative die in a state that has not modernized its inheritance laws relative to adoption. (The law of the state in which the person dies governs the distribution of the estate.) This also prevents legal challenges on the basis of adoption.

Not all attorneys are sensitive to the adoption issue, so parents may have to address the subject when preparing or updating their wills.

Consistent with the legal concept that the adoptive family supplants the birth family, if an adoptee dies leaving no will, the adoptive parents, not the birthparents, are presumed to be the heirs.

Appendix D: Birth Certificates for Foreign-born Children

It is possible and desirable to obtain a birth certificate for a child adopted from a foreign country. Birth certificates may be needed when a person starts school, applies for a driver's license, marriage license or passport, registers to vote, and in many other situations.

Because the requirements and procedures vary from one state to another, it is advisable to contact the state's office of vital statistics for information on how and when to apply for a birth certificate. The Immigration and Naturalization Service will also issue a "Certification of Birth Data" to minor children who are permanent United States residents.

Appendix E: Naturalization

United States citizenship is required to vote, obtain a passport, and hold public office (although a naturalized citizen cannot be president of the United States). Male citizens are also eligible for military service.

An adopted child can become a naturalized citizen of the United States as soon as his adoption is final. Most parents proceed with this step unquestioningly, but some wonder if they should allow the child to keep his citizenship in his country of birth. Dual citizenship is not recognized by the United States government, but it is recognized by some countries, although not by Korea, where the majority of intercountry adoptions have originated. Allowing the child to remain a citizen of his country of birth is one way to communicate that his origins are important, but parents should remember that citizenship may require the child to serve in that country's military. Parents who would like their child to remain a citizen of his country of birth, in addition to becoming a naturalized United States citizen, should:

— Check with the country's consulate in the United States to see if the government recognizes dual citizenship

— Notify their adoption agency that they intend to allow their child to retain citizenship in his country of birth so that the agency does not automatically cancel the child's citizenship when it receives notification that the child has been naturalized.

Most agencies who place children from foreign countries provide up-to-date information on the procedure for applying for naturalized citizenship. Or, the local office of the U. S. Department of Justice's Immigration and Naturalization Service can provide information on the procedure. Generally, naturalization involves filing an application, which must be accompanied by photographs that meet specific requirements. A personal interview with an immigration official is required, at which time parents will need their child's birth certificate, a certified copy of the adoption decree, as well as their own birth, marriage and divorce certificates, their child's alien registration card, and the filing fee.

The child becomes a naturalized citizen during an appearance before a judge, at which time the applicant or his parents swear loyalty to the United States. These ceremonies are not frequent, sometimes occurring only once every year or two, and may involve traveling a great distance. Only one parent need file the naturalization petition. If both do, both must attend the hearing and oath-taking ceremony.

Children probably won't understand what naturalization means until they are about seven years old and understand both adoption and abstract concepts like political boundaries. Children younger than seven or eight can be told that they weren't born where they are now living, they were born in a place "far away" or "across the ocean." They can be told that the naturalization ceremony is "a special way that we say we are glad that we live here" and that after the ceremony the child will "belong in the United States and have all the rights of other people in the United States." Most children like flags, and while young children will not understand how a flag represents a country, parents can explain that becoming a citizen means that the flag belongs to them, too. In general, it's easier for children to understand the idea of "belonging" than they can the concept of geographical boundaries.

Older children may be concerned that giving up their citizenship in the country of their birth is somehow disloyal, and may resist becoming a United States citizen for this reason. Parents can explain the difference between nationality and membership in an ethnic group; that becoming a naturalized citizen does not mean that the child will no longer be Korean or Chilean. It does mean that he will have the same rights as other people living where he lives. It may help him to attend a naturalization ceremony where he can see that many adults born in other countries want to be United States citizens. An opportunity to talk with some naturalized adults can also help him understand that becoming a citizen is not a rejection of the land of his birth, but an opportunity to participate in the government that affects him.

Selected References and Resources

GENERAL ADOPTION

A few books have so changed adoption practices or thinking they have become essential reading. At the top of the list are H. David Kirk's two books, *Shared Fate: A Theory and Method of Adoptive Relationships*, rev. ed. (Ben-Simon Publications, P.O. Box 318, Brentwood Bay, B.C., Canada V0S 1A0, 1984) and *Adoptive Kinship: A Modern Institution in Need of Reform*, rev. ed. (Brentwood Bay: Ben-Simon Publications, 1985) in which he explores the unique relationships in adoptive families and concludes that adoptive parents must acknowledge the differences between their families and families formed by birth.

Chosen Children: New Patterns of Adoptive Relationships by William Feigelman and Arnold S. Silverman (New York: Praeger Publishers, 1983) reports results of excellent research into a number of current adoption issues, and is particularly useful on the adjustment of adoptees, the importance of support to the adoptive parents, transracial and intercountry adoption, and single parent adoption. Though a research report, it is readable and useful to adoptive parents.

Claudia L. Jewett's *Helping Children Cope with Separation and Loss* (Harvard, Mass.: Harvard Common Press, 1982) describes the feelings of grieving children, and gives concrete ways to help children resolve their losses.

The Adoption Triangle: Sealed or Open Records: How They Affect Adoptees, Birth Parents, and Adoptive Parents, rev. ed. by Arthur D. Sorosky, Annette Baran, and Reuben Pannor (Garden City, N.Y.: Anchor Press/Doubleday, 1984) is the most comprehensive work on the search and reunion issue. In exploring that topic, it discusses the effect of adoption on adoptees, adoptive parents, and birthparents.

While there are many worthwhile publications for adoptive parents, two stand out because they emphasize post-placement issues and are directed at parents rather than professionals:

Adopted Child newsletter, Lois R. Melina, editor & publisher, (P.O. Box 9362, Moscow, Idaho 83843), contains interviews with adoption experts, psychologists, child development specialists, and other experts, as well as book reviews and reports on research into adoption issues.

OURS Magazine, published by OURS, Inc., (3307 Highway 100 North, Suite 203, Minneapolis, Minn. 55422) places more emphasis on special needs adoptions and intercountry adoption, and welcomes written contributions from readers.

ADJUSTMENT OF PARENTS AND THE FAMILY

The effect of adoption on the family is explored in H. David Kirk's two books *Shared Fate* and *Adoptive Kinship* (see General Adoption for a full citation). How infertility affects adoptive parents is described in Jerome Smith and Franklin I. Miroff, *You're Our Child: A Social/Psychological Approach to Adoption* (Washington D.C.: University Press of America, 1981). Patricia Irwin Johnston's booklet *An Adoptor's Advocate* (Perspectives Press, 905 W. Wildwood Ave., Fort Wayne, Ind. 46807, 1984) discusses how the adoption process could be changed to better serve the infertile client. The concept of entitlement as essential to successful adoptive parenting is developed in *How They Fared in Adoption: A Follow-up Study* by Benson Jaffee and David Fanshel (New York: Columbia University Press, 1970).

Three approaches to infant care classes are profiled in "Baby care classes aimed at adoptive parents," *Adopted Child* (April 1983).

Information about changing an adoptee's name is found in Joyce S. Kaser and R. Kent Boesdorfer, "What Should We Name This Child?: The Difficulties of Naming Older Adopted Children," *Children Today* 10 (November-December 1981): 7–8, and in "Don't rename even a young child," *Adopted Child,* (July 1982), which is based on an interview with pediatrician Vera Fahlberg. "The Special Student," a collection of essays compiled by Gloria Petersen for the Illinois Council on Adoptable Children (P.O. Box 71, Oak Park, Ill. 60303), discusses school-related problems an adoptee may face, including confusion over the surname of a recently adopted older child.

Evidence that adoptive parents may be more anxious, or more dependent on professionals is found in H.D. Kirk and K. Jonassohn, *Halifax Children: A Study of Family Structure and the Health of Children,* an unpublished 1973 report that compares adopted and non-adopted children with regard to health and psychosocial issues.

The value of support from family and friends to the success of the adjustment is discussed in Feigelman and Silverman's book (see General Adoption for full citation). Pat Holmes' pamphlet "Supporting an Adoption" (P.O. Box 1488, Gig Harbor, Wash. 98335, 1983) helps family members and friends learn how they can be more supportive to the adoptive family. While more a survey than a scientific study, Pat Holmes' *Concepts in Adoption* (Richlynn Publications, P.O. Box 1488, Gig Harbor, Wash. 98335, 1984), tackles the question of how adoptive parents work with professionals as well as how professionals view adoption and adoptive parents.

The section in this book on how siblings react to adoption was based on interviews with Laurie Flynn, Vera Fahlberg, Claire Berman, and Barbara Roberts, and several siblings of adoptees, which became a series of articles on siblings in *Adopted Child:* "Youth talk about adopted siblings," (November 1983), "Kids already in home react to new sibling," (November 1983), "Siblings need help when older child arrives," (December 1983), and "Bio children may not be eager for 'international' experiences," (April 1984). Information on the ways children born into a family are affected by adoption, as well as how to prepare children already in the home for the adoption of a child who may be sexually aggressive was derived from a presentation by Jim and Kathryn Anderson at the 1985 conference sponsored by the North American Council on Adoptable Children, which was reported in "Adoption messages may confuse biologic child" *Adopted Child* (November 1985).

ADJUSTMENT OF ADOPTEES

For a basic understanding of grief, any of Elisabeth Kübler-Ross's books on death and dying are valuable, including *Death: The Final Stage of Growth* (Englewood Cliffs, N.J.: Prentice-Hall, Inc., 1975). John Bowlby's three volume series *Attachment and Loss* is the classic work on the ways children respond to the loss of their mothers (New York: Basic Books, Inc., 1969, 1973, 1980). Among those professionals dealing with adoption, Claudia L. Jewett is recognized as an expert on the ways children grieve for the birthparents and foster parents they have lost, and how they can be helped to resolve that grief so that they can form new attachments to adoptive parents. Many of the workshops she has presented since 1977 deal with these topics, as does her book *Helping Children Cope with Separation and Loss* (cited in General Adoption). The "handing over" technique, in which adoptive parents learn the child's routine from the foster parents, and therapeutic play techniques for helping children resolve grief, were outlined in "Adopted children need more than love," *Adopted Child* (December 1981).

Carol Williams has also made major contributions to an understanding of the adjustments children must make when they are moved from one caretaker to another, chiefly through her workshops. Her views on how infants react to being moved from one home and caretaker to another became the basis for "Even babies can have adjustment problems," *Adopted Child* (June 1984). One of the few published articles on this topic is Justin D. Call's, "Helping infants cope with change," *Early Child Development and Care* 3 (January 1974): 229–247.

Guidelines for helping an adoptee adjust to a new school are found in "The Special Student" (cited in Adjustment of Parents and the Family).

ATTACHMENT

John Bowlby's three-volume work (see Adjustment of Adoptees for a complete citation) is still the definitive work on bonding and attachment and separation. A more succinct and understandable discussion is found in Frank G. Bolton Jr., *When Bonding Fails: Clinical Assessment of High-Risk Families* (Beverly Hills: SAGE Publications, 1983).

The best research on the success of attachment between mothers and their adopted infants was done by researchers at Rutgers and Yeshiva universities: Leslie M. Singer, David M. Brodzinsky, Douglas Ramsey, Mary Steir, and Everett Waters, and was reported in "Mother–Infant Attachment in Adoptive Families," *Child Development* 56 (December 1985): 1543-1551.

The attachment of parents and children adopted at an older age was discussed by Terrence J. Koller in "Older child adoptions: A new developmental intervention program," a paper presented at the annual meeting of the American Psychological Association, Los Angeles, Calif., 1981, and in "Attachment to older child has some twists," *Adopted Child* (January 1985). Vera Fahlberg's booklet, *Attachment and Separation* (Michigan Department of Social Services, 1979), is a workbook for social workers that provides a general discussion of attachment, a theory about the attachment of older children, and guidelines for assessing failure to attach. Ways to identify failure to attach as well as techniques to facilitate attachment with an unattached child were discussed by Josephine Anderson (known to many as Josephine Braden) at the

1984 conference sponsored by the North American Council on Adoptable Children, which was reported on in "Unattached child: Going through life not caring," *Adopted Child* (February 1985).

Information about breast-feeding the adopted baby is contained in both technical articles and a helpful guide. Kathleen G. Auerbach and Jimmie Lynne Avery, "Induced Lactation: A Study of Adoptive Nursing by 240 Women," *American Journal of Diseases of Children* 135 (April 1981): 340–343, discusses the reasons adoptive women choose to breast-feed and the quantities of milk produced through relactation. Ronald Kleinman, Linda Jacobson, Elizabeth Hormann, and W. Allan Walker reported that the first milk of adoptive mothers does not contain colostrum in "Protein values of milk samples from mothers without biologic pregnancies," *Journal of Pediatrics* 97 (October 1980): 612-615. *Nursing Your Adopted Baby* by Kathryn Anderson (La Leche League International, 9616 Minneapolis Ave., Franklin Park, Ill. 60131, 1983) is the most up-to-date guide for relactation. Elizabeth Hormann outlines a schedule for breast-feeding the adopted baby in "Breastfeeding: Goal is emotional, not nutritional benefit," *Adopted Child* (March 1983). Individual support and help for the adoptive mother trying to induce lactation can be provided by La Leche League members. The Lact-Aid® Nursing Trainer™ System is available from pharmacies and home health care suppliers. For more information, write: P.O. Box 1066, Athens, Tenn. 37303.

TALKING ABOUT ADOPTION

Despite the importance of the subject, little has been written about how to talk to children about being adopted. Reports and research into how adoptees feel about what they have been told about their adoption are found in Lois Raynor's *The Adopted Child Comes of Age,* John Triseliotis' *In Search of Origins,* and Betty Jean Lifton's *Lost and Found* (cited in Growing Up Adopted).

The theory that it is traumatic to tell a child of her adoption too early is put forth in Herbert Wieder's article "On Being Told of Adoption," *Psychoanalytic Quarterly* 46 (January 1977): 1–22. A child's need to know the circumstances of his or her birth is explained by Marshall Schechter in "Child needs to know birth story," *Adopted Child* (September 1982).

Terms that should be used to refer to adoptive relationships are defined in "The Terminology of Adoption," by Marietta Spencer, *Child Welfare* 58 (July-August 1979): 451–459.

One of the most illuminating reports in recent year shows how children's understanding about adoption changes with their developmental age: "Children's Understanding of Adoption," *Child Development* 55 (June 1984): 869–78, by David M. Brodzinsky, Leslie M. Singer, and Anne M. Braff of Rutgers University.

Claudia Jewett's book *Helping Children Cope With Separation and Loss* (see General Adoption for complete citation) contains detailed information on ways to explain unpleasant facts to a child. Carol Williams explains in her workshops how to talk to children about why they were placed for adoption and other questions they may have. One of these excellent presentations formed the basis for three articles in *Adopted Child:* "Child's adoption queries tied to age" (July 1982), "Help your child make a scrapbook" (May 1982), and "Talking to children about their unpleasant past" (June 1985). Talking to children about abandonment was outlined in " 'Abandonment' in Korea sometimes a pretense," *Adopted Child* (February 1986).

Although it is directed at social workers, parents wanting more detail on how to make a life book with a child should read *Making History: A Social Worker's Guide to Life Books*, by JoAnn Harrison, Elaine Campbell and Penny Chumbley (Department for Social Services, L & N Building, 9th floor, 908 West Broadway, Louisville, Ky. 40203).

GROWING UP ADOPTED

The effect of unrealistic expectations on parents is described in *Parent Burnout* by Joseph Procaccini and Mark W. Kiefaber (Garden City, N.Y.: Doubleday and Co., 1983). Their ideas were adapted to the adoptive parents' situation by Procaccini and Jean Oser in "Burn-out: Infertility, home study can lead adoptive parents to expect too much," *Adopted Child* (October 1983).

With the exception of Jill Krementz's book *How It Feels to be Adopted* (New York: Knopf, 1982), in which nineteen adopted children tell in their own words what it is like to be adopted, most of the general information about what it is like to grow up adopted is found in books that deal with the adoptee's desire to search for information about her biologic origins, such as *The Adoption Triangle* (see General Adoption for complete citation), and *In Search of Origins: The Experiences of Adopted People* (Boston: Routledge & Kegan Paul Ltd., 1973), John Triseliotis' report on seventy adoptees who requested information about their biologic origins in Edinburgh, Scotland.

The first person accounts of adoptees, such as Betty Jean Lifton's *Twice Born: Memoirs of an Adopted Daughter* (New York: McGraw-Hill, 1975), give insight into the experiences of adoptees, as does Lifton's book *Lost and Found: The Adoption Experience* (New York: Dial Press, 1979), which is based on her own experiences as well as interviews with other adoptees. How some adoptees feel about their extended family is explored by Triseliotis in *In Search of Origins,* and by Betty Jean Lifton in "Adoptees may question membership in 'clan,' " *Adopted Child* (August 1985).

Family romance fantasies are discussed by Sorosky, Baran and Pannor in *The Adoption Triangle* (see General Adoption for complete citation), and by Herbert Wieder, "The Family Romance Fantasies of Adopted Children," *Psychoanalytic Quarterly 46* (April 1977): 185–200.

The controversy over the long-term effects of adoption on adoptees began with the publication of Marshall D. Schechter's "Observations on Adopted Children," *Archives of General Psychiatry 3* (July 1960): 45/21–56/32, who concluded that adopted children were represented in his psychiatric practice a hundred times more than could be expected from the general population. H. David Kirk, Kurt Jonassohn, and Ann D. Fish, in "Are Adopted Children Especially Vulnerable to Stress?" *Archives of General Psychiatry 14* (March 1966): 291-298, question Schechter's statistics and report that in their study, adopted children were not over-represented in psychiatric populations.

More recently, Paul M. Brinich and Evelin B. Brinich looked at the representation of adoptees at a psychiatric institute from 1969 to 1978 and found a higher percentage of adoptees than expected among the children, but a lower rate among adults. Their findings are reported in "Adoption and Adaptation," *The Journal of Nervous and Mental Disease* 170 (August 1982): 489–493.

One of the best studies of a non-clinic population was undertaken in Great Britain, where 16,000 children born during one week of 1958 were followed for growth, academic performance, and social adjustment. Two books report on those in the sample who were adopted: Jean Seglow, Mia Kellmer Pringle, and Peter Wedge, *Growing Up Adopted* (Windsor, England: National Foundation for Educational Research in England and Wales, 1972), which looks at the sample at age seven, and Lydia Lambert and Jane Streather, *Children in Changing Families: A Study of Adoption and Illegitimacy* (London: The Macmillan Press Ltd., 1980), which looks at them four years later.

Another important study is Alexina Mary McWhinnie's *Adopted Children: How They Grow Up* (London: Routledge & Kegan Paul, 1967/New York: Humanities Press), wherein the author interviewed fifty-eight adult adoptees and looked at their long-term adjustment as well as factors that might have influenced their adjustment, such as the level of communication in the adoptive home about the subject of adoption.

Benson Jaffee and David Fanshel's *How They Fared in Adoption: A Follow-up Study* (see Adjustment of Parents and the Family for complete citation) reports on one hundred families who adopted children from 1931 to 1940 and evaluates their childrearing practices, how parents told the children they were adopted, parental satisfaction with adoption, and adjustment of the adoptee.

Janet L. Hoopes found adoptive parents to be more protective and less authoritarian than biologic parents, and found that adopted children had lower self-esteem and less self-confidence than non-adopted children in her examination of 260 adoptive families, which is reported on in *Prediction in Child Development: A Longitudinal Study of Adoptive and Nonadoptive Families.* (New York: Child Welfare League of America, 1982).

In a retrospective study, *The Adopted Child Comes of Age* (London: George Allen & Unwin, 1980), Lois Raynor found that adoptees and their parents were more satisfied with the adoption when they perceived themselves as similar in some way. Adoptees also were more satisfied when their parents gave them freedom to pursue their own interests.

Although the methodology they used has been questioned, Kathlyn S. Marquis and Richard A. Detweiler reported in "Does Adopted Mean Different? An Attributional Analysis," *Journal of Personality and Social Psychology* 48 (April 1985): 1054–1066, that adoptees they studied were more confident than non-adoptees and viewed their parents as more nurturing, more comforting, more helpful and more protectively concerned than biologic parents.

A major look at the academic achievements of adopted children is provided by the Collaborative Perinatal Project, which studied the pregnancies of women at fifteen hospitals throughout the United States, beginning in 1959, and followed children born to the women until 1974. Among them were 243 children who were adopted as infants. The results were published in *Early Correlates of Speech, Language, and Hearing: The Collaborative Perinatal Project of the National Institute of Neurological and Communicative Disorders and Stroke,* edited by Frank M. Lassman, Paul J. LaBenz and Elaine S. LaBenz (Littleton, Mass.: Wright-PSG, 1980).

The adjustment and academic performance of adoptees and non-adopted children six to eleven years old who were matched closely for age, sex, race, socioeconomic status, family structure and number of siblings were evaluated by the Rutgers University team of David M. Brodzinsky, Dianne E. Schechter, Anne M. Braff, and Leslie M. Singer, in "Psychological and Academic

Adjustment in Adopted Children," *Journal of Consulting and Clinical Psychology 52* (August 1984): 582–590.

A review of the literature on this subject would not be complete without Michael Bohman's *Adopted Children and their Families* (Stockholm: Proprius, 1970), and Michael Bohman and Sören Sigvardsson, "A prospective, longitudinal study of children registered for adoptions: A 15-year follow-up," *Acta Psychiatrica Scandinavica* 61 (April 1980): 339–55, and Barbara Tizard's *Adoption: A Second Chance* (London: Open Books, 1977).

Related to the issue of the long-term effect of adoption on the adoptee are studies of identity conflict during adolescence, and investigations into why some adoptees search for information about their biologic parents and why others do not. For these sources see Adolescence and Biologic Relatives and Searching.

Evidence of a greater risk among adoptees for certain behavioral problems associated with learning disabilities is detailed in "Overrepresentaton of Adoptees in Children with the Attention Deficit Disorder," by Curtis K. Deutsch, James M. Swanson, Jan H. Bruell, Dennis P. Cantwell, Fred Weinberg and Martin Baren, *Behavior Genetics* 12 (March 1982): 231–238; in *Minimal Brain Dysfunction: A Prospective Study,* by Paul L. Nichols and Ta-Chuan Chen (Hillsdale, N.J.: Lawrence Erlbaum Associates, 1981); and in "Adoption and Foster Care Rates in Pediatric Disorders," by J. Thomas Dalby, Sharon L. Fox, and Robert H. A. Haslam, *Developmental and Behavioral Pediatrics* 3 (June 1982): 61–64.

HEREDITY AND ENVIRONMENT

Further information on the medical risks of children born of incestuous relationships can be found in "Children of incest," by Patricia A. Baird and Barbara McGillivray, *The Journal of Pediatrics* 101 (November 1982): 854–857.

Several researchers have used the adoption method to study the inheritance of schizophrenia, among them Seymour S. Kety, who published some of his findings in "Mental Illness in the Biological and Adoptive Relatives of Schizophrenic Adoptees: Findings Relevant to Genetic and Environmental Factors in Etiology," *American Journal of Psychiatry* 140 (June 1983): 720–727. Evidence for the inheritance of depression and manic-depressive disease is documented in "Evidence for Genetic Inheritance of Primary Affective Disorder in Adoptees," by Remi J. Cadoret, *American Journal of Psychiatry* 135 (April 1978): 463–466; and "Genetic and Environmental Factors in Major

Depression," *Journal of Affective Disorders* 9 (September 1985): 155-164, by Remi J. Cadoret, Thomas W. O'Gorman, Ellen Heywood, and Ed Troughton.

For the non-scientist, three collections contain highly readable information about the inheritance of schizophrenia, depression, and manic-depressive disease: *The Transmission of Schizophrenia,* edited by David Rosenthal and Seymour S. Kety (London: Pergamon Press, 1968); *Genetic Research in Psychiatry,* edited by Ronald R. Fieve, David Rosenthal, and Henry Brill (Baltimore: The Johns Hopkins University Press, 1975); and *Controversies in Psychiatry,* edited by John Paul Brady and H. Keith Brodie (Philadelphia: W.B. Saunders Co., 1978). Raymond R. Crowe's article "Is Genetic Counseling Appropriate for Psychiatric Illnesses?" in Brady and Brodie is a particularly good summary of the inheritance of psychiatric disorders in addition to outlining the principles of genetic counseling.

Psychiatrists Remi J. Cadoret of the University of Iowa and Donald W. Goodwin of the University of Kansas are responsible for much of the recent research into the inheritance of alcoholism, and Cadoret has also done much research on the inheritance of antisocial personality. The most recent findings are found in "Alcoholism and Antisocial Personality," by Remi J. Cadoret, Thomas W. O'Gorman, Ed Troughton, and Ellen Heywood, *Archives of General Psychiatry* 42 (February 1985): 161-167. Goodwin provides an excellent summary of research into this issue in "Alcoholism and Genetics," *Archives of General Psychiatry* 42 (February 1985): 171-174.

Much of the work on the inheritance of intelligence has been done by Sandra Scarr and Richard A. Weinberg, and one of their most recent articles on the subject is "The Minnesota Adoption Studies: Genetic Differences and Malleability," *Child Development* 54 (April 1983): 260-67. Genetic and environmental influences on IQ are also being examined by the Texas Adoption Project, and early results of this investigation were published by Joseph M. Horn, "The Texas Adoption Project: Adopted Children and Their Intellectual Resemblance to Biological and Adoptive Parents," *Child Development* 54 (April 1983): 268-275. The Colorado Adoption Project is investigating the inheritance of a number of traits, including intelligence and personality. The first results of that study are contained in *Origins of Individual Differences in Infancy: The Colorado Adoption Project* (New York: Academic Press, 1985), by Robert Plomin and John C. DeFries. Evidence for the inheritance of vocational interests is found in "Patterns of Interest Similarity in Adoptive and Biological Families," *Journal of Personality and Social Psychology* 35 (September 1977): 667-676, by Harold D. Grotevant, Sandra Scarr, and Richard A. Weinberg.

ADOLESCENCE

The subject of sexuality in the adoptive home and how infertility may affect parents after their child becomes fertile has received scant attention in the literature or has been handled inadequately. However, Constance Hoenk Shapiro and Betsy Crane Seeber provide an excellent discussion in "Sex Education and the Adoptive Family," *Social Work* 28 (July-August 1983): 291–96. Possible tension between infertile mothers and their adopted daughters when the daughters are pregnant was the topic of "Pregnant adoptees aware of parents' infertility," *Adopted Child* (May 1985).

Information about attitudes of male adoptees to infertility and their own sexuality was derived from a workshop at the 1984 conference of the American Adoption Congress and an interview with adoptee and therapist Dirck Brown, which was reported in "Men discuss being male and adopted," *Adopted Child* (July 1984).

The vulnerability of adoptees to unwanted pregnancy was explained by Reuben Pannor in "Pregnancy: Parents worry that illegitimate kids will repeat mistake," *Adopted Child* (August 1982). Guidelines for distinguishing between teenage rebellion and adolescent adoption issues was provided by Pannor and Jerome Smith in "Teen-agers use adoption as a weapon," *Adopted Child* (February 1982). Therapist Jack Frank and Reuben Pannor affirmed the incest taboo in adoptive homes in "Incest question can stress adoptive parents," *Adopted Child* (January 1983).

The importance of parents not trying to act as therapists with their adolescents was pointed out by Frederick H. Stone in "Adoption and Identity," *Child Psychiatry and Human Development* 2 (Spring 1972): 120–128.

The ways that adolescents leave home was the topic of Claudia L. Jewett's workshop at the 1985 conference of the North American Council on Adoptable Children, which was reported in "Teens need confidence to leave home," *Adopted Child* (October 1985).

The question of identity and self-concept among adoptees has fascinated researchers and theorists, resulting in a long list of articles and books dealing with the issue. One of the earliest reports on this subject is H. J. Sants, "Genealogical Bewilderment in Children with Substitute Parents," *British Journal of Medical Psychology* 37 (1964): 133–141. There is perhaps no better insight into the adolescent adoptee and the adoptee who searches than *The Adoption Triangle,* by Arthur D. Sorosky, Annette Baran, and Reuben Pannor (cited in General Adoption), which describes the identity conflicts some adoptees have in adolescence, reasons for searching, and the impact of reunions on adoptees, birthparents and adoptive parents. Major findings on this subject are summarized in "Identity Conflicts in Adoptees," by Arthur Sorosky, Annette Baran and Reuben Pannor, *American Journal of Orthopsychiatry* 45 (January 1975): 18–27, and in "Unlocking the Adoption Files: A Social and Legal Dilemma," by Paul Sachdev, in *Adoption: Current Issues and Trends*, edited by Paul Sachdev (Toronto: Butterworths, 1984).

Among those who found that adoptees do not have difficulty with identity formation are Janet L. Hoopes and Leslie M. Stein, who continued their longitudinal study of adoptees, reporting on them during adolescence in *Identity Formation in the Adopted Adolescent* (Washington, D.C.: Child Welfare League of America, 1986).

Earlier, Melissa Norvell and Rebecca F. Guy studied thirty-eight adoptees and thirty-eight non-adopted persons and found no significant difference in self-concept: "A Comparison of Self-Concept in Adopted and Non-Adopted Adolescents," *Adolescence* 12 (Fall 1977): 443-447.

References to self-concept among transracially and transculturally adopted children are found below in Transracial and Intercountry Adoption.

BIOLOGIC RELATIVES AND SEARCHING

There is considerable overlap in accounts of identity conflicts in adoptees, reasons some adoptees search, and descriptions of the long-term adjustment of adoptees. Triseliotis (see Growing Up Adopted for complete citation) found adoptees more likely to search for their biologic parents rather than for information when information about their adoption was revealed in a hostile or evasive way or when their life was unsatisfactory. Triseliotis also describes the significant events that often precipitate a search. As the definitive work on this subject, *The Adoption Triangle* (cited in General Adoption) explores reasons adoptees search, as well as the outcome of reunions.

Though not a report of scientific research, Betty Jean Lifton's *Lost and Found* (See Growing Up Adopted for complete citation) provides insight into the search and reunion issue, as do the first person accounts of birthmothers who have searched: *Birthmark*, by Lorraine Dusky, (New York: M. Evans and Co., 1979), and *I Would Have Searched Forever*, by Sandra Kay Musser (distributed by Haven Books, a division of Logos International, Plainfield, N.J., 1979).

First person accounts of the adoption experience by adoptees, birthparents, and adoptive parents, many of which deal with search and reunion, are found in "Dialogue for Understanding, Volume I" (1981) and "Dialogue for

Understanding, Volume 2: Women's Voices," (1984), compiled by the Post Adoption Center for Education and Research (477 Fifteenth St., Room 200, Oakland, Calif. 94612).

A well-written description of the decision-making processes and experiences of birthmothers that is notable for being sensitive without being emotional is *To Love and Let Go* by Suzanne Arms (New York: Knopf, 1983).

The experiences of Lutheran Social Service of Texas, which has pioneered the practice of open adoptions, are described in *Dear Birthmother,* by Kathleen Silber and Phylis Speedlin (San Antonio: Corona Publishing Co., 1983).

Considerations adoptive parents should have when their minor children have contact with their birthparents were outlined by Barbara Tremitiere and Marietta Spencer in "Setting rules for contact with birth families," *Adopted Child* (March 1985).

The reasons against searching during adolescence are explained by Reuben Pannor and Dirck Brown in "Adolescence not the best time for reunion," in *Adopted Child* (February 1984).

TRANSRACIAL AND INTERCOUNTRY ADOPTION

Self-esteem among transracially adopted children was examined by Owen Gill and Barbara Jackson, in *Adoption and Race: Black, Asian and Mixed Race Children in White Families* (New York: St. Martin's Press/London: Batsford Academic and Educational Ltd., 1983), a follow-up study of children in the British Adoption Project. No differences in self-esteem or self-concept between black children adopted by white parents and black children adopted by black parents, nor differences between black adoptees and white, non-adopted adolescents, were found by Ruth G. McRoy and Louis A. Zurcher, Jr. in *Transracial and Inracial Adoptees: The Adolescent Years* (Springfield, Ill.: Charles C. Thomas, 1983). The book also provides anecdotal evidence of the experiences of blacks adopted transracially, including dating and friends, siblings, school, and extended family members.

Dong Soo Kim, in his doctoral dissertation, "Intercountry Adoptions: A Study of Adolescent Self Concept Formation of Korean Children Who Were Adopted by American Families" (University of Chicago, August 1976), found that the Korean adoptees' self-concepts were similar to those of the Americans in his control group.

Rita Simon reported in an interview with the author in 1984 that there were no differences in self-esteem between the black transracially adopted adolescents and the white children born into the families that she has followed since 1972. Although these latest findings have not been published, two books report on the earlier interviews with the families. *Transracial Adoption*, by Rita Simon and Howard Alstein (New York: John Wiley & Sons, 1977), reported on children's awareness of their racial identity. *Transracial Adoption: A Follow-Up*, by Simon and Alstein (Lexington, Mass.: Lexington Books, 1981), interviewed many of the parents from the original study.

Although she did not study adoptive families, Judith Porter's book *Black Child, White Child: The Development of Racial Attitudes* (Cambridge, Mass.: Harvard University Press, 1971) is a helpful look at children's awareness of their racial identity. Interviews with Rita Simon and Judith Porter were used for the articles "Racial identity forms in preschool years" and "Transracial homes foster positive images," *Adopted Child* (July 1983).

William Feigelman and Arnold S. Silverman's book *Chosen Children* (cited in General Adoption) is a source of much of the information about the support interracial families need and the extent to which they receive it, the association between postive racial identity and adjustment, and the development of racial identity among black, Colombian and Korean adoptees. Guidelines for the appropriate use of ethnic dolls were given by Karen Zelan in "Ethnic dolls: Too much of a good thing?" *Adopted Child* (December 1982).

The majority of information about the adjustment of children from foreign countries focuses on Korean adoptions. *Understanding My Child's Korean Origins* by Hyun Sook Han (St. Paul, Minn.: Children's Home Society of Minnesota, 1980) describes child care customs. Children's Home Society of Minnesota has a number of booklets and films available on Korean culture and the experiences of Korean adolescents. For a complete list, write to the Post Adoption Department, Children's Home Society of Minnesota, 2230 Como Ave., St. Paul, Minnesota 55108. Frances Koh's book, *Oriental Children in American Homes: How Do They Adjust?* (East-West Press, P.O. Box 4315, Minneapolis, Minn. 55414, 1981), is most useful for those who adopt children over the age of three. Hei Sook Park Wilkinson discussed how children feel about being Korean in a white society in *Birth is More Than Once: The Inner World of Adopted Korean Children* (Sunrise Ventures, 708 Parkman Drive, Bloomfield Hills, Mich. 48013, 1985).

Gamines: How to Adopt from Latin America (Minneapolis: Dillon Press, 1981), by Jean Nelson-Erichsen and Heino R. Erichsen, gives limited information on child care practices in Latin America, but primarily focuses on how to adopt from Latin American countries. Considerably more is needed on the customs and practices in Latin America, India, and Asian countries other than Korea.

Readily available information on the medical conditions of foreign-born children is also needed. Although it is somewhat dated, information on medical conditions that children from the International Mission of Hope in India have been vulnerable to is outlined in *Today's Child: The Health Care Needs of IMH Infants*, by Holly van Gulden Wicker and Judy Walker Haavig (Today's Child Publications, 5046 Woodlawn Blvd., Minneapolis, Minn. 55417). More recent information was obtained from a hand-out prepared by the Department of Pediatrics at the University of Minnesota. Holt Children's Services in Eugene, Oregon has had excellent materials available to its adopting parents on the medical needs of children it places, particularly Korean children.

The risk of hepatitis B among Asians was outlined by Frederick Shaw and Myron J. Tong in the article "Asians should be tested for hepatitis B," *Adopted Child* (June 1984). Guidelines for measuring growth in foreign-born children were provided by George Sterne and Robert Bilenker in "Height and weight: North American growth charts can be used for all children," *Adopted Child* (December 1984).

Linda Massey and Harold Lubin provided details on lactose intolerance in "Milk: Your child may not have to give it up," *Adopted Child* (February 1982).

Research into the reversibility of malnutrition has been published in "Malnutrition and Environmental Enrichment by Early Adoption," by Myron Winick, Knarig Katchadurian Meyer, and Ruth C. Harris, *Science* 190 (December 19, 1975): 1173–1175; "Malnutrition and Mental Development," by Myron Winick, in *Human Nutrition—A Comprehensive Treatise, Vol. 1: Nutrition—Pre and Postnatal Development*, edited by Myron Winick (New York: Plenum Press, 1979); and "Malnutrition and adoption: Two variables in child development," by Marcos Cusminsky, Luis Garcia Azzarini, Zulema Dopchiz, Maria C. Alonso, Graciela Narduzzi, and Monica Berisso, in *Early Child Development and Care* 15 (April 1984): 45–56.

A thorough and practical guide for parents of a child of unknown age is Joyce Kaser's "Parenting the Ageless Child" (Family Building Associates, 11419 Rokeby Ave., Kensington, Md. 20895).

The question of whether bilingualism is a benefit or a hindrance to children has been studied in some detail in Canada. Jim Cummins' booklet *Bilingualism and Minority-Language Children* (The Ontario Institute for Studies in Education, 252 Bloor St. West, Toronto, Ontario, Canada M5S 1V6, 1981) is an excellent review of research on the issue. And both Cummins and Wallace

Lambert of McGill University, another authority on bilingualism, were interviewed for "Bilingualism benefits foreign-born," and "Foreign children easily forget native tongue," *Adopted Child* (October 1982).

SPECIAL NEEDS ADOPTIONS

In compiling the information on children with serious behavior problems, I depended heavily on several people whose knowledge on this subject is extensive: Claudia Jewett, Barbara Tremitiere, Kathryn S. Donley, Linda Katz, James Mahoney, Josephine Anderson, and John Boyne. Most of these people use training workshops and conferences to communicate their ideas, consequently, much of the information has not been published. Much of the information discussed in Claudia Jewett's workshop on how children leave home (see Adolescence for a complete citation) also touched on how parents can deal with children who have serious behavior problems. Barbara Tremitiere travels throughout the United States speaking with authority about the large adoptive family and raising children with serious behavior problems. Some of her ideas were reported in "Tough stance taken with difficult teenagers," *Adopted Child* (November 1982). She later expanded on this topic in a personal interview for this book. Her research into the large adoptive family was presented at the 1985 conference sponsored by the North American Council on Adoptable Children, and her research on disruption at the 1984 conference of the North American Council on Adoptable Children. Many of the ideas Kathryn Donley has presented at workshops and seminars have been compiled into *Helping Placements Survive: Minimizing the Chance of a Disruption,* by Bonnie C. Bedics and Kathryn S. Donley (Social Work Department, University of West Florida, Pensacola, Fla. 32514). This work also summarizes studies of the causes of disruption. Linda Katz's ideas on the parental characteristics that enhance the success of the adoption of a child with behavior problems were presented at the 1984 conference of the North American Council on Adoptable Children and reported as "Disturbed children: Child's behavior not only factor in success of placement," *Adopted Child* (November 1984). James Mahoney presented a workshop on task-oriented therapy and how to choose a therapist at the 1985 conference of the North American Council on Adoptable Children. The importance of a therapist sensitive to adoption issues was discussed by Jacqueline Hornor Plumez and Alan Long in "Child therapy: When is it indicated?" *Adopted Child* (April 1983). John Boyne's thoughts on the risk of child abuse in adoptive homes were shared at the 1984 conference of the North American Council on Adoptable Children and reported in "Adoptive homes not immune to child abuse," *Adopted Child* (September 1984). Josephine Anderson presented ideas on how to live with the unattached child, including the "holding technique," at an institute at the 1984 North American Council on Adoptable Children conference (cited fully in Attachment).

Suggestions on dealing with children who are the same age or close in age came from "Kids close in age need individuality," *Adopted Child* (January 1983).

The one minute scolding technique is fully explained in *Who's the Boss?* by Gerald E. Nelson and Richard W. Lewak (Boulder, Colo.: Shambhala, 1985), originally published as *The One Minute Scolding* (Boulder: Shambhala, 1984), by Gerald E. Nelson.

The Toughlove theory of discipline is described by Phyllis and David York and Ted Wachtel in *Toughlove* (New York: Bantam, 1982).

Joyce S. Cohen's research on disruption, "Adoption Breakdown with Older Children," was included in *Adoption: Current Issues and Trends*, edited by Paul Sachdev (see Adolescence for complete citation).

Information on the general effect a disabled child has on parents and siblings is found in *Families of Children with Special Needs: Early Intervention Techniques for the Practitioner*, by Allen A. Mori (Rockville Md.: Aspen Systems, 1983), and *Severely Handicapped Young Children and Their Families: Research in Review*, edited by Jan Blacher (New York: Academic Press, Inc., 1984).

A general guide for parents of disabled children on subjects such as getting the right diagnosis, finding schools and programs, and organizing support services is *The Special Child Handbook* by Joan McNamara and Bernard McNamara (New York: Hawthorn Books, Inc., 1977), which contains a chapter on adoption of the special needs child. Joan McNamara also is the author of a booklet published by the North American Council on Adoptable Children, "Adopting the Child with Special Needs" (1982). The North American Council on Adoptable Children also has published Linda Dunn's "Adopting the Child with Special Needs: A Sequel" (1983). Reflections on the adoption of children with special needs and details on specific disabilities as well as practical information, such as the use of computers by children with disabilities, are found in *Commitment: The Reality of Adoption*, by Grace Sandness (Mini-World Publications, 9965 Quaker Lane, Maple Grove, Minn. 55369, 1984). J. P. Blank's *Nineteen Steps Up the Mountain: The Story of the DeBolt Family*

(Philadelphia: J.B. Lippincott Co., 1976) is the story of the adoption of special needs children by Dorothy and Robert DeBolt.

Opinions on the effect of divorce on adopted children were given by Judith Schaffer, Claire Berman, Claudia Jewett, and Judith S. Wallerstein in "Effect of divorce on adopted children not known," and "Adoptive parents feel guilty over divorce," in *Adopted Child* (August 1984). The effect of a parent's death on an adopted child was discussed in "A parent's death: each time a unique sorrow," in a special introductory issue of *Adopted Child* in 1981.

Research into single adoptive parents can be found in *Chosen Children* by Feigelman and Silverman (see General Adoption for complete citation); in "Single-Parent Adoptions" by Benjamin Schlesinger in *Adoption: Current Issues and Trends*, edited by Paul Sachdev (cited fully in Adolescence); and in "Single Persons as Adoptive Parents," by Joan F. Shireman and Penny R. Johnson, *Social Service Review* 50 (March 1976): 103–16. "The Handbook for Single Adoptive Parents" (1985), edited by Hope Marindin and available from the Committee for Single Adoptive Parents (see Organizations for address), is also helpful. The experiences of single adoptive parents were described in presentations by Donna Naclerio and Cathie Thomas at the 1985 conference sponsored by the North American Council on Adoptable Children, and by Barbara Jirik and Barbara Young at the 1984 North American Council on Adoptable Children conference.

The ways siblings help each other during the adjustment period are described in *Large Sibling Groups: Adoption Experiences*, by Dorothy W. Le Pere, Lloyd E. Davis, Janus Couve, and Mona McDonald (San Antonio: Texas Department of Human Resources, 1985) and *The Sibling Bond*, by Stephen P. Bank and Michael D. Kahn (New York: Basic Books, Inc., 1982).

LEGAL ISSUES

The inability of some adoptive parents to obtain childrearing leave comparable to maternity leave is examined in "Maternity leave sometimes denied for adoption," *Adopted Child* (March 1984) and "Feedback: Another view of maternity leave," *Adopted Child* (May 1984).

Guidelines for covering adoptees on health insurance policies and naming them as beneficiaries in wills and life insurance policies are outlined in "Check your health insurance before adopting," *Adopted Child*, special introductory issue, and "Mention adoption in will, lawyers say," *Adopted Child* (March 1982).

What young children understand about the naturalization process was the topic of " 'Citizenship' difficult concept for child," *Adopted Child* (May 1983), featuring Albert J. Solnit.

CHILDREN'S RESOURCES

Books that discuss the feelings of jealousy and displacement children have when another child comes into the house are cited in Chapter 2. Several books that mention adoption as just one way a child might be set off from her friends are listed in Chapter 4.

For preschoolers, adoption and reproduction are explained together in *Our Baby: A Birth and Adoption Story,* by Janice Koch (Perspectives Press, 905 West Wildwood Ave., Fort Wayne, Ind. 46807, 1985). *The Chosen Baby,* by Valentina P. Wasson, rev. ed. (Philadelphia and New York: J.B. Lippincott, 1977), explains the adoption of infants through agencies. Criticism of this book goes back to the 1939 edition and focuses on the title, which reflects an outdated way of talking about adoption. Although the 1939 title was retained, the adoption practices and philosophies are updated in the new edition. The theme of Susan Lapsley's *I Am Adopted* (London: The Bodley Head, 1974) is that adoption is a special way of belonging to a family, but that adopted children are not odd or different. The text is very simple and it is suitable for very young children. (Adoptive parents have had a difficult time obtaining this book, but it is now being distributed in the United States by Merrimack Book Service, 250 Commercial St., Manchester, N.H. 03101.)

Books for school-age children address the feelings of adoptees as well as the situations of the birthparents. Elaine Scott's *Adoption* (New York: Franklin Watts, 1980) contains a lengthy text with discussions of the adoption process, feelings about adoption, heredity and environment issues, and options pregnant women may choose, including abortion. Carole Livingston's popular book *Why Was I Adopted?* (Secaucus, N.J.: Lyle Stuart, Inc., 1978) covers many of the reasons children are placed for adoption. *Aaron's Door,* by Miska Miles (Boston: Little, Brown, and Co., 1977), discusses the feelings of an older child as he arrives in his new adoptive family.

For adolescents, *How It Feels to Be Adopted,* by Jill Krementz (New York: Knopf, 1982), profiles nineteen children aged eight to sixteen, who describe their feelings about adoption. This is also an excellent book for adults. Adoptees learn that their feelings and experiences are not unusual, and adults learn that adoptees often have surprisingly mature attitudes toward their birthparents.

Fred Powledge's *So You're Adopted* (New York: Charles Scribner's Sons, 1982) and *Who is David? The Story of an Adopted Adolescent and His Friends,* by Evelyn Nerlove (New York: Child Welfare League of America, 1985), are books about adolescent adoption issues. *Adoption: The Facts, Feelings and Issues of a Double Heritage,* by Jeanne DuPrau (New York: Julian Messner, 1982), is directed more at adolescents who are not adopted, but provides an accurate view of adoption.

There are a number of books that address the unique experiences of multi-racial adoptive families. *Being Adopted,* by Maxine B. Rosenberg (New York: Lothrop, Lee & Shepard Books, 1984), is a sensitive profile of three pre-teen children who are racially or culturally different from members of their adoptive families. *We Don't look Like Our Mom and Dad,* by Harriet Langsam Sobol (New York: Coward-McCann, 1984), is a photo-essay of a family with two Korean-born children, and discusses sensitively and accurately what it is like to be Asian in a Caucasian society. *Is That Your Sister?,* by Sherry Bunin and Catherine Bunin (New York: Pantheon Books, 1976), gives a six-year-old's view of what it is like to have a sister whose skin color is different from others in the family. Marjorie Waybill's *Chinese Eyes* (Scottdale, Pennsylvania: Herald Press, 1974) easily resolves a child's hurt feelings when she is teased about her almond-shaped eyes.

For a complete list of fiction and nonfiction children's books dealing with adoption, consult "What is Real? An Adoptive Parents' Guide to Children's Books," by Marilyn Cochran-Smith (1984) available from Linda Ritter, R.D. 3200, Mohnton, Penn. 19450.

MERCHANDISE

OURS Magazine advertises and sells adoption-related merchandise such as ethnic dolls (including fashion dolls), ceremonial clothing from foreign countries, ethnic Christmas tree ornaments, adoption announcements, record books for adoptees, and needlework patterns and kits with adoption sentiments. For a copy of the magazine listing these items, write: OURS Inc., 3307 Highway 100 North, Suite 203, Minneapolis, Minn., 55422.

Those selling adoption announcements in addition to *OURS* are: L. K. Thompson Designs, P.O. Box 4562, St. Paul, Minn, 55104; Jan Elsberry's Designs, 8000 60th Ave. North, New Hope, Minn. 55428; and Adoption Library, P.O. Box 1265, Culver City, Calif. 90232.

Record books suitable for adoptees include: "I Am Special," L. K. Thompson

Designs, P.O. Box 4562, St. Paul, Minn. 55104; "Your Life a Step at a Time," Chinjja Creations, 8233 Harrison Rd., Bloomington, Minn., 55437; and "Baby's First Year" and "My Memory Book," The Adoption Library, P.O. Box 1265, Culver City, Calif. 90232.

ORGANIZATIONS

Committee for Single Adoptive Parents, P.O. Box 15084, Chevy Chase, Md. 20815, provides information and support to single persons wishing to adopt.

International Soundex Reunion Registry, P.O. Box 2312, Carson City, Nev. 89702, lists birthparents, siblings, and adoptees who are willing to exchange information or meet each other and has established a medical information registry that encourages adoption agencies to notify a birth family or adoptee when critical genetic information is discovered. Enclose a self-addressed, stamped envelope when writing.

"The Loving Circle," Holt Children's Services, P.O. Box 2880, Eugene, Ore. 97402, is an organization for grandparents and extended family members of adoptive families to build understanding about adoption.

The National Committee for Adoption, 2025 M St. N.W., Suite 512, Washington, D.C. 20036, is an umbrella organization of adoption agencies that lobbies on many adoption issues, but has become known for its opposition to opening sealed adoption records.

North American Council on Adoptable Children, P.O. Box 14808, Minneapolis, Minn. 55414, is a nonprofit organization that advocates the adoption of children with special needs and is the best source of adoptive parent support groups in the United States and Canada.

OURS, Inc., 3307 Highway 100 North, Suite 203, Minneapolis, Minn. 55422, is a nonprofit adoptive parent support organization with chapters throughout the United States.

PACER (Post Adoption Center for Education and Research), 477 Fifteenth St. Room 200, Oakland, Calif. 94612, provides educational sessions and publishes information about the adoption experiences of adoptees, birthparents, and adoptive parents.

Resolve, Inc., P.O. Box 474, Belmont, Mass. 02178, is an information, advocacy, and support group for infertile couples with chapters across the United States.

Index